Studying English Literature

Edited by

Ashley Chantler

and

David Higgins

continuum

Continuum
The Tower Building
11 York Road
London SE1 7NX

80 Maiden Lane, Suite 704
New York
NY 10038

www.continuumbooks.com

British Library Cataloguing-in-Publication Data
A catalogue record for this book is available from the British Library.

ISBN: 978–0–8264–9749–9 (hardback)
    978–0–8264–9750–5 (paperback)

Library of Congress Cataloging-in-Publication Data
A catalog record for this book is available from the Library of Congress.

Typeset by RefineCatch Limited, Bungay, Suffolk
Printed and bound in Great Britain by the MPG Books Group

Studying English Literature

Related titles available from Continuum:

How to Read Texts
Neil McCaw

Literary Theory: A Guide for the Perplexed
Mary Klages

The Essential Guide to English Studies
Peter Childs

The Poetry Toolkit
Rhian Williams

Contents

Contents

Detailed Table of Contents

Notes on Contributors

Derek Alsop is a Senior Lecturer, Head of English and Teaching Fellow at the University of Chester, specializing in literature of the period 1660–1780, with a further research interest in the twentieth century. The co-author of *The Practice of Reading: Interpreting the Novel* (Macmillan, 1999), he has also published articles and chapters on Rochester, Sterne, and Handel (most recently in *The Musical Quarterly*). His interest in the relationship between music and literature has resulted in over thirty programmes for BBC Radio 3 on subjects including the musical adaptation of literary sources in the work of Monteverdi, Handel, Mozart, Vaughan Williams, Holst, Finzi, and Britten. He is currently working on textual variants in Beckett's prose and drama.

Ashley Chantler is a Senior Lecturer in English at the University of Chester, where he specializes in twentieth-century literature and creative writing. He is the Series Editor of *Character Studies* (Continuum); author of *'Heart of Darkness': Character Studies* (Continuum, 2008); and co-editor of *The Alternative A–Z of English Literature* (Alternative Press, 2008), *Translation Practices: Through Language to Culture* (Rodopi, 2009), *Flash: The International Short-Short Story Magazine*, and the forthcoming *Literature and Authenticity, 1780–1900* (Ashgate). He is currently working on Ford Madox Ford's poetry.

David Higgins is a Lecturer in English Literature at the University of Leeds. He is the author of *Romantic Genius and the Literary Magazine* (Routledge, 2005) and *'Frankenstein': Character Studies* (Continuum, 2008). His current research project is provisionally titled *Romantic Geographies of the Self*. He teaches mainly in the Romantic period and has recently completed a co-edited book on *Teaching Romanticism* (Palgrave, 2010).

Jessica L. Malay is a Senior Lecturer in Renaissance Literature at the University of Huddersfield. She is author of *Textual Constructions of Space in the Writing of Early Modern Women* (Edwin Mellen Press, 2006) and *Prophesy and Sibylline Imagery in the Renaissance: Shakespeare's Sibyls* (Routledge, 2010) and has written essays, articles, and reviews on Renaissance writers, including Milton, Shakespeare, Anne Clifford, Elizabeth Russell, and Isabella Whitney. She has also written on manuscript culture and gender. She is presently working on autobiography and abuse narratives in the seventeenth century.

Emma L. E. Rees is the Deputy Head of English and a Senior Lecturer at the University of Chester. Research and teaching interests include Shakespeare studies; early modern literature and culture; film; and gender. Her book, *Margaret Cavendish* (Manchester University Press), was published in 2004, and she has many other publications on Cavendish and on gender. She is currently working on a monograph called *Can't: Uncovering the Postmodern Vagina*, which examines how female anatomy is simultaneously displayed and silenced in filmic and literary texts. She has also contributed essays to several recent books (a chapter on Victorian gynaecology, 'Narrating the Victorian Vagina: Charlotte Brontë and the Masturbating Woman'; a chapter on *King Lear*, 'Cordelia's Can't: Uncovering Shakespeare's Vaginas'; and a chapter co-authored with Richard E. Wilson on Freudian fetishism, 'Sometimes a Guitar is Just a Guitar').

William Stephenson is a Senior Lecturer in English at the University of Chester, specializing in utopianism, science fiction, literary theory, and the literature of addiction. He is author of two books, *John Fowles* (Northcote House, 2003) and *John Fowles's 'The French Lieutenant's Woman'* (Continuum, 2007), as well as essays on J. G. Ballard, Bret Easton Ellis, Alex Garland, William Golding, James Joyce, and Irvine Welsh. He has book chapters and journal articles forthcoming on Iain M. Banks, John Fowles, David Mitchell, and Hunter S. Thompson. He is working on a book entitled *Gonzo Republic: Hunter S. Thompson's America* (Continuum).

Deborah Wynne is a Reader in English at the University of Chester. She is the author of *The Sensation Novel and the Victorian Family Magazine* (Palgrave, 2001) and *Women and Personal Property in the Victorian Novel* (Ashgate, forthcoming). She has published numerous articles in journals on aspects of nineteenth-century literature and culture, including *Journal of Victorian Culture, Dickens Studies Annual, Women's Writing*, and *19*, as well as book chapters on Ellen Wood, Jane Austen and film adaptations, and reading practices. She teaches on the MA in Nineteenth-Century Literature and Culture, as well as courses on nineteenth-century literature, women's writing and theory.

Introduction

Ashley Chantler and David Higgins

Chapter Overview

Studying Literature at Degree Level

Studying for a literature degree is a challenging but highly rewarding experience. Literature, even at its most fantastical or abstract, is concerned with how human beings relate to each other and to the world around them. It deals, therefore, with issues that are fundamental to us all and, as you relate to the texts on your course, you may well find your ideas about life changing and developing. The ways in which literature addresses these fundamental issues vary enormously: between texts, between authors, between genres, and above all between historical periods. Rather than disclosing simple eternal 'truths' about love, death, loss, belief, emotion, relationships, or whatever, studying literature reveals the irreducible complexity and variety of human experience. It requires close attention to language and to history: that we wrestle with words and meanings, and that we consider the differences between past and present, as well as their similarities. Studying literature is a journey in which the pleasures and perils of travelling are much more important than the final destination. This book is designed to help you on your way.

Hopefully you are doing an English degree at least partly because you enjoy reading and are affected by the experience. This is crucial, but it is not sufficient. English literature is an academic *discipline* that, as the term implies, makes demands on those who study it. We need to channel and focus our initial responses through analysis. Above all, as literary critics we are concerned with how texts work, so reading and re-reading should make up the bulk of your study time. Of course, you will also have important contacts with tutors and other students. Lectures, seminars and tutorials allow for the sharing of ideas and interpretations and will have a vital role in your studies. But they are not meant to tell you how to think or to provide material for you to regurgitate in essays and exams. Rather, they will present you with a variety of readings and critical approaches that will help you to articulate *your own* interpretations and arguments. Often you will find that what your lecturers and peers have to say is interesting and helpful; sometimes you may find it baffling or apparently irrelevant. But it may be that ideas that do not immediately make sense will resonate when you revisit them in the future. The first year, in particular, is foundational and will help you to acquire knowledge and develop skills that will be invaluable later in your studies.

Studying at university, above all, is about learning to be an active, independent learner and to *engage* with lectures, seminars, and literary texts. This is also the case with secondary sources: the work of scholars, critics, and theorists. Such work can help to expand and deepen your knowledge and understanding of literature. But it is important that you try to *use* secondary material in the service of your own arguments. This is not to say that you always have to disagree with critics or refine their claims, although this is important. There may be times when you simply want to use a critic to support or contextualize what you are saying. This is fine, as long as you *always* acknowledge your sources. *Never* be tempted to plagiarize; that is, to pass off another person's words as your own. Apart from the moral issues involved, if plagiarism is discovered (and many academic institutions now use sophisticated software to detect unacknowledged sources in student assignments), there can be severe disciplinary consequences. The issue of plagiarism can cause anxiety, particularly among first-year students, but a simple rule to remember is: if in doubt, provide a reference!

The volume of secondary material relating to most aspects of literary studies can be daunting, even to experienced academics. As a student of literature, you will become increasingly adept at deciding what to read and what not to read by using reading lists, contents pages, indexes, and the various helpful online resources that are available. Many important scholarly articles can now be accessed online through websites such as JSTOR or LION, to which your university may well subscribe. Be careful, though, with *open access* internet resources. Some of these are scholarly; many are simplistic or misleading. You should become able over the course of your degree to judge the academic credentials of websites, but if you are ever unsure, consult your tutor. The internet is a wonderful resource, but never neglect your university library. At their best, libraries can still offer a haven for students and occasionally even academics to escape from the distractions of emails, MP3 players, text messages, Facebook, YouTube, MySpace, and Twitter, and to engage in the careful, concentrated reading that is required for the study of literature.

This may all seem like rather a lot to take on board. However, your first year as an undergraduate is *developmental*: you are not expected to be operating at degree level straight away. Lectures, seminars, reading, writing, and feedback will all help to bring you up to speed. Study guides like this one can also be really useful, although be wary of guides that tell you what to think rather than suggesting possibilities. Access to a quality dictionary and thesaurus is crucial, as is ownership of a glossary of literary terms. You will need to develop your technical vocabulary in order to discuss and write about literature in a precise and informed fashion.

Through studying literature at university, your skills will improve, as well as your knowledge of the subject. You might be surprised by how many important skills, both subject specific and transferable, an English degree involves: a valuable list can be found on the website of the United Kingdom's Quality Assurance Agency for Higher Education (QAA). Two skills with which this book is particularly concerned are 'close reading' and 'critical thinking'. Both are complex processes. Both require that we continually analyse, rather than assume, and that we are aware of, and reflect on, our own assumptions. The academic study of English literature is dependent on think-ing self-consciously about the different ways in which we might read and interpret texts. 'Theory' is not optional: there is no approach to texts that does not have some sort of theoretical basis, as Jonathan Culler points out:

> [Theory is] an attempt to show that what we take for granted as 'common sense' is in fact a historical construction, a particular theory that has come to seem so natural to us that we don't even see it as a theory. As a critique of common sense and exploration of alternative conceptions, theory involves a questioning of the most basic premises or assumptions of literary study, the unsettling of anything that might have been taken for granted: What is meaning? What is an author? What is it to read? What is the 'I' or subject who writes, reads, or acts? How do texts relate to the circumstances in which they are produced? (pp. 4–5)

We might add two more to Culler's list of fundamental questions. What is 'literature'? And who decides how we should define it? The last twenty-five years or so have seen strong critical interest in the relationship between 'litera-ture' and 'history', and one effect of this has been an increasing awareness that the categories of 'literary' and 'non-literary' are the result of complex ideological processes that have led to the unjust exclusion of certain writers and genres from academic study. It is possible to accept this premise without, at the same time, concluding that this means that all writing is equally worthy of critical attention. In this book, we have tried to be sensitive to history, and to the increasing capaciousness of 'literature' as a category, while at the same time giving due emphasis to writers and forms that we, and most other literary academics, believe to be particularly important, even if what makes them 'important' may be over-determined and difficult to articulate. An inspiring recent attempt to address this thorny issue can be found in Derek Attridge's *The Singularity of Literature* (2004).

As you begin your university studies, you will no doubt be keen do well in your assessment, and eventually to gain a strong degree, and hopefully a good job. However, the way to do well is not to be obsessed by these outcomes but instead to immerse yourself in the processes of learning. There are a wide variety of interesting, fertile approaches to literary texts, many of which we discuss in this book. It is ultimately up to you to find your own ways of engaging with the texts that you encounter. This is what makes literary study so stimulating, exciting and, yes, fun: the freedom and inventiveness of reading and writing.

How to Use This Book

Studying English Literature is very intentionally *not* a door-stopping guide to English literature from the Renaissance to the present day. Legions of them have already been published and most do not teach you how to study literary texts, they tell you stuff that you might regurgitate: dates, facts, biographical anecdotes, and so on. A sub-title to *this* book could be: *How to Do It Yourself*.

As mentioned above, studying literature at university is about your own interpretations and arguments, and learning how best to articulate them in seminars and assessment. Each chapter here is written to help you to do your own close reading of *any* literary text and to construct your own ideas about them. In the 'Case Study' on Pope's poetry, for example, there is a discussion of iambic pentameter*. It helps you understand Pope's use of that poetic line, but also prompts you to think about its use when studying other poets. Each chapter also introduces you to a wide range of critical and theoretical writing, not to tell you when you must use it but to suggest how you might use it. There are many books, articles and websites that tell you what to think. *Studying English Literature* will show you how to be an independent researcher and interpreter of texts. The students who do best at university are not those who repeat what they are told by their tutors, but those who develop their own personal responses to literature. This might, of course, sound rather intimidating. Do not let it be. The first year is foundational. You are not expected to dazzle your tutors from the outset – and reading *Studying English Literature* will help you learn how to engage with English literature at degree level.

One of the things that might seem different about studying literature at university is the engagement with historical context: considering when literary texts were written and how this might help us better understand them. *Studying English Literature* has been structured chronologically in order to give you a sense of the broad sweep of literary history and to emphasize the importance of historical context to understanding any literary text. There are four main sections:

- Studying Shakespeare
- Studying Seventeenth- and Eighteenth-Century Literature
- Studying Romantic and Victorian Literature
- Studying Twentieth-Century and Contemporary Literature.

In order to keep this book to a manageable length, we have focused particularly on the texts, authors, and periods that you are most likely to come across in the first year. As you go through your degree, you will probably encounter important areas of literary study that we do not cover in detail, such as medieval literature and postcolonial* literature. We hope, though, that this book will have helped to equip you with skills that can be applied to all literary texts, regardless of whether or not we discuss them in this book.

Shakespeare opens *Studying English Literature* because his comedies and tragedies are considered to be fundamental to studying English literature at university: if you can get to degree-level grips with a Shakespeare play, you are well on your way to becoming an excellent student. The Shakespeare section begins with a general essay on 'Shakespeare and the Renaissance', which covers the historical context and other key writers of the period. It will help you see Shakespeare as of his time, rather than as a 'genius' whose plays are somehow ahistorical, transcending time and place, speaking 'universal' truths. The opening essay is followed by chapters on the comedies and the tragedies, which are split into four parts: 'Key Texts'; 'Criticism and Literary Theory'; 'Case Study'; 'Further Reading'. See below for an outline of each part.

The other three sections of the book consider particular periods: the seventeenth and eighteenth centuries; the Romantic and Victorian periods; and the twentieth century to the present day. Each section is divided into the following parts.

Historical Context
This part might sound slightly off-putting, either because at school or college you had to discuss only the text in isolation, or because history textbooks, with their dry-as-dust lists, charts, graphs, dates for this, dates for that, can be tedious. The thought of spending days in the library and memorizing statistics about national debt or emigration probably does not appeal. You do not need to worry.

In your first year, you are not expected to be an expert in the period you are studying, nor are you expected in seminars to be able to robotically regurgitate numerous facts, but you are expected to show an awareness of *some* dates and have a sense of why certain texts are as they are: why they came into being at a particular time and how they relate to their historical period. A simple example is First World War poetry. Siegfried Sassoon's and Wilfred Owen's war poetry is obviously related to events that occurred at the time; Owen's 'Gas! GAS! Quick, boys!', for example, in 'Dulce Et Decorum Est' (Silkin, p. 194), refers *specifically* to German mustard gas, a new weapon in warfare, so the line is of its time: it came into being because of historical events. We might not say that Virginia Woolf's *To the Lighthouse* (1927) is *about* the War, but when we read, in one of the short paragraphs placed in square brackets, '[Mr Carmichael brought out a volume of poems that spring, which had an unexpected success. The war, people said, had revived their interest in poetry.]' (p. 183), the 'war' reference is to the First World War, and this helps us towards a better understanding of the other square-bracketed paragraphs.

An awareness of certain dates also helps us avoid making erroneous claims. An obvious example is Ford Madox Ford's novel *The Good Soldier*. Its title and first publication date (1915) might suggest that it was Ford's early response to the First World War, when actually it was written 1913–14. Furthermore, a bit of research will reveal that Ford planned to title it *The Saddest Story*. Similarly, T. S. Eliot's poetry collection *Prufrock and Other Observations* was first published in 1917, but to interpret 'The Love Song of J. Alfred Prufrock', for example, as being about a man feeling acutely mortal because of the First World War would be to misread the poem, which Eliot completed in 1911.

Some knowledge of history also helps us avoid making generalizations, usually about religion, class, gender, and sex. 'Before Darwin, everyone believed in God.' 'The working classes were all illiterate.' 'Women were oppressed due to patriarchy.' 'The Victorians were sexually repressed.' A bit of secondary reading would expose these statements as far too vague and sweeping.

Remembering that texts are of a particular time and about a particular time also helps us be more careful when we discuss character. It is inevitable that we respond to and judge literary characters as we do real people – you will find one character irritating, another confusing – but we should not let our responses lead to unscholarly statements. When writing about D. H. Lawrence's short story 'The Odour of Chrysanthemums' (1911), for example, we might say that Elizabeth is heartless and selfish to think in a business-like way about money and her children rather than worry about their feelings if their father has been killed. But if we remember that Lawrence is writing about a working-class mining family in Nottinghamshire at the turn of the twentieth century, where the death of the father would mean the children would grow up (if they managed to) in *dire* poverty, then our view of Elizabeth changes: her seemingly cold thinking it is actually born of love and unselfishness.

Reminding ourselves of the differences between the past and the present helps us be sensitive to and understand different beliefs, ideas, assumptions and ways of life: different ways of thinking and being. It also helps us with humour. It is not uncommon for students to say that Shakespeare's comedies, for example, do not make them laugh. But by thinking about historical context we can make the leap between the present and the past, and so have a much better understanding of the *use* of the comic. When Malvolio, in *Twelfth Night* (1602), says, 'These be [Olivia's] very c's, her u's, and her t's, and thus makes she her great P's' (2.5.83–84), we might miss the joke if we are not aware that 'cut' was slang for women's genitals. Shakespeare's audiences would have got the gag, which comically reveals that the supposedly straight-laced and chaste Malvolio probably thinks about Olivia's vagina; 'cut' cuts his façade.

'Historical Context' gives an overview of chapter's period, discussing key events (historical, social, and cultural) that influenced the writing and thinking of the major authors at the time. It stresses the importance of knowing that the texts you are studying are the products of a particular time and place, and that placing them in context is necessary for degree-level interpretation.

Key Authors and Texts

This part gives you an overview of the major writers and texts of the period, and indicates some of the links between their works. It stresses the importance of making connections between texts, rather than studying each in isolation, and engaging in a considered and extended way with themes and issues. As with historical context, you are not expected to have a detailed knowledge of every author or text mentioned, but you might find yourself inspired to read, say, a poem by an author not on your reading list and refer to it in an essay. Doing so will not only impress your marker, it will give you a stronger understanding of the complexity and richness of literary history.

Criticism and Literary Theory

In seminars and lectures, your tutors will probably encourage you to do some 'secondary reading', by which they certainly mean literary criticism (articles and books about the primary texts you are studying) and probably literary theory as well (articles and books about ideas and approaches to the study of literature; texts that get us thinking about ways of reading). Again, this can seem rather daunting, especially given the volume of the material available: stand in the Shakespeare section of your library and look at all the books that have been written about his plays. Do not be put off. You are not expected to read everything, and, as mentioned above, you will become increasingly adept at working out what to read, and how and when to use it in your assessment. 'Criticism and Literary Theory' introduces you to a selection of critical and theoretical writing that you might find useful when discussing the literature of the period. It shows you how engaging with secondary texts can lead to more nuanced interpretations.

Case Studies

Studying English Literature, as we have said, could be sub-titled: *How to Do It Yourself*. Each case study does not tell you what to think about the chosen text or texts; they are not short overviews, nor are they comprehensive guides. You should see the case studies as illustrations of possible ways of analysing *all* texts: how to do close reading of any text; how to use the critical techniques and terms at your disposal when analysing any text; how you might draw on criticism and literary theory when writing about any text. After reading a case study, think about what its author did with the primary text and how you might do the same, initially with other parts of the same text and then with other texts. Use them to help you become a better and more independent critic of English literature.

Further Reading

This part lists six texts and two websites that you will find useful when *starting* to do further research into the literature of the period. Also use the 'References' section at the end of *Studying English Literature*.

Glossary of Terms

Throughout *Studying English Literature*, you will see that certain terms (mainly literary, critical, and theoretical) are followed by an asterisk (*). This indicates that there is a brief definition of the term at the back of the book.

If you are unsure of the meaning of a term that has not been asterisked, see if it is in Chris Baldick's *The Oxford Dictionary of Literary Terms* (2008); for detailed definitions of poetic terms, see John Lennard's *The Poetry Handbook* (2005). And as always: if in doubt, ask your tutor.

References

This section lists all the books referred to in each chapter. It is similar to the bibliography you will be expected to give at the end of every essay you write. Use it, and similar lists in other secondary texts, as a resource to support your research.

Part I
Studying Shakespeare

1 Shakespeare and the Renaissance

Emma L. E. Rees

Chapter Overview

The Renaissance

> In the Middle Ages both sides of human consciousness – that which was turned within as that which was turned without – lay dreaming or half awake beneath a common veil. The veil was woven of faith, illusion, and childish prepossession, through which the world and history were seen clad in strange hues. [. . .] [I]n Italy this veil first melted into air; an *objective* treatment and consideration of the state and of all the things of this world became possible. The *subjective* side at the same time asserted itself with corresponding emphasis; man became a spiritual *individual*. (Burckhardt, p. 98)

The term 'the Renaissance', used to describe the massive, gradual alteration in thought and representation which took place in Europe in the early modern period, was actually coined in the nineteenth century by a Swiss-born historian called Jacob Burckhardt, who published *Civilization of the Renaissance in Italy* in 1860. Burckhardt established the view (still held by many critics and historians today) that the Renaissance (the term roughly equates to the word 'rebirth'), in its recovery of Classical (ancient Greek and Roman) modes of thought, marked an emergence from the superstitious 'dark ages' where people identified themselves principally as part of a community, to a period where people thought of themselves principally as individuals.

Pinning down the Renaissance to a precise set of dates is impossible. Its arrival in northern Europe is generally accepted to be later than its first flourishing in the south, particularly in Italy, in the fourteenth and fifteenth centuries, and in terms of English Literature it approximates to the period from 1550 to 1660 (but even these dates are debated by scholars). As Burckhardt described, it was a period of seismic change in the way in which human beings regarded themselves and their universe. Humanism, that key intellectual and educational system with its emphasis on the *studia humanitatis*, or 'the humanities' as we might term them today, was in the ascendant, and the visual, literary, and musical arts slowly developed from concentrating on 'God' to making humanity (as the epitome of God's creation) their focus. At the same time the very universe was being reconsidered: there was a shift in humanity's view from a Ptolemaic formulation (which had Earth as central to the cosmos), to Copernicus' heliocentric (sun-centred) model.

At the same time that such scientific and cultural progress was being made, however, a darker movement of religious intolerance and persecution was on the rise. This was the era of the witchcraft phenomenon, a concerted campaign that effectively allowed communities to find an ideologically-sanctioned focus for their frustrations and anxieties. That focus was usually any woman who refused to conform to the Renaissance ideal of femininity, which presented chastity, silence, obedience, and domesticity as the watchwords of her life. Individuals scapegoated as witches were usually women who lived on a community's peripheries, being subject to gossip and rumour. A central paradox* of the phenomenon was that society forced the role of victim onto these persecuted women, and some suspects confessed that they had started practising 'witchcraft' in order to get revenge against those same neighbours who had excluded and ridiculed them in the first place.

One of the two monarchs who ruled in Shakespeare's lifetime, James VI of Scotland and I of England (ruled 1603–25), was fascinated by the witchcraft phenomenon, publishing his *Daemonologie* in 1597. James was at pains to show how 'witchcraft' differed from, for example, more conventional medical practices by affecting people's health through words rather than actions. Ideas such as these grew popular because to the early modern mind the universe was full of mysteries – failed harvests; sick cattle; sudden deaths – which seemed only able to be explained by citing magic as their origin and cause. Shakespeare, of course, also saw in the witchcraft phenomenon a creative opportunity. *Macbeth*, with its bold (and, to some members of the original audience, genuinely frightening) opening stage directions, pays several partially concealed compliments to King James, and it was probably first performed at Hampton Court Palace in 1606. The power of magic or enchantment is also evident in other Shakespeare plays: in *Othello* Brabantio accuses the hero of bewitching his daughter, Desdemona, causing her to fall in love with him; in *A Midsummer Night's Dream* another disgruntled father, Egeus, accuses Lysander of doing something similar with his daughter, and the fairy world is a place of magic and enchantment. Other literary witches included the hags in Ben Jonson's *Masque of Queens* (1609); Hecate in Thomas Middleton's play *The Witch* (1612); and the real-life Elizabeth Sawyer, the eponymous* *Witch of Edmonton* in the collaborative play written by William Rowley, Thomas Dekker, and John Ford (1621).

Elizabeth I

The idea of femininity in the Renaissance period was, as the witchcraft phenomenon vividly illustrated, beset by a variety of cultural anxieties about sexual, social, and political disorder. It is particularly compelling, then, to consider that, in terms of the English Renaissance, no figure was so dominant as a woman: Queen Elizabeth I (ruled 1558–1603). As well as being a highly educated and articulate individual, Elizabeth had a profound effect on almost all aspects of English Renaissance life. A woman in charge of a country whose very identity was characterized by a deep-set patriarchy*, she was the embodiment of paradox*. In religious terms she felt an immense obligation to ensure the continuation of her father's (Henry VIII's) establishment of the Church of England, and she successfully guided her country through a series of threats and difficulties thanks to her exceptional intellect and acute awareness of the paradoxical vulnerability she experienced as a female monarch. She encouraged and, in her own writing, developed, a remarkably powerful representation of herself as the 'Virgin Queen'. Her refusal to marry or to name an heir kept courtiers and citizens in a state of unease about what would happen on her death. In one of her own poems, 'On Monsieur's Departure' (c. 1582), she expresses the powerful split between private love and public duty in an ambiguous phrase ostensibly about the Duke of Anjou's departure, but equally possibly about her self-image: 'from myself another self I turned' (p. 303). Issues of marriage and succession came to dominate Elizabeth's reign. Had she decided to marry an Englishman she would have been seen by certain of her courtiers as siding with a particular faction over the interests of others. However, had she married a foreign ruler like Anjou she would have been accused of making England subservient to an alien or even an enemy power. Marriage was, therefore, less a matter of personal choice than a tool of foreign policy for Elizabeth.

Literary and visual artists competed to represent their Virgin Queen in a favourable light. Throughout her reign the project of Elizabeth's artists was twofold: they had to represent a woman of seemingly cosmic power and importance; and they had to perpetuate that representation when age and frailty became physical realities for the monarch. This conjunction of art and power is central to any notion of an English Renaissance, and Elizabeth's image was more widely disseminated than that of any previous ruler. Complex allegorical paintings were circulated, ensuring that Elizabeth became the stuff of legend, being both illustrated and created by visual and literary portraits. Painters represented the iconic qualities Elizabeth was keen to propound – thus William Segar's 'Ermine' portrait of 1585 symbolizes chastity, and George Gower's 'Armada' portrait (c. 1588) brilliantly depicts Elizabeth's imperial power.

In the literary field Edmund Spenser and Philip Sidney were chief among the courtier poets. Spenser's *Faerie Queene* (1590–96) set out to represent human virtues in the persons of worthy knights. In the first Book of this long allegorical poem, the victory of the Protestant reformation is celebrated. Later books focus on 'Concord' and 'Chastity', and Elizabeth is portrayed both as muse and as political and religious reformer. In Book 3 she is represented by the figure of the powerful Britomart, a woman disguised as a knight. This complicated gendered representation of Elizabeth recalls the Queen's own speech to her troops at Tilbury docks on the eve of the battle against the Spanish Armada in 1588. It was here that she uttered the famous words that in so many ways have come to epitomize both her reign and her sense of gendered ambiguity: 'I know', she said, 'I have the body but of a weak and feeble woman, but I have the heart and stomach of a king and of a king of England, too' (Elizabeth I, p. 326). The cult of the individual fostered by the Renaissance found perhaps its most profound expression in the person of Elizabeth. She exemplified many of the attributes of the ideal Renaissance monarch in her management of all aspects of her nation – political, religious, military, and imperial – and she managed all this through her careful control of herself and of the accompanying iconography which circulated about this self. In many ways she *was* the English Renaissance.

Renaissance Thought

Elizabeth's court was home to many of the period's leading thinkers and artists, whose creativity impacted upon, and helped to form, 'the Renaissance'. New forms of writing emerged, chief among them the pithy, meditative, and often didactic (instructive) essay form. Popularized in France by Michel de Montaigne, it was the form to which the philosopher Francis Bacon turned his attention in England in the 1600s. The essay was ideally suited to thinkers who wanted to formalize their musings about what it meant to be living in a world where long-held preconceptions were under intense scrutiny. In terms of thinking about William Shakespeare and his place in the Renaissance, Montaigne's essay 'Of the Cannibales' is particularly informative. In this essay, parts of which Shakespeare reproduces almost word-for-word in *The Tempest* in the loyal Gonzalo's utopian* musings in Act 2, Montaigne held up a mirror to the New World (those countries, particularly those in South America, colonized by Europeans such as Columbus) in order to reflect on what he regards as the faults of Southern Europe, the Old World. 'I am not sorry', wrote Montaigne, 'that we notice the barbarous horror of such acts [cannibalism], but I am heartily sorry that, judging their faults rightly, we should be so blind to our own' (p. 155). Bacon was rather less self-absorbed than Montaigne in his essays, and many of his observations have a kind of freshness even today. In his essay 'Of Marriage and Single Life' he urges men to consider how having a family may jeopardize their career plans. 'He that hath wife and children hath given hostages to fortune', wrote Bacon, 'for they are impediments to great enterprises, either of virtue or mischief. Certainly the best works, and of greatest merit for the public, have proceeded from the unmarried or childless men; which both in affection and means, have married and endowed the public' (p. 353). Such a sentiment has a startling modernity to it, as anyone who has tried to juggle career success and domestic life will indicate. Bacon's own 'Virgin Queen', Elizabeth, had to make precisely such a choice, metaphorically marrying her public, endowing her people, to use Bacon's words, 'both in affection and means'.

The writings of Niccolò Machiavelli had a profound influence on Renaissance dramatists, and many of Shakespeare's most memorable characters owe a debt to him. Machiavelli's most influential work, published in 1532, was called *Il Principe* (*The Prince*). In the first decade of the sixteenth century Machiavelli became acquainted with Cesare Borgia, the powerful Italian soldier and politician, and he came to admire his courage, ambition, autocracy, and secrecy. Machiavelli quickly realized that such qualities were necessary for maintaining power in Renaissance Italy, and he began to develop a philosophy around them. In observing Borgia's rise and fall, Machiavelli made both Fortune and 'virtú' (the self-serving ability to act appropriately in threatening circumstances) the cornerstones of his political philosophy, speculating that too inflexible an attitude on the behalf of a ruler led to failure. 'Fortune', wrote Machiavelli, using an unapologetically misogynistic metaphor, 'is a woman, and if you want to control her, it is necessary to treat her roughly. And it is clear that she is more inclined to yield to men who are impetuous than to those who are calculating' (p. 87). A ruler, therefore, should change his mind and approach – always with a specific goal in mind – to suit the circumstances. This audacious pragmatism is what drives many of the Machiavellian characters of Renaissance drama, too, from scheming, self-interested malcontents such as Edmund in *King Lear*, to Iago, the ruthless, ambitious manipulator of *Othello*.

Courtly Love

The courtly love tradition was significant in the Renaissance court. Although their ways of finding answers to the 'big' questions of life may differ from our own, Renaissance writers were preoccupied with the same sorts of concerns that trouble us today. In literature the problem of how we know what 'love' is, and of how we articulate intense and personal feelings, was a key concern. Some of the clichés about love which are familiar to us are drawn from a medieval courtly love tradition where men were brave and women needed protecting. It was a tradition which fascinated Renaissance writers not least because of the powerful presence of Elizabeth, the highest, least attainable, paradoxical representation of the beloved: had she not existed she would have had to have been made up to fulfil the poet-courtiers' needs.

The courtly love tradition was a literary mode which extended far beyond mere words on the page, becoming a style of writing which described and enacted a way of behaving in a courtly, chivalric, knightly fashion. Critics debate its authenticity – in other words, how far it existed outside the badinage and playful literary exercises of a few bored aristocratic men in Elizabeth's court – but this highly stylized form was designed to demonstrate to ladies and to lovers how to behave. Its origins lay in the lyrics* of the French troubadours (eleventh-century singer-songwriters) and the thirteenth-century allegorical *Roman de la Rose*, which had represented the lover pining for his lady. Courtly poets like Edmund Spenser were influenced by the deeply allegorical dream-vision narratives of texts like *The Romance of the Rose* (c. 1275) and Chaucer's *Book of the Duchess* (c. 1370). The courtly love tradition borrowed not only images and phrases, but also social and gendered hierarchies, from both feudal and religious discourses. Thus the spurned male lover is subject to his Lady as though she were his social superior – the Knight *serves* his courtly lady, who is in complete *rhetorical* control. The overarching irony, of course, was that in real Renaissance society women were actually disenfranchised; the power that the beloved women have in the poetry is granted to them by the male lover, and this act of gifting is in itself an assertion of power.

Other required reading for the young men of Elizabeth's court included Baldassare Castiglione's *Book of the Courtier* (*Il Cortegiano*). Written over many years and first published in 1528, this was effectively a Renaissance 'How to' book – in this case, how to be the perfect courtier. Well-read writers of the Renaissance who wanted to write about love would also have been familiar with the work of the Roman poet Ovid who, in his *Ars Amatoria* (c. 1 BC) portrayed a powerless lover. In his *Amores* (16 BC) Ovid argued that a man could only be virtuous if he were also a lover: in other words, love ennobles the human spirit. 'Love', then, was as much about networking and power as it was about emotion. Elizabeth's Renaissance court was a place of fashion and influence where to speak the right language and to have the right manuscripts* to show off were seen as necessary socially aspirant qualities. The courtly love genre had provided exactly the language and mode of behaviour needed to impress – something poets like Walter Raleigh, Christopher Marlowe and Edmund Spenser were very keen to do.

In the fourteenth century the Italian poet Petrarch had described in his sonnets his unrequited love for Laura. Indeed, it is Petrarch's poetic treatment of courtly love which is perhaps the most influential in terms of English Renaissance literature. The Petrarchan take on the courtly love convention moves us away from the 'reality' of love as an emotion to thinking about love more as a psycho-social phenomenon influenced by courtly-literary fashion. In his famous Sonnet 130, Shakespeare acknowledges the Petrarchan mode in his wholesale parody* of it: 'My mistress' eyes are nothing like the sun'. Here the volta (the 'twist' or 'turn' in the progress of an argument) saves Shakespeare from thoroughly insulting the silent addressee, instead serving as a brilliant riposte to the inequalities of the Petrarchan mode: 'And yet, by heaven, I think my love as rare / As any she belied with false compare' (p. 2458). In extolling the human, recognizable qualities of his beloved, Shakespeare has turned Petrarchan idealism on its head. His lover is *real*, and, to him, is as unique or 'rare' as the women who are unrealistically depicted ('belied with false compare') in Petrarchan rhetoric.

Shakespeare

Most biographical summaries of Shakespeare begin with a phrase along the lines of 'remarkably little is known about the playwright's life'. In a sense, however, his poems and plays tell us as much as we need to know. To go beyond those in search of elusive autobiographical nuances or echoes is to engage in potentially interesting but fruitless speculation. In a quite brilliant short story called 'Everything and Nothing', the South American writer Jorge Luis Borges expresses how the conflation of the writer and his characters is an inevitable result of the extraordinarily vivid style of Shakespeare's characterization. 'No one', writes Borges, 'has ever been so many men as this man who like the Egyptian Proteus could exhaust all the guises of reality' (p. 77).

The ways in which Shakespeare's texts were produced and distributed can seem quite alien to a twenty-first-century reader or playgoer. The playwright himself wrote a draft set of 'foul papers' which would become, once transcribed and annotated with stage directions, a 'fair copy' which functioned as a prompt book. This would be made available for approval by the Master of

Revels, the man from the Lord Chamberlain's office who had the ultimate power of veto over what could and could not be performed in the London theatres (the three most influential of these were on the South Bank of the Thames: the Rose, the Swan, and the Globe). During Shakespeare's lifetime, individual pamphlet-like versions of some of his plays (called 'Quartos' because of their size – a folio sheet folded to make four leaves or eight pages) were printed but they were not approved by the author and so often contain inaccuracies or inconsistencies. The Quartos might have been transcribed from memory by actors in the plays and then pirated, or could have been taken from notes made by audience members. The first 'complete works' appeared in 1623, some 7 years after Shakespeare's death, and was edited by John Heminges and Henry Condell. Because of its size and shape the edition has become widely known as the 'First Folio'.

The generic subdivisions of Shakespeare's plays which are predominantly in circulation today are derived directly from the First Folio's system of grouping the plays into three categories: comedies, tragedies, and histories. As thinking about genre has developed since the Renaissance, these classifications have increasingly been questioned. At the end of the nineteenth century, in *Shakespeare and His Predecessors*, F. S. Boas coined the term 'Problem Play' to describe those of Shakespeare's plays which have ambiguous endings or which are permeated by serious concerns despite having ostensibly comic main themes. Boas originally intended the term to be applied to *All's Well That Ends Well, Troilus and Cressida, Hamlet*, and *Measure for Measure*, the plays which explore social issues that extend far beyond the immediate lives of their central protagonists*. Perhaps the most famous of these is *Measure for Measure*, a play in which the themes of death, corruption, and tyranny are scarcely offset by moments of light heartedness, and in which the would-be nun Isabella remains ominously silent when the dictatorial Duke asks her to marry him at the end of Act 5. The 'problems' of 'comedies' like this are both ethical and aesthetic.

The role of Isabella, indeed of all of Shakespeare's female characters, is further complicated for us by the fact that until 1660 no women were formally permitted to act on the English public stage; this had an impact on the kinds of female roles dramatists created. The complexities of Shakespeare's female characters would, therefore, have to be conveyed by specially trained boy actors. This was a widely-accepted Renaissance convention but many members of the theatre audience would have been well aware of the paradox* that was appearing onstage where boys dressed as girls, who often, as the plot demanded, disguised themselves as boys in order fully – but temporarily – to participate in public life.

An outbreak of the bubonic plague in 1593 led to the temporary closure of the London theatres in an attempt to contain the spread of this deadly and highly contagious disease. For this period of around eighteen months Shakespeare focused his efforts on poetry, often inspired by his reading of Ovid, and his long, erotic poem *Venus and Adonis* was published. It was followed in 1594 by *The Rape of Lucrece*. Ironically, given today's cultural concentration on Shakespeare's *plays*, these two narrative poems* were the only real bestsellers he knew in his lifetime. Indeed, as Jonathan Bate and Eric Rasmussen, editors of the *Complete Works* (based on the First Folio, and the edition I use throughout this section of *Studying English Literature*), write: 'Shakespeare became famous as a poet before most people knew that he also wrote plays' (p. 2393). The poems for which he is probably best known today, his Sonnets, were also written in the 1590s, but they were not published (and then probably without the poet's supervision) until 1609, although documentary evidence suggests that before then Shakespeare shared some in manuscript* form with friends. The 154 poems that comprise the sequence have been seen by many critics as falling into three groups. Sonnets 1–126 are often discussed as being addressed to a young man of higher social status than the poet (although the addressee of many of the Sonnets after 17 is ambiguous); in them, the speaker meditates on love, desire, commitment, fear, and mortality. A 'dark lady' (a term coined by critics, not by Shakespeare) dominates Sonnets 127–152, which are characterized by a sexual and scornful tone. Sonnets 153 and 154 concern Cupid, 'the little Love-god' (Sonnet 154). For further information about the sequence, start with Colin Burrow's excellent introduction to *The Complete Sonnets and Poems*.

Shakespeare did not only work in isolation but, in keeping with the literary practice of his time, collaborated with several other writers. Indeed, it is possible that his first performed work was one scene in the play *Arden of Faversham* (c. 1590), and at around the same time he may have written sections of the anonymous *Edward the Third*. Bate and Rasmussen suspect co-authorship of sections of 2 and 3 *Henry VI* (probably composed in 1591 and published in 1594 and 1595 respectively); and of several others of his plays, culminating in three plays which he probably co-wrote with John Fletcher between 1612 and 1614: *Cardenio, Henry VIII*, and *The Two Noble Kinsmen*. Shakespeare's dramatic predecessors had experimented with tragic forms before him, and we should be aware that he was, in addition to his collaborators, one of several extremely popular playwrights of the era. Christopher Marlowe, for example, had great success with his *Tamburlaine the Great* in 1587, consolidating this with *Doctor Faustus* a year later. Thomas Kyd had used motifs in his *Spanish Tragedy* (c. 1586) similar to those with which Shakespeare was to experiment in his tragedies of the 1590s, and the tragic mode was continued under King James by John Webster in his bloody and nightmarish plays *The White Devil* (1612) and *The Duchess of Malfi* (1613). Shakespeare's comic dramatic writing should not be considered in isolation, either. Here, it is informative to consider the highly successful career of his immediate contemporary Ben Jonson, perhaps best known today for *Volpone* (1606) and *The Alchemist* (1610). Jonson was also involved in the writing and production of court masques*. These were extravagant and visually stunning short plays put on by the well-connected for the amusement of their peers.

We may be surprised by how some ingredients of Shakespeare's comedies initially appear similar to those of the tragedies. We frequently need to look to the end of the plays to see the differences between them in terms of genre – in comedy obstacles are overcome such that the main characters leave us with a sense that an equilibrium has been achieved, and a happiness restored. By contrast, in tragedy the obstacles have proven insurmountable – even fatal – and while we may leave the theatre with a sense of a rebuilding being promised, we are still dazed by a profound feeling of darkness. Those obstacles are different, too, depending on the type of play it is that we are watching: in a comedy they may be merely minor human shortcomings (vanity, inflexibility, impatience), but in a tragedy these same shortcomings become deadly impediments. The pessimistic world of the tragedies permeates the characters' speeches and actions; in the comedies there is often a playful optimism in the language, and the 'bigger', preoccupying questions of life – Who am I? Who controls my destiny? What does life mean? – do not cast the sinister shadow over the action that they do in the tragedies.

Shakespeare's multifaceted world is, then, both strikingly similar to, and radically different from, our own. In his plays we can identify joy, despair, love, hatred, reconciliation, and loss because they are emotions which we will all, at some point in our lives, experience. In situating Shakespeare's plays in their historical context we can recognize in them characters, plots, and preoccupations which would have had an immediate resonance for their first audiences, and which might have been lost to us without our own careful contextualization. As twenty-first-century literary critics we breathe life into the plays, simultaneously recalling their Renaissance origins and contexts, and seeing in them a fascinating freshness, relevance, and charm.

Further Reading

Greenblatt, Stephen (2005), *Renaissance Self-Fashioning: From More to Shakespeare*. Chicago: Chicago University Press. First published in 1980, this highly influential study examines personal identity in the literature and culture of the English Renaissance; a foundational text of New Historicism.

Hadfield, Andrew (2001), *The English Renaissance, 1500–1620*. Oxford: Blackwell. A useful, clear introduction to the period, divided into four sections: 'A History of the English Renaissance'; 'Writers'; 'Key Texts'; 'Topics'. Also includes a guide to further reading.

Hattaway, Michael (2005), *Renaissance and Reformations: An Introduction to Early*

Modern English Literature. Oxford: Blackwell. An insightful and wide-ranging introductory study. Covers canonical* and less well-known authors and includes extracts from significant texts of the period.

Hebron, Malcolm (2008), *Key Concepts in Renaissance Literature*. Basingstoke: Palgrave. Short, lucid entries on a range of topics, split into sections on 'Contexts', 'Literature' and 'Criticism'.

Hopkins, Lisa, and Matthew Steggle (2006), *Renaissance Literature and Culture*. London: Continuum. An introductory guide to the period from 1533 to 1642; includes a section on critical approaches, a chronology, a glossary, and a guide to further reading.

Norbrook, David (2002), *Poetry and Politics in the English Renaissance* (revised edition). Oxford: Oxford University Press. An important and influential study first published in 1984. Particularly focuses on Sidney, Spenser, Jonson, and early Milton.

'Luminarium (Renaissance English Literature)': http://www.luminarium.org/renlit/. A comprehensive guide to authors and topics of the period.

'Early Modern Resources': http://www.earlymodernweb.org.uk/emr/. A useful gateway site that brings together a wide range of online resources that are all free to access.

Do not forget to keep a record of *all* the texts and websites you look at when researching for an assignment: you will need to list them in your bibliography.

2 The Comedies

Emma L. E. Rees

Chapter Overview

Key Texts

In Heminges and Condell's First Folio, fourteen plays by Shakespeare are presented as 'Comedies'. While it is certainly true that the body-count in them is virtually nil, and while love seems to be the overarching theme uniting the characters, the trajectory of the five acts is such that by the end of Act 3, it can feel as though the action could go either way. It is less a question of how the potential for tragedy in the opening acts is neutralized than one of how the realization of that potential is postponed, as we often leave the plays feeling that a trace of the opening acts' menace endures. This makes the endings of the plays extremely problematic, since behind every dance, celebration, or joyous union lurks the possibility that the disorder of the opening acts may erupt again. The designation of 'comedy' is further complicated by the fact that our modern expectations as to what makes a play 'funny' are probably very different to those of Shakespeare's original audiences. Whereas public entertainment in the Renaissance included bear-baiting and dog-fighting, today we may well find such activities barbaric and unnecessarily cruel. Similarly, what was the stuff of 'comedy' then may not be as amusing to many theatregoers today. However, a careful reading of the comedies can reveal to us complex punning, subtle wit, or even slapstick and crude jokes, which may cause us at the very least to smile.

In this section, we will think about the main characteristics and themes of Shakespeare's comedies before moving on to see how these are apparent in a specific play, *Twelfth Night*. 'Comedy' is incredibly difficult to define. People often talk about 'low' and 'high' comedy: one of the interesting things about Shakespeare's plays is that they combine these two modes. 'Low' comedy can border on farce*, which relies on bawdiness, improbability, and exaggeration; by contrast, 'high' comedy relies on greater linguistic sophistication and more complex characterization. Satire*, the exposé of social ills through their absurdly comic presentation, is one kind of 'high' comedy. Another difficulty in trying to define 'comedy' is that it is highly culturally specific. Put simply, what makes you laugh may not make me laugh at all because I may bring to the joke or situation an entirely different set of cultural experiences and expectations from those you bring to it. So, comedy must be about more than laughter; if we do not find ourselves rolling in the aisles at puns that seemed hilarious to members of Shakespeare's first audiences, then the amusement must come from other sources.

While some of the plays categorized as 'comedies' in the 1623 First Folio might struggle to fulfil many comic criteria, three stand out as being, to some twenty-first-century critics at least, almost impossible to categorize as belonging to the comic genre. They are *The Merchant of Venice* (probably written 1596–97; Quarto 1600); *The Taming of the Shrew* (probably written 1589–92; Folio 1623); and *The Winter's Tale* (probably written 1611; Folio 1623). Indeed, once we start applying our postmodern* sensibilities to the plays, even more of them seem sinister and appalling: *The Tempest* (probably written 1611; Folio 1623); *Measure for Measure* (probably written 1604; Folio 1623); and *Twelfth Night* (probably written 1601; Folio 1623). The rest have a dark undertow: *A Midsummer Night's Dream* (probably written 1595–96; Quarto 1600); *The Two Gentlemen of Verona* (probably written 1591–92; Folio 1623); *The Merry Wives of Windsor* (probably written 1600–01; Quarto 1602); *The Comedy of Errors* (probably written 1594; Folio 1623); *Much Ado about Nothing* (probably written 1598; Quarto 1600); *Love's Labour's Lost* (probably written 1595; Quarto 1598); *As You Like It* (probably written 1599; Folio 1623); and *All's Well That Ends Well* (probably written 1605; Folio 1623).

Repeatedly in the comedies the would-be humour derives from situations where the norms of society have been shaken up. We call this process 'transgression' or inversion, and in Shakespeare's comedies characters repeatedly transgress the gender or class boundaries which society has established for them. This is often done through the use of disguise. So, Viola disguises herself as Cesario in *Twelfth Night*; Portia as Balthasar in *The Merchant of Venice*; and Rosalind as Ganymede in *As You Like It*. Often characters adopt psychological (rather than literal) or more subtle disguises. Thus Katherina *appears* to acquiesce to Petruchio's demands in *The Taming of the Shrew*; Paulina hides Hermione for fifteen years in *The Winter's Tale*; and Isabella substitutes Mariana for herself in the 'bed-trick' in *Measure for Measure*. You will be struck in reading this list of examples by how often disguise is a technique used by Shakespeare's *female* characters. I mentioned in the previous chapter how the roles of female characters in Shakespeare's day were additionally complicated because they were taken by male actors. We see repeatedly in the comedies how female characters must pretend to be men in order to gain access to social worlds where they can make things happen, rather than have things simply happen to them. Tellingly, this transgression is always temporary: for some members of Shakespeare's audience, perhaps, the sight of a woman engaging independently with society would have been more troubling than amusing had the final act of the comedy not reinstated the woman's 'typical' social role, more often than not by marrying her off.

Disguised as men, Shakespeare's female characters adopt new names. More broadly, naming is used by Shakespeare to comic effect. In *Measure for Measure*, for example, the Madam of the Viennese brothel at the centre of Angelo's clean-up campaign is called 'Mistress Overdone'; that her servant is called Pompey Bum does not suggest that he is to be taken seriously. Indeed, Pompey Bum is a clownish character, one of the stock theatrical types on which Shakespeare drew. Similarly, Bottom's literally asinine behaviour in *A Midsummer Night's Dream* (he has been transformed into a man with the head of an ass by Oberon, King of the Fairies) comes as little surprise to an audience who have picked up on his name: the expectation is not that someone called 'Bottom' will be an Athenian senator or a tragic king. In the study of *Twelfth Night* we will be looking at the character of Feste, the 'fool' or 'court jester' figure who wanders with ease between the different households and social worlds of the play. His name, like the play's title, is suggestive of festivity and entertainment. Another Shakespearean fool, Touchstone in *As You Like It*, is a character against whom the behaviour of other characters is measured: the fool may actually expose the foolish vanities or artificialities of others. If we do not understand the important social role that the fool plays, and regard him as a mindless entertainer with little serious comic function, then we might be surprised to find a fool in our analysis of a serious play, *King Lear*. The function of Lear's fool, however, is not unlike that of the other fools we might meet in Shakespeare's plays: he can speak truth and offer guidance in a way which is barred to other characters.

Often Shakespeare interweaves two or more plots, each providing a commentary on the others. We call plots which run concurrently with the main action 'sub-plots'. Both of the plays we will be looking at in more detail in the case studies use their sub-plots to emphasize and enhance the themes and concerns of the main plots. In *Twelfth Night*, as we shall see, while the main characters perform their elaborate rituals of courtship, 'below stairs', as it were, less central characters also pair up. This structural characteristic of the sub-plot is not limited to the comedies, and in *King Lear* the family breakdown experienced by the king is both echoed by and, to some extent, the cause of, Gloucester's own terrible misfortunes at the hands of his son Edmund. In the comedies, sub-plots offer a useful contrasting illustration of the dominant themes of the action. Thus in *A Midsummer Night's Dream* the Athenian Duke Theseus and his wife-to-be Hippolyta have counterparts in Oberon and Titania of the fairy world; their worlds are linked by the antics of the amateur artisanal acting troupe who, in rehearsing a play for the ducal wedding, crash into the magical world of the Athenian woods. In reading any of Shakespeare's comedies, then, it is often informative to think about how seemingly unrelated characters cast a light on the activities of their more prominent counterparts.

Unsurprisingly, Shakespeare delighted in the theatricality of life, and it is the philosophical character Jaques in *As You Like It* who best summarizes this. 'All the world's a stage', he declares, 'And all the men and women merely players' (2.7.142–43) (all my references to Shakespeare's plays are to Bate and Rasmussen's 2007 edition). Jaques' speech, in which he details the metaphorical journey of an individual from cradle to grave, strikes a solemn but familiar note in what is a principally light-hearted play, but it serves well to show how in both his comedies and his tragedies, Shakespeare had an awareness of life as role-playing. The use of the play-within-a-play motif in works as generically diverse as *Hamlet*, *A Midsummer Night's Dream*, and *1 Henry IV* forces us to ask questions about what it means to be a human being with a specific role in a culture or community.

Finally, while we must not read Shakespeare's plays solely in terms of their destinations, the adage that tragedies end with a pile of bodies on the stage, and comedies with a marriage and a dance, seems, broadly speaking, to hold true. In Shakespeare's plays marriage is a source of conflict. It is in the comedies that it most forcefully comes to signify reconciliation and the resumption of social norms. Thus not one but three weddings are celebrated at the conclusion of the problematic comedy *The Taming of the Shrew*; Valentine and Proteus look forward at the end of *The Two Gentlemen of Verona* to their weddings; and in *Much Ado about Nothing*, a dual wedding is arranged. In many comedies revelations come before the anticipated unions: thus in *The Merchant of Venice* (one of the darkest of the First Folio's 'comedies', as I have already pointed out) Portia and Nerissa reveal their ring trick to their new husbands; and in *Twelfth Night* the twins are reunited as Cesario is revealed to be Viola. The feeling we have when we watched one of Shakespeare's comedies, then, is often one of relief at obstacles having been overcome with little injury or pain to any character in which we feel we have made a significant emotional investment. As should by now be becoming clear, however, in some of the comedies this optimistic feeling is not untainted, if the journey to the end of the final act has been particularly fraught: in the 'Case Study' below we will think about this in relation to *Twelfth Night*. Such concerns might strike you when reading others of the 'comedies', too: viewed from a feminist* perspective, for example, the long speech the previously rebellious Katherina gives at the end of *The Taming of the Shrew* presents all kinds of difficulties since her sense of self seems to have been so radically and forcibly changed by the abuses visited upon her by her new husband. Similarly, Isabella's refusal to respond to the Duke's proposal in the final scene of *Measure for Measure* might be interpreted by us as troubling: were this really a comedy (rather than a 'problem play') then we would experience a less ambiguously 'happy ever after' ending than the one that Shakespeare has given us.

Criticism and Literary Theory

There are many books and journal articles which focus on Shakespeare's comedies. In this section I have chosen those texts from the twentieth and early twenty-first centuries which I regard as being the most influential and which demonstrate how differing critical and theoretical approaches can be brought to bear on the plays. Despite these critics' diverging literary-political standpoints, there is a continuum in that later writers do build on (either through incorporation or dismissal of the core tenets) what has gone before. Remember when reading critical texts that no one view necessarily has any more validity than another, provided the writer has made careful, close, and frequent reference to the plays they discuss. You should come up with your own ideas about a play before seeking out what others have published on it. Often this critical or secondary reading will open up possibilities of interpretation which you had not imagined on a first reading.

The classic text in the history of criticism of Shakespeare's comedies is C. L. Barber's *Shakespeare's Festive Comedy: A Study of Dramatic Form and its Relation to Social Custom* (1959). Barber looks at some of Shakespeare's early plays (*A Midsummer Night's Dream, Love's Labour's Lost, As You Like It, The Merchant of Venice, Twelfth Night*, and *Henry IV*) and identifies in them echoes of the patterns and rituals of Elizabethan festivals (Easter, May, Whitsuntide, Midsummer, Harvest, and Christmas) and folk traditions. Barber is keen to separate Shakespeare's comedies, which affirm 'not man's possible perfection but his certain imperfection' (p. 229), from romantic comedies or satire*, and key to the festive traditions he discusses is the carnival. In the period of carnival (we might do well to remember here the Christmas time festival of 'twelfth night') folly is temporarily allowed to rule and opposing forces are brought together so as to produce startling dramatic effects. Thus in the *Henry IV* plays Hal moves easily between 'low' tavern and 'high' palace, engaging both with robbers and with the King. We can apply this idea to other Shakespeare plays, too, seeing how in *Measure for Measure* the world of the prison and the brothel sits cheek-by-jowl with the Ducal palace and the nunnery. In the 'Case Study' below I will consider how Barber's ideas can help us make sense of the many confrontations *Twelfth Night* dramatizes between the rebellious festive spirit of Sir Toby Belch and the puritanical restraint of Malvolio.

We have already seen how difficult it is to come up with one coherent definition of Shakespearean comedy, and the idea of a unifying theme holding together the plays was questioned by Kenneth Muir. In *Shakespeare's Comic Sequence* (1979) he identified significant phases in Shakespeare's comic writing, as the playwright matured, and his awareness of the fluidity of genre and form increased. Muir describes these phases in sections entitled 'Experiment', 'Maturity', 'Problem Comedies', and 'Tragicomedies'. In an earlier work Muir had already differentiated between what he saw as Shakespeare's 'Early Plays' (*Romeo and Juliet, A Midsummer Night's Dream*, and *The Merchant of Venice*); his 'Mature Comedies' (*Much Ado about Nothing, As You Like It*, and *Twelfth Night*); and his 'Problem Plays' (*Troilus and Cressida, All's Well That Ends Well*, and *Measure for Measure*). Muir is alert to how the playwright must guide the audience as to the genre of a drama, writing of Shakespeare's introduction of the clownish Dogberry in *Much Ado* that 'as the play was to be a comedy, Shakespeare had to inform the audience before the church scene that Don John's villainy would come to light; and for this purpose he created Dogberry' (2005, p. 53).

Shakespeare was not a genius working in isolation: like his peers, he was engaging with established literary traditions. Robert Miola has examined how Shakespeare's writing in many ways continues a classical comedic tradition. In *Shakespeare and Classical Comedy: The Influence of Plautus and Terence* (1994) Miola uses the work of Roman playwrights Plautus and Terence, and that of the earlier Greek writer Menander, to show how aware Shakespeare was of comedic convention. These early playwrights 'form and enrich the dialogues that constitute drama in western civilization' (p. 1). Miola looks at the Roman dramatic themes of errors, intrigue, *alazoneia* (arrogance or boastful pride), and romance*, in reading eight of Shakespeare's plays: *The Comedy of Errors, Twelfth Night, The Taming of the Shrew, Much Ado about Nothing, The Merry Wives of Windsor, All's Well That Ends Well, Pericles* (probably written 1608; Quarto 1609), and *The Tempest*. Interestingly, Miola also looks at *Hamlet* and *King Lear* (which are discussed below in the 'Tragedy' section) in a chapter called 'Heavy Plautus': his argument is that in both plays classical comic principles are set up but then 'the whirling progress of the play shatters the inscribed comedic structure' (p. 178). Miola's book is in many ways a continuation of the work started by Leo Salingar in *Shakespeare and the Traditions of Comedy* (1974). Salingar, like Barber, focused on the role of festivities in Shakespeare's comedies, and identified links to classical antecedents. According to

Salingar, connections between characters' disguises and the workings of fate or serendipity are fundamental to the structure of Shakespeare's comedies: 'He uses the convention to draw together the various themes and strands of his plots, to represent an aspect of life outside the theatre, and at the same time to emphasize the immediate reality of the play as stage performance' (pp. 25–26).

In *Friends and Lovers: The Phenomenology of Desire in Shakespearean Comedy* (1985), W. Thomas MacCary follows the male hero's development in the plays from self-absorption, to love of one like him, to love for a disguised woman, to love for the woman who has cast off her disguise. In this psychoanalytical* reading of the comedies, MacCary argues that so great is the power of love that only by experiencing it can characters delineate their own identities: 'the lover comes into being as a conscious subject by his pursuit of an object' (p. 107). He focuses particularly on the power of those characters who are girls-disguised-as-boys, who reflect back on the amorous heroes a non-threatening version of masculinity (some feminist* critics have argued that this is an extremely limited kind of 'power' as the female characters are objectified in MacCary's account), and uses Freud's texts 'Of Mourning and Melancholia' and 'On Narcissism' to illuminate the relationship of *Twelfth Night*'s particularly self-reflexive lovers. On the journey to heterosexual union and a harmonious ending for the comedies, then, the male protagonists* journey through a period of indeterminacy and homosocial* (if not actually homosexual) desire.

Valerie Traub also engaged with this idea of same-sex desire in the comedies in *Desire and Anxiety: Circulations of Sexuality in Shakespearean Drama* (1992). Barbara Freedman, too, uses psychoanalysis* as a theoretical framework in *Staging the Gaze: Postmodernism, Psychoanalysis, and Shakespearean Comedy* (1991). She brings to the plays a wealth of critical insights, employing film theory, feminism*, cultural materialism*, and psychoanalysis* (particularly the ideas of the French philosopher Jacques Lacan), as her tools. Freedman uses contemporary documents to reconstruct the specific cultural character of the Renaissance; such documents are often scientific, to do with vision and perspective. Seeing, not seeing, and pretending to see are key to the comedies and the experience of watching them, according to Freedman's argument, since 'by tracing [. . .] misrecognitions, Shakespearean comedy centers and decenters the subject as it circles about in fantasied appropriation of its mirror image, thereby staging the rivalry between ego and persona in the construction of subjectivity' (p. 35). We can see these uncertainties at work in a play such as *Twelfth Night*, where the twins' identities are repeatedly mistaken; whatever makes 'Viola' essentially 'Viola' seems not to be fixed, but to be constructed out of others' attitudes, opinions, and beliefs. Such a fluid notion of subjectivity should be familiar to us as we watch the play: think about the versions of yourself that you project according to setting. The language you use in front of your lecturers, for example, is almost certainly different from that which you adopt when with a group of your friends; your 'persona' is made up of a myriad of subtle characteristics which are influenced by circumstance and audience. Shakespeare delighted in the dramatic exaggeration of this idea.

R. W. Maslen, in *Shakespeare and Comedy* (2005), examines how Shakespeare responded to contemporary critics (like Stephen Gosson) who complained about what they perceived to be the immorality of comic drama. Indeed, 'from the 1570s onwards, playwrights seemed to take a perverse delight in dramatizing Gosson's fears about the deleterious effects of comedy' (p. 39). Maslen shows how plays like *The Two Gentlemen of Verona* and *The Comedy of Errors* are actually 'tragic-comedies', observing that an atmosphere of aggression or of looming tragedy is present, a fact that he attributes to the hostility to the form shown by Gosson and other detractors. He illustrates this idea by showing how very close in themes, characterization and setting are *The Two Gentlemen of Verona* and *Romeo and Juliet*. Maslen's book is a superb and accessible study of the context, reception, and themes of Shakespeare's comedies.

Finally, a text which brings together over half a century of criticism on Shakespeare's plays is Russ McDonald's edited volume *Shakespeare: An Anthology of Criticism and Theory* (2004). Every important English language critic is excerpted here, and the dominant theoretical movements of the last 60 years are represented too. Thus one can read sections from Northrop Frye and Barber on comedy as well as dipping into psychoanalytical*, feminist*, or postcolonial* approaches to the plays.

The same plays, then, produce wildly differing critical interpretations. The raw material of the comedies affords us the opportunity to take to them whatever critical tools seem to us to be most appropriate or interesting. While you may not agree that psychoanalysis* is a useful tool for thinking about the plays, or while you may not see the relevance of using 'carnival' as a way into understanding them, you are free to find a critical angle that you find rewarding and which, importantly, you can adopt and adapt in formulating your *own* responses to the plays' vivid worlds.

 Twelfth Night

Twelfth Night can be seen as a 'typical' Shakespearean comedy, not least because of its potential for revealing to us, in the midst of the humour, some important truths about the darker side of life. As with so many of

Shakespeare's plays, plots interweave in a rich and illuminating way. As the play opens we are presented with the figure of a young man who, it is quickly ascertained, is a Duke. Rather than being a powerful, authoritative figure, however, this Duke has been rendered powerless by his unrequited love for the beautiful Olivia. 'If music be the food of love', he reflects as the play opens, 'play on': he wants to feed his melancholy pining for the unattainable countess (1.1.1). Underpinning this quickly established theme of romantic love is the idea of the extraordinary power of sibling love; the reason why Olivia will not return Orsino's affections is that she is in mourning for her drowned brother. Into this plot comes the recently shipwrecked figure of Viola. Landing in Illyria, Viola (incidentally also believing that she has lost her brother, Sebastian, to the sea) decides to disguise herself as a young man, Cesario, so as to protect herself in a strange land.

We have already considered how important disguise – both literal and psychological – is in Shakespeare's comedies. When Olivia falls in love with Cesario, we can begin to understand why the play is ripe for psychological interpretation. Who is it that Olivia has fallen for? Can she really be so shallow as to have fallen for Cesario merely on the basis of 'his' appearance? The question would have been even more pressing for members of Shakespeare's original audience because, you will recall, Viola was played by a boy actor, so we have a boy playing a girl, acting as a boy, who in turn is desired by a boy actor pretending to be a female character called Olivia. We might choose in our interpretation of the play, then, to consider latent and frustrated homosexual desires, or we may believe that in performance such gender confusion is merely comedic. Meanwhile, Viola-as-Cesario has fallen for Orsino, who loves Olivia, believing Viola to be a boy. Several times Viola's cover is almost blown when she is disguised as Cesario. 'Now Jove in his next commodity of hair send thee a beard' (3.1.32), says the wise and mysterious fool, Feste, to Cesario, hinting that he sees through Viola's disguise and knows that he is not talking to a 'real' man.

Indeed, Feste, Olivia's jester, is a fascinating character whose ambiguous social status allows him to slip easily between households, classes, and characters. When other characters would be ill-advised to make candid observations about powerful people like Olivia and Orsino, Feste's unusual status allows him to do just that. 'Good madonna, why mourn'st thou?' (1.5.49), asks Feste of the recently bereaved Olivia. What may on first hearing seem to be an insensitive and unnecessary question (especially since it is followed by Feste's declaration that he believes Olivia's brother's 'soul' to be 'in hell' (1.5.51)) actually takes on a forceful logic of its own: if Olivia's brother has really gone to heaven then he is in a better place so it is not necessary to mourn for him. 'Take away the fool, gentlemen' (1.5.54), declares Feste of Olivia. Olivia understands Feste's point; her unbendingly humourless steward, Malvolio, however, does not. He does not appreciate the peculiar philosophizing of Feste, and he envies the intimacy this 'barren rascal' (1.5.62) has with Olivia.

It is precisely this inflexibility and bitterness which makes the cold Malvolio the victim of a practical joke arranged by a group of the other characters. Malvolio is tricked into believing that Olivia desires him, so wears an absurdly and uncharacteristically colourful outfit of cross garters and yellow stockings. Olivia, however, scorns him, and he is temporarily imprisoned by the other characters, led by Olivia's boisterous relative, Sir Toby Belch. The treatment these characters mete out to Malvolio can, depending on the decisions made by director and actors, seem utterly disproportionate when set against Malvolio's actions against them. However, Robert Miola argues that Malvolio, the *agelast* (someone who experiences a sense of humour failure), is a stock comic figure who is laughable in his intransigence. 'Feste's quicksilver changes', writes Miola, 'contrast with Malvolio's idiotic performance previously, his laborious and unsuccessful metamorphosis into a smiling lover. Feste [. . .] has the ability to act, to lose one self (but not one's self) and become another; Malvolio remains rigidly himself, even in cross garters and yellow stockings' (p. 46). Using Miola's assertion we can see how the play is concerned with the clash of opposites: while Feste is comfortable in unpredictable situations, Malvolio, by contrast, is not, as his natural habitat is one of order and logicality. Even when he *tries* to step outside of this persona, Malvolio fails, providing the other characters (and, indeed, members of the audience too) with a source of entertainment as they take a vindictive delight in his failure.

The name of the play, along with its subtitle of *What You Will*, offers another possible reason for the animosity between Malvolio and the group made up of Sir Toby, his friend Sir Andrew Aguecheek, Feste, and Olivia's maid Maria. The title *Twelfth Night* probably refers to the Christian festival of the Epiphany, the 6th of January, the day which marked the coming of the magi (the Three Wise Men) to visit Jesus. 'Epiphany' derives from the Greek 'epiphainein', which means 'to manifest, show, or reveal'. Having read the play we should be able to see straight away how important such themes of revelation are. At the play's conclusion, for example, Cesario is revealed to be Viola, and Orsino can at last reveal his love for her; Olivia, too, can legitimize her potentially problematic desires (remember that she is in love with a woman whom she believes to be a man) when Sebastian, Viola's twin brother, is revealed to be alive and well.

The setting of the play at this time of year has other important implications, and Barber's *Shakespeare's Festive Comedy* (1959) is useful in this context. If you think about your behaviour at festive times of the year (Christmas, Chanukah, Eid, Diwali, or similar), you may note that you over-eat, sleep in late, or watch too much TV. Were you to behave in such a 'festive' way all year round you would not get a lot of studying done. Societies and communities function, then, because of a shared awareness of when the 'letting off steam' festive times are, and when the 'getting back to everyday life' secular times are. Twelfth night marks the shift from one of these phases of being to another; from festivity to the everyday. While Malvolio is relieved to see an end to what he regards as the riotous partying he has observed in Olivia's house, however, other characters who revel in excess – Sir Toby and Sir Andrew – want to hang on to the party atmosphere for as long as possible. Malvolio's frosty resistance to this – 'My masters, are you mad?' he asks, 'Do ye make an alehouse of my lady's house?' (2.3.66, 68) – is one key reason why the other characters seek such a humiliating revenge on him as they do.

We can, then, be creative in our interpretations of the play. Following Barber, we might perceive the characters to symbolize opposite ends of the festive spectrum, choosing to read Malvolio, for example, less as a 'real person' with thoughts and feelings than as an embodiment of ideas. We might decide, perhaps having read the psychoanalytical* approach of MacCary, that sexuality is key to understanding the play. Thus Orsino comes across as a ruler weakened by his love for the idea of Olivia and confused by his desires for Cesario – this confusion is, of course, legitimated by the rapid pairing off at the end of the play once Sebastian has reappeared and Viola has shed her disguise. Renaissance, modern or postmodern* approaches have an applicability and a resonance when applied to specific moments in the play. Take Orsino's address to Cesario in Act 1, for example:

> they shall yet belie thy happy years,
> That say thou art a man: Diana's lip
> Is not more smooth and rubious, thy small pipe
> Is as the maiden's organ, shrill and sound,
> And all is semblative a woman's part. (1.4.30–34)

This moment in the play might be played just for laughs: Viola might fear that her disguise is about to be revealed (Feste, as we have seen, also plays with this fear); perhaps we might interpret the 'small pipe', 'maiden's organ' and 'woman's part' as some members of Shakespeare's own audience would have done, as bawdy jokes about genitalia. But we might think that the humour of this speech is secondary to its socio-political resonances: Orsino, we might argue, is unconsciously expressing a repressed desire for the young man who stands before him. It is a desire, of course, on which he cannot act in the heteronormative* confines of Illyria. Alternatively we might pursue the reference to the Roman goddess 'Diana' in Orsino's speech, recalling that Elizabeth I was sometimes compared to her, and investigating the importance of her association in popular mythology with chastity, hunting and the moon. These five lines alone could, in theory – and *with* theory – unlock for us the dominant concerns of the entire play.

Finally, in thinking about what the characteristics of a 'comedy' are, we must consider the play's ending. On the surface of things, *Twelfth Night* is a play that ends happily ever after, with a dance and a double wedding. The characters from the upper classes appear to have found happiness: the Duke with Viola, and the Countess with Sebastian; additionally, Maria and Sir Toby are married. However, as with so many of Shakespeare's comedies, there may well be a bitter after-taste in our mouths if we think about which characters are *not* in a celebratory mood at the end of the play. A minor, yet important character, Antonio, for example, has been shown throughout the action to be a faithful friend of Sebastian. Some critics have, with justification, identified his love for Sebastian as homosexual desire ('I do adore thee', he says in Act 2). If the end of the play is about the reinstatement of dominant ideologies after a period of relative chaos, however, then the heterosexual status quo celebrated by the two central marriages does not allow a space for Antonio, and so we are left wondering what becomes of him. Another character who troubles our sense of comfortable closure at the play's end is, of course, Malvolio. The last words we hear him utter – 'I'll be revenged on the whole pack of you' (5.1.360) – can, if we allow them to, cast a threatening shadow over the supposed happiness of the concluding moments. The ending of a comedy by Shakespeare often implicitly complicates the more explicit sense of completeness and harmony.

Further Reading

Atkin, Graham (2008), *'Twelfth Night': Character Studies*. London: Continuum. A very good introduction to the play. Each major character is considered in detail as Atkin explores how the playwright makes them both credible and entertaining.

Bate, Jonathan (2009), *Soul of the Age: The Life, Mind and World of William Shakespeare*. Harmondsworth: Penguin. An important intellectual biography by the co-editor of the recent Macmillan/RSC edition of the *Complete Works*; pays close attention to Shakespeare's cultural contexts.

Dutton, R., and Jean E. Howard (eds) (2005), *A Companion to Shakespeare's Works, Volume III: The Comedies*. Oxford: Blackwell. Examines Shakespeare's comedies from a variety of critical positions. François Laroque's 'Shakespeare's Festive Comedy' is a reassessment and updating of C. L. Barber's influential work. Phyllis Rackin contributes a compelling essay on 'Shakespeare's Crossdressing Comedies', and in 'Shakespeare's Comic Geographies' Garrett A. Sullivan investigates how 'errors' in Shakespeare's geographical accuracy should be reconsidered as deliberate imaginative and symbolic dramatic devices.

Leggatt, A. (ed.) (2002), *The Cambridge Companion to Shakespearean Comedy*.

Cambridge: Cambridge University Press. A recent, accessible introduction. Leggatt's contributors examine the comic tradition out of which Shakespeare wrote, and look at specific comic themes and motifs in his plays. David Galbraith's essay 'Theories of Comedy' is a useful starting point for understanding the classical origins and definitions of 'comedy', and how these impacted on Shakespeare's writing.

McDonald, Russ (ed.) (2004), *Shakespeare: An Anthology of Criticism and Theory* Oxford: Blackwell. Every important English-language critic is excerpted here, and the dominant theoretical movements of the last sixty years are represented too.

Smith, Emma (ed.) (2003), *Shakespeare's Comedies: A Guide to Criticism*. Oxford: Blackwell. After an overview of how critics from Shakespeare's day to the twentieth century have talked about his plays, the book is divided into sections on genre, language, gender and sexuality, history and politics, and performance.

'Touchstone': http://www.touchstone.bham.ac.uk/. An online tool for Shakespeare research; particularly useful for students is the information on past, current, and future Shakespeare productions.

'Bardbox': http://bardbox.wordpress.com/. A website that brings together 'some of the best and most interesting of original Shakespeare-related videos' available online; includes a wide range of material divided into categories from 'Animation' to 'Feature films' to 'Rap'.

Do not forget to keep a record of *all* the texts and websites you look at when researching for an assignment: you will need to list them in your bibliography.

3 The Tragedies

Emma L. E. Rees

Key Texts

Twelve of the plays reproduced in the 1623 First Folio were called 'Tragedies' by the editors. The earliest (in terms of the date of composition) is *Titus Andronicus* (in all likelihood written in 1591–92; first being performed and appearing in Quarto in 1594). *Romeo and Juliet* came next (1595–96; Quarto 1600). The composition of *Hamlet* can be dated to 1600–01 (it was printed in a Quarto edition in 1603 and again in 1604–05); *Troilus and Cressida* was probably written in 1601–02 (it appeared in Quarto in 1609); *Othello* was written in 1604 (Quarto 1622); and *King Lear* in 1605–06 (it was performed in 1606, and was published in Quarto in 1608). Six of the tragedies were first published in the 1623 Folio: *Julius Caesar* (probably written in 1599); *Antony and Cleopatra* (probably written in 1606–07); *Timon of Athens* (composed 1605); *Macbeth* (probably written in 1606); *Coriolanus* (which probably dates from 1608); and *Cymbeline* (probably written in 1610). Recent editors and critics have redefined the genres of some of these plays – and of two in particular. *Cymbeline* is often classified as a 'Romance' (the term is less to do with love or affection than it is to do with a chivalric, courtly love tradition); *Troilus and Cressida* is reclassified too. In *Cymbeline* optimism certainly outweighs tragedy, thanks in no small part to the extraordinarily strong Imogen, and only the repulsive character, Cloten, dies. Of all Shakespeare's plays *Troilus and Cressida* is perhaps the most difficult to pin down in terms of genre. This Trojan tale is more properly thought of as a 'problem play' but the satirical treatment of both lovers and soldiers can verge on the comic in performance.

Many of Shakespeare's tragic heroes have their origins in Classical or Chronicle histories. *Hamlet, Cymbeline, King Lear* and *Macbeth* have some similarities with characters described in the sixteenth-century chronicler Raphael Holinshed's works. The Roman plays (*Titus Andronicus, Julius Caesar, Antony and Cleopatra,* and *Coriolanus*) owe a considerable debt to the writings of the Greek historian Plutarch, as does *Timon of Athens.* Finally, the writings of the Italian writer 'Cinthio' (Giovanni Battista Giraldi) provided source material for both *Othello* and *Romeo and Juliet.*

The great Shakespearean critic G. Wilson Knight wrote in his influential *The Wheel of Fire* (1930) that 'the wonder of Shakespearian tragedy is ever a mystery – a vague, yet powerful, tangible, presence; an interlocking of the mind with a profound meaning, a disclosure to the inward eye of vistas undreamed and but fitfully understood' (p. 182). This is a powerful claim that deserves our attention: can watching one of Shakespeare's tragedies really have such a profound psychological effect on us as Knight seems here to suggest? For many critics and commentators it is the theory of tragedy advocated by the Greek writer and philosopher Aristotle that most easily explains how a Shakespearean tragedy can enter our consciousness at such a deep level that it has an almost transformative impact on who we are. Key here are ideas of *peripateia** and *catharsis**. Central, too, is the notion of the main protagonist's* 'fatal flaw' – a psychological weakness or predisposition present in the great men (and I use that word 'men' advisedly) of whom Shakespeare writes.

In an Aristotelian tragedy circumstances seem to conspire to make the central character's flaw let loose an unstoppable torrent of destruction. However, while Aristotle also tells us about the three dramatic 'unities' (of time, place, and action) which characterize tragedy, we may be less able to define these in Shakespeare's plays, some of which ignore them altogether. Another influence on Shakespeare's tragic writing was the Roman playwright Seneca. The Senecan mode of revenge tragedy incorporated ghosts, witches, and bloody acts of violence. Shakespeare's earliest tragedy *Titus Andronicus*, in its extreme violence and bleak portrayal of human endeavours, certainly owes much to the Senecan tradition. In some ways, too, this play functions as a blueprint for the later and more mature *King Lear*, the subject of this chapter's 'Case Study'.

Shakespeare's tragedies follow the misfortunes of a central figure. That central man (and it is almost always a male character who is the main focus of the action) will often be someone in a position of power, but someone whose experiences are on some level recognizable for members of the audience. Thus Lear is a king, but he seeks reassurance that his daughters love him; Othello is a leading military figure but he suffers from extreme jealousy; Hamlet is a prince, but he cannot commit to a course of action when circumstances demand he make specific choices. So familiar to us are less extreme versions of these human imperfections and follies (insecurity, jealousy, indecision) that we find ourselves caught up in, or identifying with, the emotional worlds of the characters.

A key device Shakespeare employs precisely to cause us to identify with the characters is the soliloquy*. Some of the most accomplished soliloquies Shakespeare wrote appear in his tragedies, and some of these have taken on a life of their own in the popular imagination. Thus many Westerners would know the opening words of Hamlet's 'To be or not to be' speech without knowing necessarily where it comes from, and the same is true of Macbeth's 'Is this a dagger which I see before me?' There is a universality to great soliloquies like these that urges us to be moved by, or to recognize, the thought processes being revealed to us (both of the examples quoted shows a man desperately trying to gear himself up to do something he knows at a fundamental psychological level to be morally wrong).

Shakespeare's tragic heroes, then, require from us an emotional investment and their actions profoundly impact on our responses to the play. I have already mentioned the Aristotelian notion of *peripateia** as a characteristic of Shakespeare's tragedies. For Romeo and Juliet, for example, the world seems a happy place as they lie in their marital bed, and Juliet's greatest concern is to convince Romeo to stay longer: 'Wilt thou be gone?' she asks him, 'It is not yet near day. / It was the nightingale, and not the lark, / That pierced the fearful hollow of thine ear' (3.5.1–3). The lovers' happiness is soon reversed, however, and the play ends with them both dead. As *Titus Andronicus* opens, the hero is triumphant, having defeated the Goths; by the end of the play he has murdered his son Mutius, his beloved daughter Lavinia, and is himself slain. Othello's joy at his military promotion and his marriage to Desdemona is short-lived as his aide, Iago, poisons his mind, preying on his predisposition to insecurity and worthlessness. Othello kills his wife before turning his knife on himself to, as he puts it, smite 'the circumcisèd dog' (5.2.398).

*Peripateia** comes about for a variety of reasons: forces extrinsic to the protagonist* appear to conspire against him. Thus Coriolanus is rejected by the plebeians who cannot overcome their distrust of the Senate, and in *Timon of Athens* Timon, as the philosophical Apemantus warns him, is deceived by insincere friends. Additionally, the hero will – and this is the idea of the 'fatal flaw' – take ill-advised courses of action which contribute to the calamities that befall him. Othello's own insecurities and possessiveness lead him to believe the rabidly deceitful and self-seeking figure of the Machiavellian Iago, and Cymbeline has to endure much on account of his psychological failings, relying on his daughter Imogen for the play's happy ending. Finally, a supernatural force is often blamed in these plays for the moment of *peripateia**:

Macbeth focuses responsibility for the events which befall him not on his own greed and ambition, but on the three witches, and Gloucester, in *King Lear*, instead of recognizing how poor a judge of character he is, initially blames Fate, here personified by the gods: 'As flies to wanton boys are we to th' gods: / They kill us for their sport' (4.1.41–42).

If all that the tragedies left us with was a sense of emptiness and doom, however, they would not make for particularly enlightening viewing. Aristotle's ideas about *catharsis** can help us to understand why watching the appalling sufferings of characters with whom we feel an emotional bond is not only a worthwhile but also a necessary process. While as spectators of the tragedies we experience strong emotions of pity and fear, we also undergo a release of emotional tension: we have witnessed terrible distress but, crucially, we have come through it. This experience of fear being purged renews us spiritually: we have undergone a process of *catharsis**. Thus in *Hamlet* we may mourn the death of an intelligent and troubled young man, but we are also reassured by Fortinbras requesting full military honours for Hamlet, and by Horatio waiting to recount the full story of what has happened. More young lives are lost in *Romeo and Juliet* but as the play draws to a close we sense that a community previously split by ancient feuding will now unite – as the Prince declares in the last speech of the play, 'a glooming peace this morning with it brings' (5.3.315). That notion of 'a glooming peace', apparently paradoxical (we might even say oxymoronic*) as it is, neatly sums up the ambiguity of the tragedies' endings: they simultaneously offer us darkness and redemption. It is the redemption which enables us to enjoy the *catharsis** or purging of the gloom.

A. C. Bradley made the point that in Shakespeare's tragedies the suffering extends beyond the hero. The price of his thwarted ambition is despair and death not only for himself but, in a domino-like effect, for those around him too. In *Titus Andronicus* it is not only the eponymous* hero who dies, but his daughter, sons, and son-in-law too. Add to this Titus' enemy Tamora, Tamora's husband, her three sons, a nurse and a clown, and we see that the ripple-effect of the tragedy is deeply inscribed. We can trace similar patterns in others of the tragedies too: morally good and bad characters die alike, and the barbarity of those deaths can strike us forcefully. Titus, Romeo, Julius Caesar, Hamlet, Cordelia, Desdemona, Macbeth, and Coriolanus are murdered; Juliet, Ophelia, Othello, Lady Macbeth, and Antony and Cleopatra take their own lives; and Lear dies of grief.

Earlier in this section I quoted from G. Wilson Knight's *The Wheel of Fire*. The book's title comes from *King Lear*: 'I am bound', the King says upon being reunited with his daughter, Cordelia, 'Upon a wheel of fire, that mine own tears / Do scald like molten lead' (4.6.46–48). Shakespeare's tragedies can – and do – have a profound effect on us precisely because that imaginary wheel, and the torturous progress of fate or fortune it represents, cannot be stopped from turning. Watching *Romeo and Juliet* we might inwardly scream 'No!' when Romeo – believing mistakenly that Juliet is dead – drinks the poison, but the power of the tragedies is that there is nothing we can do but watch. As Edmund, realizing that all his scheming has come to nothing, declares shortly before the end of *King Lear*, 'The wheel is come full circle' (5.3.187).

Criticism and Literary Theory

Scholarly work on Shakespeare's tragedies has had just such a long and varied history as we saw in the section on critical works on the comedies. A key point of disagreement for critics is whether the characters of the tragedies should be thought about as though they were 'real' people. Should we worry about what these characters were doing before the play began? Or what might happen to them once the play has drawn to a close? A number of critics have seen character as just one ingredient in a tragic whole; others direct their readers to find meaning in the power of Shakespeare's language alone. In the twentieth- and twenty-first centuries, feminist* critics have returned to Shakespeare's tragic women, understanding them not merely as support acts to the headline male characters, but instead as significant in their own right. If male characters can engage in evil acts which precipitate their downfalls then what does it mean when female characters appear to transgress Renaissance expectations by engaging in evil deeds? In this section I look at a variety of works on Shakespeare's tragedies which have, for one reason or another, been particularly influential and enduring.

Probably the most important study remains A. C. Bradley's *Shakespearean Tragedy: Lectures on 'Hamlet', 'Othello', 'King Lear' and 'Macbeth'* (1904). Bradley's thinking had at its base the Aristotelian formulation of tragedy, particularly the idea that the main protagonist* has a 'fatal flaw', a personality trait which will be exacerbated by the action of the play, and which ultimately will lead to his downfall. As a tragedy opens, Bradley argued, we are presented with an exposition, a scene-setting; next, conflicts arise; and finally there is a catastrophic finale. That fatal flaw means that the protagonist* is not solely at the mercy of external forces, but is at least in part responsible for his own fate. What can make a tragedy particularly compelling is when the character's fate seems disproportionately harsh compared with his flaw. *King Lear* is an example of this, and Bradley wrote that the play had a 'peculiar greatness' because of its 'mass and variety of intense experience which it contains; the interpenetration of sublime imagination, piercing pathos*, and humour almost as moving as the pathos*; the vastness of the convulsion both of nature and of human passion' (p. 247).

The tragedies are also considered in G. Wilson Knight's *The Wheel of Fire*. Knight responds to the plays imaginatively and almost spiritually as he argues that the atmospheres they invoke are at least as important as plots and characters: these are all part of the same dramatic scheme. We might find Knight's tone not one that we are used to when we read a work of literary criticism because it often reads like creative writing in its own right. For example: 'Each incident, each turn of thought, each suggestive symbol* throughout *Macbeth* or *King Lear* radiates inwards from the play's circumference to the burning central core without knowledge of which we shall miss their relevance and necessity' (p. 11). Knight's ambition was to 'get to the heart' of the plays (p. 11), a 'heart' of death in *Hamlet*; of evil in *Macbeth*; and of negation versus creation in *Othello*. He also made some important claims about the issues of genre in his chapter on '*King Lear* and the Comedy of the Grotesque'. '[T]here is a humour that treads the brink of tears', he wrote, 'and tragedy which needs but an infinitesimal shift of perspective to disclose the varied riches of comedy' (p. 181). Knight discussed at length the four major tragedies (*Hamlet, Macbeth, King Lear,* and *Othello*) as well as considering *Troilus and Cressida, Measure for Measure, Julius Caesar,* and *Timon of Athens*. *The Wheel of Fire* is a remarkably readable, idiosyncratic and important milestone in the history of the criticism (or, to use Knight's preferred term, the 'interpretation') of Shakespeare's tragedies.

Just three years after Knight published his influential work, another critic, L. C. Knights, published a long essay called 'How Many Children Had Lady Macbeth? An Essay in the Theory and Practice of Shakespeare Criticism' (1964), which was a critique of what Knights regarded as the speculative and ultimately unproductive interpretative tendencies of A. C. Bradley (who had famously asked in *Shakespearean Tragedy*, 'Where was Hamlet at the time of his father's death?' (p. 403)). Knights attempted to shift the focus of criticism of Shakespeare's tragedies away from thinking about Shakespeare's characters as though they were 'real people' and towards considering 'themes' as larger structural and symbolic* entities instead. He emphasized the importance of paying close attention to the language of Shakespeare's plays. 'We have to elucidate the meaning', he wrote, 'and to unravel ambiguities; we have to estimate the kind and quality of the imagery and determine the precise degree of evocation of certain figures [. . .] we have to decide exactly why the lines "are so and not otherwise" ' (1966, pp. 16–17). Indeed, Knights treats the Elizabethan audience as though they were literary interpreters themselves, with 'an educated interest in words, a passionate concern for the possibilities of language and the subtleties of poetry' (p. 17). Elsewhere, in a refinement of his critical stance, Knights emphasizes in a brilliant analysis of *Hamlet* what he regards as the importance of moving away from a Bradley-ite character-based analysis: 'Hamlet's state of mind', he writes, 'the Hamlet consciousness, is revealed not only at the level of formulable motive, but in its obscure depths; and it is revealed through the poetry' (p. 192).

Half a century after Bradley's pioneering *Shakespearean Tragedy* the structuralist* critic Northrop Frye published *The Anatomy of Criticism* (1957). In this he set out five phases through which a tragedy passes. Even though his ideas are now themselves more than half a century old they can still provide us with a useful framework for thinking about Shakespeare's tragedies. The first phase is 'Encroachment'. Here the central protagonist* embarks on an ill-judged course of action which exceeds their given social role. Having set out on their mistaken path the protagonist* enters a phase of 'Complication'; obstacles appear which will, in his or her attempt to overcome them, lead to the protagonist's* tragic demise. The futility of this project necessitates a period of 'Reversal', where just how ill-judged the initial course of action was becomes painfully clear. The dramatic drive is towards a phase of inevitable 'Catastrophe'; the personal and wider tragic effects are intensely felt. Finally, as the play closes, a bittersweet 'Recognition' is effected. The protagonist* undergoes a poignant and vivid realization of his or her mistaken path and beliefs, and the play draws to a salutary end. In reading Shakespeare's tragedies we can identify these phases which serve to provide a structure for thinking about all of the plays, no matter how different they on first reading appear to be.

Echoes of Frye's tragic phases can be seen in Tom McAlindon's *Shakespeare's Tragic Cosmos* (1991), in which he argues that Shakespeare's tragedies have chaos at their core. The protagonist's* personal or microcosmic world is thrown into a disarray which is picked up and mirrored by the macrocosm, family or state. For McAlindon, then, the natural and supernatural worlds work in tandem in these plays both to echo and to exacerbate the hero's agonies. Cristina León Alfar's *Fantasies of Female Evil: The Dynamics of Gender and Power in Shakespearean Tragedy* (2003) is a feminist* re-evaluation of how in five of his plays (*Romeo and Juliet*, *King Lear*, *Macbeth*, *Antony and Cleopatra*, and *The Winter's Tale*) Shakespeare created female characters who have traditionally been thought of as 'evil'. Alfar uses Renaissance conduct books as one way in to understanding the complexities of Shakespeare's female characters. Thus 'Lady Macbeth's encouragement of her husband's regicide [may be read] as Shakespeare's parodic depiction of wifely duty. Set within a structure of power dependent on violence for stability, Lady Macbeth's behavior adheres to rather than transgresses her gender role' (p. 113). This is an unorthodox approach to the character, and one which demands of us as critics either an agreement or a rejection. Indeed, one of the joys of reading criticism of Shakespeare's plays is that we are empowered – *if* we know the plays themselves well enough – to situate ourselves in the critical debate, bringing to it our own interests and interpretations, and representing our own views forcibly in response to that criticism which has gone before. This is an approach perhaps most clearly exemplified by postcolonial* critics who have found a relevance and inspiration in Shakespeare's tragedies, acknowledging their composition at a time of global expansion, exploration, and colonization, while simultaneously stressing their relevance to our own diverse and, at times, racist and oppressive world. As Ania Loomba and Martin Orkin put it: 'we must not flatten the past by viewing it entirely through the lens of our own assumptions and imperatives. However, neither is it desirable, or even possible, entirely to unhook the past from the present' (pp. 5–6). Once again, it would seem that to understand Shakespeare's work we must look both to his contemporary context and to our own.

 ### King Lear

King Lear is perhaps the greatest of Shakespeare's tragedies. Its key theme is family breakdown and it asks important questions about the origins of evil and about the role of an individual's free will in an unpredictable universe where the possibility of the existence of a benign divinity is often called into question. Set in ancient Britain and based on an anonymous late sixteenth-century play, *The True Chronicle History of King Leir and his Three Daughters*, *King Lear* taps into Renaissance ideas about the interrelatedness of all things in its examination of the relationship between the individual and the cosmos. On a microcosmic (a 'microcosm' is a 'local', small-scale version or reproduction of the wider universe) level, the family, the building-block of patriarchy*, is in jeopardy; this resonates in the macrocosm, where storms rage as though they are both directly caused by, and echoing, human suffering. Knights argued that '*King Lear* has the three characteristics of the very greatest works of art: it is timeless and universal; it has a crucial place in its author's inner biography; and it marks a moment of great importance in the changing consciousness of the civilization to which it belongs' (1964, p. 74). We will now briefly turn to the play in an attempt to understand why, for Knights and other critics, it is such an influential tragedy.

King Lear is very much in keeping with the bloody Jacobean* plays that were in vogue in the early years of the sixteenth century. In *Macbeth* we do not witness the murder of Duncan, the smothering of Desdemona in *Othello* is bloodless, and the poisonings and stabbings at the end of *Hamlet* take place in a courtly, duel-like setting. However, the barbarity of the violence meted out in *King Lear* as Gloucester's eyes are torn out onstage is without parallel: 'Out, vile jelly!' snarls Cornwall as he prises out Gloucester's remaining eye at Regan's instigation, 'Where is thy lustre now?' (3.7.88–89). In *Titus Andronicus*, the early play that in some important ways functions as a kind of literary draft for the much later *King Lear*, we see the after-effects of the rape and mutilation of Lavinia, but the acts themselves are consigned, mercifully, to the stage's wings. In Trevor Nunn's acclaimed 2007 RSC production of *King Lear*, starring Ian McKellen in the lead role, Gloucester's eyes were forced out mid-stage and, as though to heighten the drama's exposure of inhumanity, Lear's Fool was hanged onstage too.

Indeed, the Fool is a key character who has much preoccupied critics. Like the clown, Feste, in *Twelfth Night*, Lear's Fool has access to truths to which other characters are often oblivious, offering, paradoxically perhaps, a sane commentary on a world turned upside down. This is most in evidence as Lear reaches his lowest psychological point as he rages against the storm on the barren heath. Gently but insistently the Fool attempts to anchor his master in reality by reminding him of how the dramatic events were set in train, and of how chaos and inversion in Lear's familial and psychological world have led to disorder in all aspects of Lear's external world. 'When nobles are their tailors' tutors', says the Fool, 'When every case in law is right / When [. . .] bawds and whores do churches build, / Then shall the realm of Albion / Come to great confusion' (3.2.82, 89–91).

Running alongside the main plot of the play is the sub-plot of Gloucester and his sons, Edgar and Edmund. In a culture governed by the strict rules of primogeniture (whereby wealth and title pass entirely to the oldest legitimate male in a family), Edmund is an outsider, excluded from the social system by his legal status as a bastard. Simply to read this character as somehow 'evil', however, is to overlook the complexities with which Shakespeare endows him. Much in the pattern of the extraordinarily pragmatic rulers described by Machiavelli in *The Prince*, Edmund is a charismatic, plausible, and articulate manipulator. Acting in counterpoint to this wickedness is the extreme loyalty and love Edgar eventually shows his father, leading him literally to safety, and metaphorically to spiritual peace and reconciliation.

Some of the play's richest language is given to Edmund, and his soliloquy* which sets the tone for Act 1 illustrates this. 'Thou, nature, art my goddess', muses Edmund:

> to thy law
> My services are bound. Wherefore should I
> Stand in the plague of custom and permit
> The curiosity of nations to deprive me
> For that I am some twelve or fourteen moonshines
> Lag of a brother? Why bastard? Wherefore 'base'?
> When my dimensions are as well compact,

My mind as generous, and my shape as true,
As honest madam's issue? Why brand they us
With base? With baseness? Bastardy? Base, base? (1.2.1–10)

If you read these lines out loud you will notice how the last two lines, with their repeated 'b' sounds, can be spat out. The harsh alliteration* amply reveals Edmund's bitter rage. Indeed, in interpreting Shakespeare we must remember that these were plays to be seen, not to be read. In reading this speech out loud, even if we at first do not pick up on every precise meaning, we certainly do sense the strong emotion which is threatening to erupt. We might also notice the interrogative structure of the soliloquy*: we can easily note the unusually high number of questions, and we might as a result decide that not only is this an angry character, but that this is a character intent on getting answers – by any means necessary. We might also be struck by the addressee of this soliloquy* (which may, given a soliloquy's* solo status, at first seem like a contradiction in terms): 'nature'. The natural world and its laws are being conjured up in that opening personification*. If natural law is Edmund's 'goddess', then social constructions of illegitimacy or 'bastardy' are irrelevant to him: what difference do a few months either way ('twelve or fourteen moonshines') make to him as a person? If we know a little about the social context of the play we will quickly identify Edmund as a Machiavellian character: almost magnetic in his use of language; determined; and with a chip on his shoulder. He is a man who cuts straight through social niceties in order to reach his goal. In this speech he effectively distances himself from his own community's traditions and belief systems ('the curiosity of nations') in order to establish a system of his own making where illegitimacy, far from being a social handicap, becomes both a motivation and a justification. Thus Edmund declares at the end of the soliloquy*: 'Now, gods, stand up for bastards!' (1.2.22). This can only make us anxious and curious about what impact such rage is going to have as the play gets underway.

Edmund pursues his goal in full sight of the other characters, *seeming* to be the dutiful son, loyal subject, or faithful lover as appropriate. Other characters are metaphorically blind to his machinations. The Fool's prophecy of the third act may be interpreted in the context of a play where 'vision' has many meanings (it is multivalent), both literal and symbolic*. Key characters have to learn the hard way: 'I stumbled when I saw' (4.1.21) muses the blinded Gloucester as he reflects on his former almost wilful ignorance of his sons' true characters. Similarly, Lear could not 'see' beyond the veneer of his older daughters' flattering and hyperbolic* speeches in the love test of the first act. Indeed, Lear is a somewhat ambiguous character. His vanity and desire for control lead to his downfall – this is the idea of Aristotle's 'fatal flaw', and this hubris (excessive pride) is a trait evident in Goneril and Regan, too.

Representations of the female are central to an appreciation of the play. Cordelia was a particular favourite of critics in the late nineteenth and early twentieth centuries, some of whom saw in her Christ-like qualities of forgiveness and serenity. Cristina León Alfar (see 'Criticism and Literary Theory', above) is deeply suspicious of the patriarchal* control Lear attempts to exercise over his daughters, even reading the halcyon vision he conjures up of his imprisonment with Cordelia as influenced by his controlling personality. Newly reunited with his daughter Lear urges her: 'Come, let's away to prison. / We two alone will sing like birds i'th'cage' (5.3.9–10). You may choose to see in this a poignant and moving declaration of an old man's last-gasp attempt at happiness with his most-loved daughter. Others, in line with Alfar, however, might believe that 'Lear looks forward to his period of imprisonment with Cordelia as an interval during which he owns his daughter completely and thus achieves the desires that motivated his division of the kingdom' (Alfar, p. 184). If we adopt Alfar's view, we are presented with an even more bleak view of *Lear*'s tragic cosmos since it would seem that that one redeeming possibility – of self-betterment and repentance – is not unproblematically present in the person of the old King here. He is not as changed as Frye, for example, using the notion of the protagonist* entering the final phase, of Recognition, might suggest. The same passage from the play, then, can generate radically different interpretations, depending on the critical prism through which we choose to view it.

Finally, and perhaps somewhat ironically given its literary form, this is a play which functions as an examination of the inadequacies of language. This knotty dilemma (of words being used to say that words cannot say anything meaningful because they are always at least one step removed from reality) is most famously articulated in *Hamlet*, in that eponymous* hero's musings of 'To be or not to be'. The very public love-test which Lear engineered at the start of *King Lear* is confounded by his most-loved, youngest daughter's refusal – or inability – to participate. Paradoxically (but, of course, logically, given the topsy-turvy universe the play inhabits), then, Cordelia's 'Nothing' of the opening scene reverberates throughout the entire play as a very powerful 'something'.

Further Reading

Bate, Jonathan (2009), *Soul of the Age: The Life, Mind and World of William Shakespeare*. Harmondsworth: Penguin. An important recent intellectual biography by the co-editor of the recent Macmillan/RSC edition of the *Complete Works*; pays close attention to cultural context.

Dillon, Janette (2007), *The Cambridge Introduction to Shakespeare's Tragedies*. Cambridge: Cambridge University Press. A methodical discussion of ten plays from *Titus Andronicus* to *Coriolanus*. Dillon provides a clear and intelligent overview of the plays.

Dollimore, Jonathan (2004), *Radical Tragedy: Religion, Ideology and Power in the Drama of Shakespeare and his Contemporaries* (third edition). Basingstoke: Palgrave. First published in 1984, this highly influential cultural materialist* study of Shakespeare and other dramatists of the period pays close attention to how literature relates to the ideological contradictions of its time.

Dutton, R., and Jean E. Howard (eds) (2006), *A Companion to Shakespeare's Works, Volume I: The Tragedies*. Oxford: Blackwell. Contains some essays concerned with Shakespearean tragedy in general, and others offering detailed readings of specific plays. Particularly useful essays include David Scott Kastan's 'Shakespeare and the Idea of Tragedy' and Sasha Roberts' 'Reading Shakespeare's Tragedies of Love'.

Marsh, Nicholas (1998), *Shakespeare: The Tragedies*. Basingstoke: Macmillan. A clear and concise guide to reading and thinking about the plays. Marsh uses close readings of key sections from *Hamlet, King Lear, Othello* and *Macbeth* to illustrate his exploration of the plays' openings, endings, characters, societies, use of humour, and imagery.

McEachern, Claire (ed.) (2002), *The Cambridge Companion to Shakespearean Tragedy*. Cambridge: Cambridge University Press. An excellent collection of essays by a variety of contributors. The essays take in the four major tragedies as well as looking at *Titus Andronicus, Coriolanus, Romeo and Juliet, Julius Caesar, Antony and Cleopatra* and *Timon of Athens*. Tom McAlindon's essay 'What is a Shakespearean tragedy?' is a first-rate introduction to the topic.

'Touchstone': http://www.touchstone.bham.ac.uk/. An online tool for Shakespeare research; particularly useful for students is the information on past, current, and future Shakespeare productions.

'Bardbox': http://bardbox.wordpress.com/. A website that brings together 'some of the best and most interesting of original Shakespeare-related videos' available online; includes a wide range of material divided into categories from 'Animation' to 'Feature films' to 'Rap'.

Do not forget to keep a record of *all* the texts and websites you look at when researching for an assignment: you will need to list them in your bibliography.

Part II
Studying Seventeenth- and Eighteenth-Century Literature

4 Literature 1600–1660

Jessica L. Malay

Historical Context

In 1601, Elizabeth I of England executed Robert Devereux, the second Earl of Essex, on a charge of treason. This event provides the most extreme example of the increasing disruption of government because of rivalries within Elizabeth's court. These rivalries were exacerbated by the certainty that Elizabeth's life was nearing its end and uncertainty concerning who would replace her. In the end, James VI of Scotland was accepted as Elizabeth's successor after her death in 1603. Yet, despite a smooth transition, many continued to be anxious about the new king. He was a foreigner and brought with him Scottish courtiers who raised suspicion and jealousy amongst the English. His manner of governance differed from Elizabeth as well. James was an ardent believer in his divine right to rule. As a male monarch he did not feel the need for the more reciprocal tone Elizabeth had used in her dealings with her courtiers and government. His demeanour at times alienated his subjects and created discontent. Thus, those that hoped the long-awaited male monarch would establish discipline and order within court and country were soon disappointed.

Some of this disappointment was the inevitable result of the expectations of the differing religious factions. There had been religious unrest in the country even before Henry VIII's famous break from the Catholic Church in the 1530s. Catholic families, after decades of persecution, expected their situation would improve under James I. This was not the case, and a few Catholics unhappy with his policies attempted the destruction of Parliament in the Gunpowder Plot of 1605. At the opposite end of the religious spectrum, the radical Protestant factions (often called Puritans) believed religious reform had not gone far enough in ending Catholic abuses of the Christian Church. Many of these called for a complete overhaul of the Church, ending the hierarchy of Church governance, as well as discarding the *Book of Common Prayer* that had established a unified order of worship throughout England and Wales. James, like Elizabeth before him, believed the Church was fundamentally an agent of social stability and tried to maintain a compromise position that was acceptable to the vast majority of society. Throughout James' reign, religion remained one of the most important and often divisive issues in the three kingdoms over which he ruled (Scotland, Ireland, and England). The immense quantities of religious poetry and prose written in the period reflect this vital concern.

In addition to these religious issues, James inherited a series of domestic and foreign difficulties that left the country in a perilous financial situation. In order to bolster the economy, James quickly ended hostilities against Spain. He also encouraged the expansion of mercantile ventures such as the East India Company (est. 1600), the Virginia Company (est. 1606) and the Massachusetts Bay Company (est. 1629). A number of colonies were also established in North America and exploration of this continent and beyond continued to be supported. These ventures generally benefited the country financially, while at the same time they expanded public knowledge of diverse cultures and gave people a sense of a much larger world. Poets like John Donne and playwrights including William Shakespeare integrated the imagery and themes of exploration and colonization into their poems and plays.

Unfortunately, some of James' money-making strategies led many to feel that the court was riddled with favouritism and corruption. These activities included the selling of monopolies and royal duties (collected at ports) as well as the selling of titles. There was also disapproval concerning James' penchant for installing royal favourites in positions of unrivalled power, especially George Villiers, the Duke of Buckingham. A number of scandals also tarnished the royal court. This subject of corruption, both at court and in society, became a favourite amongst Jacobean* playwrights and satirists.

James' court also had a reputation for lavish and costly display. And while this led to criticism, it also provided an opportunity for playwrights such as Ben Jonson, Samuel Daniels, and others who were commissioned to write court masques*. Many professional acting companies received royal patronage and were summoned to court to perform plays. The most famous of these were the King's men, the company to which Shakespeare belonged. This court support of dramatic productions also resulted in a loosening of the restrictions against the performance of adult companies within the city of London. This allowed for the performance of plays in more elite indoor venues, stimulating innovations in dramatic forms to suit this environment. The vibrant literary culture of the court helped poets secure patronage and maintained an environment favourable to the production of innovative literature.

Away from the court, an increasingly diverse and accessible print culture was developing. At the most affordable end of the market were the pamphlets (small booklets with no binding) and broadsides (one printed sheet of text). Certain forms of literature (including ballads* and other popular poetry, sensation narratives, and essays on topical subjects) obtained a large circulation, providing opportunities for writers as well as readers. Manuscripts* continued to be created, by paid scriveners as well as private individuals, and were disseminated widely. The practice of keeping commonplace books, where one copied out literary and other texts thought to be of value, shows a widespread interest in contemporary literary forms which often served as models for individuals in the composition of their own poetry and prose. The opportunities for producing inventive literary texts continued, and even flourished despite the increasing political tension that resulted in the English civil war, or as it is sometimes termed, the War of Three Kingdoms.

James, while not always a popular monarch, managed to maintain a peaceful relationship with the various factions within his three kingdoms. However, his son, Charles I, was not able to achieve this. Charles acceded to the throne in 1625 and, like his father, believed in his divine and absolute right to rule the country as he pleased; this included imposing his religious and political beliefs upon the citizenry. Like his father, he depended on a few select individuals to advise him and to enforce his will. These included his queen (the French Catholic princess Henrietta Maria), Thomas Wentworth (the Earl of Strafford) and William Laud (the Archbishop of Canterbury).

Charles also had financial problems, and sought to alleviate these with unpopular taxes. He also tried to impose a form of religious practice, Arminianism, upon the people, through his installation of William Laud as Archbishop of Canterbury. Theologically, Arminianism rejected the widely held Calvinist belief (developed by John Calvin) in predestination (that only those selected by God would be allowed into the kingdom of heaven and that all salvation emanated from God). Jacob Arminius, a Dutch theologian, rejected this, contending that God's grace could redeem everyone, and that good works could influence divine judgement. Arminianism as a practice also placed a greater emphasis on ceremony, ritual and the privileges of clergy.

51

This struck many, especially Puritans, as a way of reintroducing Catholicism through the backdoor. These conflicts led Charles to dissolve Parliament in 1629 and begin an eleven year period of personal rule.

This period ended when Charles tried to introduce the English *Book of Common Prayer* in Scotland. The Scots practiced a more austere form of Protestantism – Presbyterianism – and saw Charles' attempts to introduce a set form of ritualized worship as an assault on their religion. They responded in a violent series of uprisings called the Bishop's Wars of 1639–40 (the opening military action in what would come to be known as the War of Three Kingdoms). Fearing a Scottish invasion, Charles was forced to recall Parliament in 1640. This Parliament expected Charles to address their grievances before they agreed to subsidize war against Scotland. Charles was not willing to do this and dissolved Parliament after only three weeks. Later that year the King was forced to call Parliament again. The so-called 'Long Parliament' nullified the King's power in 1642, announcing that its laws and ordinances were legally binding without the King's approval, and beginning the civil war. The Battle of Naseby in 1645 was the decisive battle where the King's army was defeated.

In 1649, Charles was publicly executed and a period called the Interregnum began. The most dynamic leader of this period was Oliver Cromwell, who through the force of his personality managed to inspire his troops, the New Model Army, and return some form of stability to the country. However, after his death in 1658 the government was not able to govern effectively. Charles II (son of Charles I) outlined in the Declaration of Breda the terms upon which he would agree to return as King, resulting in the Restoration of the monarchy in 1660.

The English civil war was certainly a period of conflict, but also provided opportunity for many writers to produce works of poetry, autobiography, political essays, and other texts. Andrew Marvell and John Milton composed poetry exploring the ideals of the new forces in government while others like Richard Lovelace and Katherine Philips wrote in support of the Royalist cause. The turmoil of war provided an opportunity for marginalized people, especially women and those with non-mainstream views, to write and have their work distributed in some form. The public theatres were closed in 1642, but scholars like Sue Wiseman (see 'References') have found ample evidence for dramatic activity in private venues as well as part of public events and displays.

Literature reflected and engaged with the social and cultural movements and upheavals of this particularly tumultuous period. Dramatists enacted society's concerns and interests on the stage, while poets grappled with the conflicts between their own individual interests and the expectations of society. It is important to consider the effects of events, attitudes, traditions, and powerful individuals when working on literature written from 1600 to 1660, or indeed during any literary period.

Key Authors and Texts

In the sixteenth century, a variety of literary techniques were developed. Early in that century a number of courtier poets, most famously Thomas Wyatt and Henry Howard, appropriated the Italian (or Petrarchan) sonnet form, customizing it in a variety of ways. An important selection of their work was printed in a volume popularly called 'Tottel's Miscellany' (collected by Richard Tottel and published in 1557 as *Songes and Sonettes*). This publication made the poetic innovations developed by Tudor court poets accessible to a wider audience. These poems not only provided models but also encouraged innovation with poetic forms that was enthusiastically taken up by later poets of the seventeenth century. By 1600, poets had a rich and diverse poetic heritage from which to draw in their own creative endeavours.

One of the best known of early seventeenth-century poets was Ben Jonson. Jonson crafted poetry that has a clear sense of proportion and clarity. His poems are often restrained and carefully structured, though at times they contain a more extravagant tone, accompanied by a satirical* impulse. His song 'To Celia' (1616) is formed through the alternation of tetrameter* and trimeter* lines, which expresses a restrained sexuality conveyed through simple but sensual images. This ability to express abundance with concise poetic imagery also served him well when commissioned to write masques* for court. Jonson's poetic economy proved well suited to the genre, supporting rather than competing with the visual imagery. Some of his most famous masques* include *The Masque of Blackness* (performed in 1605) and its sequel *The Masque of Beauty* (1608). Jonson practiced another type of economy in his satirical dramas for the popular stage. In these plays, including *Volpone* (1606), *Bartholomew Fair* (1614), and *The Alchemist* (1610), he often adopts a strict classical form, eschewing the innumerable sub-plots popular with many of his contemporaries. Upon this uncomplicated structure he displays his characters and progresses his plot with a biting wit. Jonson, like many writers of the period, possessed a virtuosity that allowed him to write in many literary genres.

Mary Wroth (niece of the famous sixteenth-century poet Philip Sidney) also wrote plays and various forms of poetry and prose. Her most famous work is a long prose romance*, *Urania* (1621), which appropriates elements of chivalric and pastoral romance* popular in the previous century (including her uncle's *Arcadia*, c. 1590) and reshapes them into a compelling tale intermingling the rituals of romance* with the steady realism* of her characters. Her female characters especially are dignified and resilient in the face of betrayal and misfortune. This quality of character is also evident in her sonnet sequence

Pamphilia to Amphilanthus (1621). Here, Wroth provides an interesting counterpoint to the many male-authored sonnet sequences, exploring the experiences of love and its effect upon a female speaker. Wroth also composed a play, *Love's Victory* (c. 1615), which allegorizes love and its power through the figures of Venus and Cupid and four pairs of lovers.

Poetry, especially in the early part of the seventeenth century was dynamic and innovative. Where Jonson chose elegance and simplicity in much of his poetry, John Donne favoured a complexity that could communicate simultaneous ideas, sensations, thoughts, and emotions (see the 'Case Study', below). Other poets of the period embraced a mixture of these approaches, though many often chose to work predominantly in one form. Those poets who favoured elegance and simplicity are often described as the Sons of Ben, or more generally Cavalier poets. Their poetry is characterized by the use of colloquial language and a playful tone that is affectionate, casual, and irreverent. Robert Herrick's poem 'Upon the Loss of His Mistresses' (1648) illustrates this well. His mock melancholic tone is belied by the very number of the women he has loved. His secular poems are often sensual and even erotic, and he delights in the rhythms and fertility of the year with poems that celebrate Mayday celebrations and Harvest homes. Herrick, who was ordained as a minister in 1623, also wrote a collection of religious poems *His Noble Numbers* (1647). Stylistically, these religious poems share much with his secular poetry as he expresses his faith with an innocent simplicity, as can be seen in his lyrical poem 'To His Saviour, by a Child' or his sonnet 'To His Sweet Saviour' (both 1648). Other Cavalier poets include Thomas Carew, John Suckling, and Richard Lovelace. The poetry produced by these poets often celebrates the pleasures of the moment, but could also express endurance and faith. Richard Lovelace's 'To Althea, from Prison' (1649) employs a simple structure to voice a steady resistance to political adversity.

Much poetry of the period concerns religious experience. In a time of repressive government control of religious activity, the poetic moment allowed individuals to express an unmediated religious experience with God. George Herbert's religious poetry, while sometimes termed metaphysical*, is perhaps better described as contemplative. He uses imagery loaded with mystical significance derived from the parables of Jesus. His poems often work as a narrative conveying the reader from the secular present to a sacred eternity. Henry Vaughan's secular and religious poetry relies much more on the intricate and at times obscure imagery shared by metaphysical* poets. His poem 'Regeneration' (1650) allegorizes the Calvinist concept of the elect through an interplay of images drawn from both biblical sources and the natural world. Aemilia Lanyer also engages in a combination of natural and religious imagery in her long verse narrative of the passion of Christ *Salve Deus Rex Judæorum* (1611). In this poem she explores the nature of women and their relationship with both God and men. She employs complex imagery that reveals the influence both of sixteenth-century pastoral poetry as well as the more complex or metaphysical* imagery developing amongst some of her contemporaries.

The intense personal and yet universal nature of metaphysical* poetry, and the playful, irreverent tone of Cavalier poetry with its easily accessible tropes, can both be identified in the drama of the period. Jacobean* drama is a rich collection of plays that appropriate a myriad of sources, and exhibit diverse imagery, intriguing characterization, and a variety of plot structures. As already mentioned, Ben Jonson chose to follow classical models in structuring his plays, maintaining simplicity in plot construction. He was almost unique in this, though Elizabeth Cary also chose a classical plot style in her *Tragedy of Mariam* (1613). Cary contains the play in one place, one day and in one unrelenting action that moves the characters to their destruction at the hands of the tyrant Herod. On the public stages, however, the audience generally delighted in multiple plots. This element of Jacobean* drama has its roots in medieval and folk drama, and allowed playwrights greater freedom in plot development.

Much of William Shakespeare's work appeared in the early seventeenth century. His late plays, especially those often labelled the Romances – *Cymbeline* (1609), *The Winter's Tale* (1610), and *The Tempest* (1611) – show the influence of changing court tastes and the popularity of masques*. Other playwrights catered to the popular taste for savage and often political revenge tragedies. In John Ford's *'Tis a Pity She's a Whore* (c. 1630) an atmosphere of depraved self-assertion permeates the drama. The governing figures pursue their self interest, while other characters abandon themselves to their sexual desires. This results in murder and reveals the inadequacies of a judicial system that places the interests of powerful men above justice. Ford's plot revolves around the story of two unfortunate lovers. Their impediment to happiness is not, in a perverse appropriation of elements of *Romeo and Juliet* (1594), feuding families, but rather that they are brother and sister. And yet despite their incestuous relationship they remain the most sympathetic characters in the play. Ford places them within a maelstrom of corruption and deceit which ultimately destroys them. Thomas Middleton and William Rowley in *The Changeling* (1622) also explore the way a corrupt aristocracy entices the innocent only to destroy them. This play contrasts the virtuous and active integrity to be found in the local mad house, in the person of the asylum's keeper's wife, with the sexually and morally depraved Beatrice Joanna, daughter to Vermandero, governor of Spanish Alicante. Thomas Middleton's *The Revenger's Tragedy* (1606) also explores governmental corruption and the destruction of individuals and society when those in power succumb to the demands of their appetites for sex, power, and wealth. This play is particularly stark, with many of the characters exhibiting a grotesque depravity. Brothers murder brothers, a mother encourages her daughter to enter into a liaison for money, rape is committed with impunity, while most heinously, the Duke, who should dispense justice and maintain order, murders a woman he craves sexually, and later is so deceived by these sexual desires that they lead him to his own death. The revenger, Vindice, plays upon the appetites of his enemies in order to restore justice, though the price of this is his own life. These plays were influenced in part by the works of the Roman playwright Seneca, who at the beginning of the first century wrote plays that reveal an increasing anxiety with corrupt government in Rome. Likewise, many Jacobean* plays reveal a general concern about corruption in society generated by the scandals of James' court, along with its opulence and impression of moral laxity.

However, this concern was not confined to tragic dramas, nor was it simply focused on the court. A sense of a general malaise in society brought on by increasing wealth, especially apparent in the city, also became fodder for the satirical comedies of the period, often set in London. Several of Ben Jonson's plays, including *Volpone* (1605), *Epicoene* (1609), *The Alchemist* (1610), and *Bartholomew Fair* (1614), reveal a deep cynicism concerning the nature of humanity. His characters follow their greed, sexual appetites, petty pride, and even religious beliefs (often portrayed as hypocritical) into ridiculous and demeaning situations that often destroy their illusions and leave them broken. Other comedies, including Thomas Dekker's *The Shoemaker's Holiday* (1599) and Middleton's *A Chaste Maid in Cheapside* (c. 1613), are not as unrelentingly harsh as Jonson's satiric comedies; however they do playfully participate in satirizing the pretensions and appetites of the merchants and minor gentry of London.

Many other texts of the period also explored the state of society. These include the edifying sermons and essays that were popular with the reading public. One of the most famous of these is Francis Bacon's *Essayes or Counsels, Civill and Morall* (first published 1597; expanded 1612 and again 1625). This collection ranges widely across the spectrum of human concern including essays as diverse as 'Of Death', 'Of a Regiment of Health', 'Of Building', and 'Of Deformity'. Lancelot Andrewes' *XCVI Sermons* (1629) provide a careful analysis of scriptural texts. John Donne's sermons and theological essays proved even more popular with contemporary audiences than his poetry. Donne avoids the overuse of complex rhetorical strategies common in prose essays, instead employing compelling and accessible stylistic techniques.

The upheaval of the civil war and the Interregnum inspired many to write autobiographical accounts of their experiences. Lucy Hutchinson wrote the *Memoirs of the Life of Colonel John Hutchinson* in the 1670s (first published 1806) as a defence of her husband, who was imprisoned in the Tower of London (and died there in 1664) because of his involvement in the execution of Charles I. The royalist Lady Anne Halkett also produced a manuscript* memoir (composed 1667–68) as well as a massive twenty-one volumes of autobiographical writing, her *Meditations* (composed 1644–99). Both works reveal a lively and dynamic personality struggling with the crises of social and civil conflict. Edward Hyde also wrote of the conflict in a historical work, *History of the Rebellion and Civil Wars in England in the Year 1641* (1671–72), which discusses both the events contributing to the conflict as well as considers political theory and just governance, and in his memoirs, *The Life of Edward Earl of Clarendon* (first published 1759), which provide a more personal insight into the events of the period.

Literature produced between 1600 and 1660 was expressive and experimental, while at the same time steeped in traditional forms and devices. This diversity created a climate that allowed authors to explore and appropriate themes, styles and imagery in the creation of their own texts. Court patronage supported writers, while concerns generated by the behaviour of court provided much subject matter. The work of many writers was also influenced by the political upheaval caused by the civil war, and the discussions regarding social, political, and theological issues emerging in the Interregnum. It is important to consider the way in which writers and their works influenced each other. Writers read each other's works and watched plays written by others, and often incorporated or extended ideas they found there. One should, therefore, always consider how a particular text may have been influenced by other writers.

Criticism and Literary Theory

A number of approaches to the analysis of literature have successfully engaged with texts written between 1600 and 1660. Formalist* approaches, associated particularly with the New Critics* of the 1940s and 1950s, have proven particularly useful as writers of the period were acutely conscious of the interplay between structure, word order, rhythm, symbolism*, imagery, and various other literary devices. Cleanth Brooks produced some important formalist* analysis of seventeenth-century poetry in *The Well-Wrought Urn* (1947), especially the poetry of John Donne, contending that Donne's metaphysical* conceits* were often extreme forms of the use of paradox* that could also be seen in the works of other writers. Kenneth Burke, in *The Philosophy of Literary Form* (1941), argues that all human language, including the literary, was in some way rhetorical, or deliberately shaped for particular situations or the demands of particular genres. Criticism of the New Critics'* practice of treating the text as a self-contained unit, without reference to the cultural milieu in which it was created, led to a movement away from purely formalist* approaches to these texts, as will be discussed below. However, this type of practical criticism continues to provide a useful analytical tool.

The experimentation with poetic forms such as the sonnet, the lyric*, and the epic*, as well as particular rhythmic styles, and classical imagery, was widespread. Poets crafted their texts in ways that engaged imaginatively with conventional practice. Thus an analysis of the formal properties of a literary text can usefully reveal much about a text's engagement with contemporary poetic trends. Indeed, many formal qualities of these texts were part of a poetic discourse that created or enhanced meaning through an intertextual* relationship with other texts. For example, Thomas Carew's country-house poem 'To Saxham' (c. 1624) playfully engages with Ben Jonson's earlier 'To Penshurst' (1616). Carew replicates Jonson's structure, while at the same time inverting Jonson's imagery. He also inserts a tone that gently mocks Jonson's more earnest poem of praise. Jonson, one of the early writers of English poems celebrating place, appropriated structures and imagery from classical Latin poems by Martial and Horace, expecting his audience to understand his allusions* and the meanings attached to them. Thus, an awareness of the structural affinities between the two poems allows for a more developed analysis.

A formal analysis of a text also allows the reader to consider symbolic* systems, such as numerology. The use of particular metrical patterns by many writers allowed the insertion of a particular numerological meaning. In many poems the numbers three, five, and ten bear particular symbolic* significance, often in reference to contemporary beliefs regarding religious salvation and the second coming of Christ. (For further information, see Alastair Fowler.) Many poets consciously subverted expected metrical forms in order to re-orientate traditional imagery. Others chose to appropriate a form traditionally associated with a particular human experience and deploy it unconventionally, as was the case with writers like John Donne, who expresses his intense religious experience through the creation of a sonnet sequence, which was typically used to express passionate love for a woman.

However, though this practice of close reading is often necessary and useful, many object to the analysis of a text that relies solely on formal properties. They argue that a text is a product of the society in which it was written, and to ignore this fact is to ignore important elements contributing to its meaning and function. Cultural materialism* is a critical approach that considers the influence of culture upon a literary text. A materialist approach considers the way in which texts, as products of a society, reveal the exercise of power and social control. This type of analysis seeks to identify how texts internalize social practice. At the same time, cultural materialists* are keenly aware that each society is dynamic and complex. Thus, rather than seeking to identify a static world view within a literary text, they explore the way in which texts participate in this complexity. Some of the most influential of these critics include Jonathan Goldberg, Alan Sinfield, and Jonathan Dollimore, all of whom wrote important critical studies of seventeenth-century literature. Indeed, the complexities, anxieties, and upheavals of seventeenth-century society make this critical approach especially fruitful.

A cultural materialist* analysis often explores texts for gaps and contradictions which may indicate a resistance to prevailing conditions or expectations. It also tries to identify how texts aid in the consolidation of societal beliefs and perpetuate prevailing power structures. An example of this can be seen in Ben Jonson's 'To Penshurst'. In this poem Jonson presents the material production of crops and the labour of agricultural workers as natural and reciprocal: 'But all come in, the farmer and the clown / [. . .] Some bring a capon, some a rural cake' (1996, p. 96, ll. 48, 51). However, just previous to this presentation of gifts is a reference to social unrest within society in relation to enclosures: 'And though thy walls be of the country stone, / They're rear'd with no man's ruin, no man's groan' (ll. 45–46). Enclosure was a sensitive issue in the period as landowners appropriated for their own use land that had been held in common and used by the poorer members of society for grazing or small plot farming. The results were often riots and destruction of property. Jonson's juxtaposition of a reciprocal celebration of gift giving with an allusion* to social disorder is one of those poetic moments that can be usefully analysed to reveal the complexity of seventeenth-century culture.

Closely related to cultural materialism* is New Historicism. The two critical approaches have much in common, interested as they are in the way a text reveals the functioning of society and the role of individuals in maintaining and challenging prevailing social norms. The most influential New Historicist critic is Stephen Greenblatt, whose *Renaissance Self-Fashioning* (1980) is seen as the study which established this approach. Greenblatt and Svetlana Alpers also founded the journal *Representations*, where other scholars applying a similar approach published essays. Louis Montrose published several important essays on sixteenth- and seventeenth-century poetry in this journal. New Historicists contend that the boundary between literary texts and other historical texts is artificial, and that neither provides empirical truth about a particular historical period. In the same vein, they also question the concept of a consistent or transcendent individual. Instead they consider the ways in which the individual is constructed within society, and how evidence of this manifests itself within the literary (or other) texts. New Historicists are keenly aware of the way in which they themselves are influenced by the culture within which they live, and attempt to make clear their own theoretical position as they analyse a text.

Other cultural criticism focusing on particular experiences are also useful when analysing a literary text of the seventeenth century. This includes feminist* criticism (and its corollary, gender criticism) and postcolonial* criticism. Feminist* criticism considers the position of women within a particular society. The political aim of feminist* criticism is to reveal social attitudes concerning women in order to redress inequalities and secure equal status for women. Tina Krontiris and Louise Schleiner are two feminist* critics who explore the way gender inequalities in seventeenth century are revealed in literary texts. This type of analysis can also reveal the objectification of women, as can be readily seen in many sonnets of the period where the female is reduced to a representation of male desire. Literary texts are often explored to reveal female participation in society and the contributions made by women, as can be seen in the work of Anne M. Haselkorn and Betty Travitsky, as well as Helen Hackett. A feminist* analysis can also reveal the methods through which women perpetuated prevailing social attitudes concerning gender as well as challenged them.

A particularly rich vein of literature for feminist* analysis is the participation of men and women of the seventeenth century in the *querelle des femmes*, or the dispute over the nature of women, that had been raging in texts for centuries. This genre of polemic literature began in earnest with Christine de Pisan's *The City of Women* (1404), which presents women as virtuous and intelligent in response to many misogynist texts circulating at the time. In the seventeenth century, Rachel Speght's *A Muzzle for Melastomus* (1617) and *Certain Queries to the Baiter of Woman* (1617) covered similar ground, while Esther Sowernam (probably a pseudonym) wrote *Ester Hath Hang'd Haman* (1617) in response to Joseph Swetnam's attack on women, *The Araignnment of Lewde, Idle, Froward and Unconstant Women* (1615). These and many other prose texts, as well as poetry and dramatic productions from the seventeenth century, present various arguments that reveal there was no consensus regarding the true nature of women, or even their appropriate place and behaviour within society. Feminist* criticism also works to recover women's voices and explores the ways in which female-authored texts participated in prevailing literary practices. This critical approach identifies the role of education and cultural prohibition in restricting women's full participation in some literary genres.

Postcolonial* criticism considers literary texts produced in relation to the colonizing activities of Western cultures. This analysis includes identifying and exploring the attitudes and belief systems of the colonizers as well as the voices of the colonized. Philip Boucher explores seventeenth-century European representations of indigenous peoples, while Richard Helgerson discusses the way in which British national identity in the seventeenth century was in some way defined through the otherness of newly discovered lands and peoples. Much postcolonial* analysis attempts to discover and reveal areas of resistance in texts as well as evidence of conformity and assimilation. Closely related to cultural materialism* and New Historicism, it uses similar methodologies and theoretical positions, but more finely focuses these to explore the complexities of the colonial experience. The goal of post-colonial* criticism, as with feminist* criticism, is to bring to light prejudice and injustice which has been internalized and perpetuated in cultures affected by European (and later American) colonization.

Postcolonial* criticism is an especially useful tool in the analysis of Renaissance texts because several colonization projects, in Ireland and the Americas, were first conceived and then robustly prosecuted in the seventeenth century. It was also a period when the powerful trading companies which were to shape so much of British imperialism* were first formed, most especially the East India Company. Works like Richard Hakluyt's *The Principal Navigations, Voyages and Discoveries of the English Nation* (1589) and Edmund Spenser's *A View of the Present State of Ireland* (1595), along with several literary and historical texts, attempted to engage, construct, or assimilate the rapidly accumulating experiences of unfamiliar cultures fostered by colonial projects, exploration, and trading expeditions. Postcolonial* criticism attempts to discover within these texts the effects of colonialism upon individuals and cultures as well as their responses.

Critical and theoretical approaches like those discussed above can enhance literary discussion. They can extend and develop ideas that emerge from close reading and they are most effective when applied after careful study of a text where the purpose of the analysis is clearly stated and defined. It is important when employing any of the approaches discussed above to consider their appropriateness for the particular text, as well as the goal of the discussion. It is also useful to note that much literary analysis often employs elements of several critical approaches.

 ## John Donne's Poetry

John Donne's poetry covers many diverse and even contradictory themes. His love poetry celebrates a passionate sensuality, while his satires* condemn the corruption he observed in his society. His religious poetry constantly rehearses the desperation of man trapped in his sinful nature, who intensely desires a union with God. However, despite the differing sentiments, all Donne's poetry shares similar elements. His tone is engaging and colloquial, with the rhythms and structures of the poems supporting rather than contributing to the subject of the text. Donne depends on a dramatic presentation to intimately engage the reader. Many of Donne's metaphors develop through the appropriation of philosophical and scientific discourses as well as imagery derived from world exploration. Donne's poetry often attempts new ways of understanding and reading the human condition, in both its secular and its spiritual endeavours. All of these qualities can be seen in his religious poem, 'Good Friday, 1613, Riding Westward' (c. 1613).

Donne's complex metaphorical constructions require close attention not only to their initial construction and deployment but also to their transformation within the poem. Thus analysing the formal qualities of the poem is usually necessary before further cultural analysis. In this poem it is useful first to identify the scene as Donne often incorporates or even constructs a metaphorical scheme through the use of setting. Here the poem is set on a road heading to Wales. The most important element of this journey is the westward direction of travel, as the title makes clear. It is this movement that informs the extended metaphor of the entire poem.

The opening line – 'Let man's soule be a sphere' (p. 241, l. 1) – is a good example of what has come to be termed a metaphysical* conceit*. Donne generally avoided more conventional metaphors and chose instead to compose complex and often paradoxical conceits* formed of unusual comparisons. In this case, his metaphor begins by comparing the soul of an individual to a sphere. The sphere is both the concept of wholeness and a celestial sphere. Donne utilizes traditional philosophical and theological understanding of celestial bodies, as well as recent discoveries in astronomy. These recent discoveries contradicted traditional understandings of the movement of celestial bodies, discovering that their orbits were elliptical, not spherical. Donne uses this contradiction in the development of his metaphor: individuals, like planets, are pulled out of their divinely set, or spherical orbits by foreign bodies, which he represents as the hurrying concerns of everyday life. They can only regain their right movement through the aid of a divine 'intelligence' that ideally guides the spheres in a perfect circular orbit or motion. This intelligence is the *primum mobile*, or first mover, identified in Christian theology as God. Through this close reading of the opening metaphor, the subject of the poem is revealed as an individual's relationship with God.

The poem develops this primary theme by layering metaphor and imagery that contributes to the completion of the metaphor of westward movement, while also engaging the reader in a powerful sensual experience. Donne's poetry often presents the reader with original and sometimes startling ways of experiencing the events he portrays. He does just this here through a depiction of the Passion of Christ. Donne invites us to experience visually the crucifixion, paradoxically by withholding it: 'Yet dare I almost be glad, I do not see / That spectacle of too much weight for me' (ll. 15–16). Five lines later, Donne forces the reader to see what initially he withheld: 'Could I behold those hands, which span the poles / And tune all spheres at once, pierced with those holes?' (ll. 21–22). These two lines form a complex matrix of physical sensation, theological disputation and geographically derived metaphor which all serve to communicate Donne's understanding of the meaning of crucifixion. The poles are the physical crossbar of the cross, but they are also the geographic poles of the earth. This sphere infers the previous microcosmic sphere that opened the poem, the human being. The hands of Christ represent salvation but also the invitation to salvation and thus God's grace. The reference to the tuning of the spheres again engages with the earlier metaphor of the celestial spheres in perfect motion through harmony with the *primum mobile*. Donne asserts that Christ's death reharmonizes the physical disharmonies in the universe identified by astronomers, and this also alludes to the disharmony created by the fall of humanity in the Garden of Eden, which Christ's death redeems.

Donne's poetry requires this close analysis in order to experience fully the emotions and to understand at least in part the themes he attempts to communicate. Donne expects his reader to have some knowledge not only of contemporary scientific discoveries but also of systems and philosophies from the medieval and classical philosophers. He is not concerned with the authority of either, but rather the way they can serve the theme of the poem. It is also useful to understand that Donne's Protestantism was underpinned by the belief in Calvinist predestination. The self-examination often practiced by Calvinist Protestants could be excruciating, and explains Donne's use of violent imagery in his own metaphors of salvation.

This is evident in 'Good-Friday, 1613, Riding Westward'. Returning to the metaphor of the movement west, Donne asserts in the poem that he turns his back on the East, and thus the crucifixion of Christ. However, this is not because he cannot bear to witness it; he has now acknowledged that Christ's passion exists continually in his memory due to his own role as sinner and thus that he is complicit in Christ's crucifixion, another Calvinist belief. Rather, he has turned his back so that he can be scourged, or beaten into submission to God's divine grace, so that he can truly repent and thus be sure of his membership among the elect. Through this chastisement he will be able to turn his face to God, and paradoxically die to live. Thus, by moving west, he invites the scourge and ensures his salvation. Donne transforms what initially appears to be a metaphor representing humanity's rejection of God into a metaphor for solicitation of and submission to God's will.

This use of practical criticism to identify and analyse meaning communicated through metaphor, syntax, and other literary devices provides a useful exploration of the poem. However, it can also provide support for a more materialist reading. Cultural materialists*, as discussed previously, are interested in not only the internal function of a text but its relationship to a wider cultural discourse and its role in supporting, challenging, or subverting prevailing social norms. One might initially think this approach would yield little from a poem like 'Good-Friday', given its intensely personal nature and complex metaphorical structure. However, this is not the case. Donne's poem situates him within a particular social discourse. Thus a materialist analysis can consider the ways in which the Calvinist doctrine underpinning this text supported the prevailing power structures. The practices of the Church of England under James were not strictly speaking Calvinist but allowed for a less absolute understanding of predestination and the workings of grace that would become more pronounced in the Arminianism of Charles I's reign. Donne's poem could be seen as challenging James' religious beliefs, or even the concept of kingly authority. On the other hand, Donne's poem could be seen as supporting powerful social forces committed to Calvinist doctrine. Through a materialist approach one can analyse the relationship this and other poems have with their culture.

Other cultural criticism, including a postcolonial* analysis, can also be usefully applied to this poem. Here, the world is constructed through a European philosophical, theological, and scientific understanding. The world functions as a sphere whose sole purpose is to bring the Christian sinner to divine redemption in an apocalyptic Jerusalem. A postcolonial* analysis might ask: what are the implications for indigenous people with divergent belief systems when colonized by those who share Donne's Calvinism and the essentialist world view it presents? What room is there, in Donne's westward movement, for the many peoples and belief systems he would encounter in his metaphorical travels west, to reach the east?

And what would a feminist* approach to this poem reveal? Certainly the importance of the individual as primarily a soul apart from the world could suggest a form of equality between the sexes, at least upon a spiritual plane. However, the oppressively authoritarian and even violent construction of God could be seen as perpetuating and authorizing a patriarchal* society that denied the individual agency of women. Research related to women's involvement in Calvinist households, their construction of the experience of salvation within their own writings in response to Calvinists beliefs, could also form the basis of a discussion concerning this poem.

In analysing Donne's poetry it is important to carefully explore his deployment of metaphor and to tease out its relationship to theme and its role in creating an engaging experience. It is often necessary to explore his references to contemporary knowledge and attitudes related to philosophy, science, and exploration to identify the matrix of meanings he constructs. It is most important to have some familiarity with the various religious beliefs of the period, especially when analysing his religious poetry. Though possessing a unique voice, Donne can be situated among other contemporary poets and writers who also shared his concerns, interests, and poetic practices. Thus the approaches discussed above can also be usefully applied to the texts of other poets of the period.

John Milton's Poetry

Another influential poet writing on both secular and religious subjects is John Milton. Milton's work spans the Jacobean* period (he was born in 1608) beyond the Restoration of Charles II. His early poetry at Cambridge in the 1620s already showed poetic maturity. Some of these early poems include 'On the Morning of Christ's Nativity' (1645), 'Epitaph on the Marchioness of Winchester' (1645), and 'On Shakespeare' (1632), his first published poem, which accompanied the second folio publication of Shakespeare's plays. However, Milton was not content to simply participate in popular literary forms but also shaped them into unique works that presented his own artistic vision, often influenced by political or religious concerns. One example of this is his masque*, *Comus* (1634). The masque* as a dramatic form was associated with the excesses of James' court and later Charles I's. Milton employs the form in such a way as to extend the artistic potential of the masque*, while inserting an alternative political message critical of the excesses and religious affiliation of Charles' court. Milton also wrote numerous political, religious, and social pamphlets. These include an explanation of the necessity for the execution of Charles I, which nearly led to his own execution, and a pamphlet, inspired by a more personal calamity, concerning the necessity for divorce. Milton ended his career with the most ambitious epic* in the English language, *Paradise Lost* (1667). In this epic* poem Milton returns to themes he had visited often in his other work, most especially the nature of God and the right relationship of humanity to the divine. Humanity, through Adam and Eve, are shown as fallible, but also retain the ability to choose their destiny. God is presented as justified in giving them challenges because through these a richer life is possible. Milton ultimately rejects the rigidity of Calvinist predestination, admitting the possibility of universal salvation through his plot structure where Adam and Eve are able to move from sin to repentance and finally to willing subjection to God.

However, *Paradise Lost* is much more than simply a repentance narrative. Milton also challenges traditional theological arguments, inserts political debate, and creates a text that touches on a number of social issues. *Paradise Lost* is an epic* made up of twelve books that draws on the epic* tradition of Virgil's *Aeneid*, and Homer's *Iliad* and *Odyssey*, the purpose of which is to tell

of the heroic moment in the founding of nations. Edmund Spenser's epic*
romance* *The Faerie Queene* (1596) was also an important source of imagery
and inspiration for Milton. However, Milton ambitiously attempts more than
the construction of a foundation narrative of a particular people. Instead, his
Paradise Lost is concerned with the foundation narrative of the human race at
its very inception. In this poem he attempts to explain the basis for a Christian understanding of human identity – what is the nature of humanity – and
how this identity was shaped. Included in this is also an understanding of
human destiny and the connection between this destiny and the role of good
and evil within it. This exploration of good and evil is most clearly presented
in the character of Satan. In Milton's early work, especially *Comus* (1634), he
explored the nature of temptation and evil. And while his Satan figures in
Comus, and more especially in *Paradise Lost*, are ultimately destroyed within
the narrative, they remain intensely intriguing because of the impossibility of
discovering and thus defining the true essence of evil. In *Paradise Lost* Satan is
a character of infinite layers of conflicting elements. His many monologues
and soliloquies*, rather than illuminating his character, further complicate it.
This becomes apparent in Satan's first speech to his followers in Book I of
Paradise Lost (ll. 622–63), which will be discussed here. All of Satan's
monologues are complex. They both reveal and conceal, compelling the
reader to constantly reconsider the impressions and judgements made concerning Satan's message and character. This complexity invites many critical
approaches.

Again, a practical and formalist* approach to Satan's early monologue
in *Paradise Lost* is a useful way to begin the analysis. It is helpful to note
that much of the power of this speech comes from its structure as a dramatic
narrative. John G. Demara discusses how these early speeches of Satan may
have been lifted from an unfinished play on the subject, *Adam Unparadiz'd*.
Milton provides a compelling setting for the delivery of this speech. His
Satan surveys the utter devastation of defeat, perhaps best expressed in the
condition of his followers who are represented as being like forest oaks
burned and deformed: 'With singèd top their stately growth, though bare, /
Stands on the blasted heath' (p. 30, I, ll. 614–15). With tears 'bursting forth' (I,
l. 626) Satan begins his speech. Milton here alludes to Agamemnon in the *Iliad*,
who under similar circumstances also wept, thus positioning Satan as a
classical hero, at least for this moment in the poem. Satan begins his address
with a series of rhetorical questions designed to elicit a particular response
from both the fallen angels and the reader. He suggests with these that defeat
could not have been envisaged for so great an army made up of such noble
entities. He goes on to place the blame for their attempt upon God who, in
hiding his might, invited their rebellion: '[It was] his strength conceal'd, /
Which tempted our attempt, and wrought our fall' (I, ll. 640–41). The final

turn of the speech offers consolation in their continued ability to resist, albeit covertly, the power of God:

> New warr, provok't; our better part remains
> To work in close design, by fraud or guile,
> What force effected not: that he no less
> At length from us may find, who overcomes
> By force, hath overcome but half his foe. (I, ll. 645–49)

This speech therefore follows the form of the heroic leader's speech to his troops in times of despair much repeated in both classical sources and contemporary texts. However, it is the final exhortation to action that is intriguing. Here, Satan suggests, in a departure from the form he has appropriated, that cunning should replace heroic courage. This strategy of disrupting conventional form in order to destabilize accepted understandings of a particular moment occurs often in Milton's work. He imbeds a vast array of poetic forms in *Paradise Lost* (and other poems) including lyrics*, dramatic monologues*, epic* speeches and elegies*. Thus, in Milton's poetry, it is always useful to consider what a particular poetic form is supposed to communicate – for example, an elegy* is a poem that honours the worthy dead – and then to see if Milton employs the form in some other way.

Cultural materialist* criticism can also provide fascinating insights into Milton's poem and the wider cultural discourse in which it participated. During the Interregnum, in his position as Secretary of Foreign Languages, Milton attempted to justify the execution of Charles I to foreign governments. He also wrote many pamphlets and poetry of an overt political nature that supported governmental reform. Thus many of his texts richly portray the workings of his culture, as David Loewenstein discusses in his book, *Milton and the Drama of History* (1990). Loewenstein persuasively argues that Milton's poetry and his political writing are fundamentally concerned with the nature of humanity and humanity's right relationship with God. The restoration of the monarchy in 1660 forced Milton to retire into private life, and nearly resulted in his execution. *Paradise Lost* as well as *Paradise Regained* (1671) and *Samson Agonistes* (1671) were written in a period of reflection, disappointment, and perhaps even confusion. They present a Milton attempting to come to some sort of understanding concerning the great social upheavals he had experienced in his life. Satan's speech discussed above illustrates the manner by which the individuals and groups can be persuaded to wrong action through the manipulation of positive qualities of courage, fortitude, and determination.

A cultural materialist* analysis, then, concerned as it is with the workings of society, could consider Satan's early speech in relation to the way in which it masks the exploitation of the individual in order to secure and/or sustain a particular social order. Satan's speech attempts to reconstruct a fellowship with the fallen angels predicated on their shared victimization. Yet, this victimization and thus fellowship is made by Satan's clever fallacy where he asserts God tricked them into rebellion, while later in the poem it becomes clear Satan's jealousy was the motivation for this rebellion:

> [Though Satan was held] In favour and præeminence, yet fraught
> With envie against the Son of God, that day
> [. . .]
> Deep malice thence conceiving and disdain,
> Soon as midnight brought on the duskie houre
> Friendliest to sleep and silence, he resolv'd
> With all his Legions to dislodge, and leave
> Unworshipt, unobeyed, the throne supreme. (V, ll. 661–62, 666–70)

Thus, one could consider the relationship between Satan's motivation for rebellion in *Paradise Lost* and the turbulent political environment of the middle and late seventeenth century. One might ask, in what way does Milton's depiction of power, order, and rule illustrate or try to conceal the political systems that functioned in the period? Indeed, Milton portrays, through caustic irony, a disdain for monarchic or even authoritarian power:

> But he who reigns
> Monarch in heav'n, till then as one secure
> Sat on his throne, upheld by old repute,
> Consent or custom (I, ll. 637–40)

In these lines Satan asserts disdainfully that God's reign in heaven is maintained by his reputation, the consent of his followers, and customary practice. The inference is that God is the passive receptor of power, and therefore the allegiance of the fallen was never compulsory. This can be carried further to conclude that a ruler so maintained is not deserving of their allegiance. The lines, though, also remind the reader that Satan can only maintain his right to rule through the consent of his followers, a consent he achieves through duplicity. These lines touch on the political debates concerning monarchic power that fuelled the civil war and played a role in the execution of Charles I. Throughout *Paradise Lost*, as in much of his prose work, Milton explores the concept of right rule, and thus reflects the attitudes and concerns within his culture relating to power structures both worldly and celestial.

Throughout Milton's lifetime, his poetry participated in contemporary discussions concerning poetic practice, the nature of the individual, the workings of power, and the relationship between humanity and a Christian God. He deployed poetic forms, literary devices and imagery in inventive ways that embraced both a rich literary heritage and contemporary practice. When analysing Milton's poetry or prose work, one should consider carefully the interplay of his techniques, interests, and concerns. A close reading, or formalist* approach, is generally an essential starting place as Milton was interested in the way in which poetry could be constructed so as to create an effect on its readers. Other critical approaches are useful in identifying and discussing the relationship between Milton's construction of a poem and the poem's relationship with Milton's broader social concerns.

Further Reading

Corns, Thomas N. (ed.) (1993), *The Cambridge Companion to English Poetry: Donne to Marvell*. Cambridge: Cambridge University Press. A useful overview of texts and contexts; includes general essays on topics such as 'Politics and Religion' and 'Genre and Tradition', and essays on Donne, Jonson, Herrick, Herbert, Milton, Crashaw, Vaughan, Marvell, and the Cavalier poets.

Daems, James (2006), *Seventeenth Century Literature and Culture*. London: Continuum. An accessible introductory guide; includes a chapter on key critical approaches, a chronology, and a guide to further reading.

Hattaway, Michael (2005), *Renaissance and Reformations: An Introduction to Early Modern English Literature*. Oxford: Blackwell. An insightful and wide-ranging introductory study. Covers canonical* and less well-known authors and includes extracts from significant texts of the period.

Hebron, Malcolm (2008), *Key Concepts in Renaissance Literature*. Basingstoke: Palgrave MacMillan. Short, lucid entries on a range of topics, split into sections on 'Contexts', 'Literature', and 'Criticism'.

Hopkins, Lisa, and Matthew Steggle (2006), *Renaissance Literature and Culture*. London: Continuum. An introductory guide to the period from 1533 to 1642; includes a section on critical approaches, a chronology, a glossary, and a guide to further reading.

Wynne-Davies, Marion (2003), *Sidney to Milton, 1580–1660*. Basingstoke: Palgrave Macmillan. An accessible introductory guide to the poetry, prose, and drama of the period; includes a chronology and annotated biliography.

'Luminarium (English Literature: Early Seventeenth Century)': http:// www.luminarium.org/sevenlit/. A comprehensive guide to authors and topics of the period.

'The Women Writer's Project': http://www.wwp.brown.edu/index.html. An electronic collection of early modern women's writing.

Do not forget to keep a record of *all* the texts and websites you look at when researching for an assignment: you will need to list them in your bibliography.

Literature 1660–1714

Derek Alsop

Chapter Overview

Historical Context

For students of literature, knowledge of historical context in this period is particularly important because some of the main authors were directly involved in the politics of the age, and wrote explicitly political tracts, pamphlets, and satires*.

Our story begins with an emphatic change of direction after a period of civil war and interregnum (meaning 'between reigns', without King or Queen). On 29 May 1660 – his thirtieth birthday – Charles II entered London, to jubilant celebrations, to reclaim the throne for the Stuart dynasty, eleven years after the execution of his father, Charles I, and two years after the death of Oliver Cromwell. After one of the most turbulent and bloody periods in British history, it is hardly surprising that the 'Restoration' of the monarchy was greeted with general enthusiasm. The people would have their Christmas back (previously banned), and the court was ready to party. The flourishing of Restoration stage comedy is itself a sign of the times: not only was the theatre (also previously banned) thriving again, but real, sexy, women (rather than boys) were playing the female roles in plays full of scandal and sexual freedom. The King himself was leading the way with a string of glamorous mistresses, though it was a problem for his credibility that he seemed more committed to the bedchamber than to good government. Here is the King's friend, John Wilmot, Earl of Rochester, taking liberties in 'A Satyr on Charles II' (written 1673):

> I' th' isle of Britain, long since famous grown
> For breeding the best cunts in Christendom,
> There reigns, and oh! long may he reign and thrive,
> The easiest King and best-bred man alive.
> [. . .]
> Peace is his aim, his gentleness is such,
> And love he loves, for he loves fucking much.
>   Nor are his high desires above his strength:
> His scepter and his prick are of a length;
> And she may sway the one who plays with th'other (p. 60, ll. 1–4, 8–12)

With friends like this, who needs enemies? Charles excelled in such peaceful pastimes, but his reputation for foreign policy took a blow in a humiliating war with the Dutch (1665–67). And the mid 1660s brought other disasters well beyond the King's control. The Great Plague of 1665 killed tens of thousands of Londoners in one year, and haunted the imagination for decades to come. Daniel Defoe was only five when it struck, but its impact remained, inspiring his *A Journal of the Plague Year* (1722):

> The swellings, which were generally in the neck or groin, when they grew hard and would not break, grew so painful that it was equal to the most exquisite torture; and some, not able to bear the torment, threw themselves out at windows or shot themselves, or otherwise made themselves away. (p. 94)

The following year was infamous for the Great Fire of London, which more or less destroyed the business area of the city. Though John Dryden, in his poem *Annus Mirabilis: The Year of Wonders 1666* (1667), pictured the King as a kind of spiritual superhero, 'outpraying saints', urging God (successfully) to forgive the nation and douse the flames, many associated these natural disasters with the King's own sins. There was thought to be something rotten in the state of England.

For many, the corruption was a matter of religion. Charles was showing increasingly evident sympathy for the Catholic cause – a distinct problem in governing a nation almost entirely Protestant, with a general prejudice against Popery. To add to the concern, Charles' brother, later James II, made his Catholic faith public in 1673 and married a Catholic Princess. Things came to a head in 1678 when the moral reprobate Titus Oates announced his (fabricated) insider knowledge of a 'Popish Plot' to overthrow Charles and establish a Catholic monarchy. The hysteria that followed fuelled the Exclusion Crisis, as the Parliamentary opposition to the King tried, in three Parliamentary sessions from 1679–81, to 'exclude' James from the throne. It was this political issue that gave rise to factions of 'Whigs' (in favour of exclusion) and 'Tories' (against it), which was to dominate British politics for decades (and inspire many satiric attacks in the literature). Charles managed to overcome the challenge, and instituted one of many new persecutions of the 'dissenters'. For the Anglican majority, the whole period is characterized by, on the one hand, a fear of Catholic ascendancy and, on the other, by the dangers of seditious sects of 'Dissenters' or 'Non-conformists' (Protestant, but not Anglican, religious groups such as Baptists and Quakers). Jonathan Swift, in his *A Tale of a Tub* (1704), ridiculed the excesses of both groups against the comparative (though imperfect) moderation of the Church of England. Defoe, himself a Dissenter, in his *The Shortest Way with the Dissenters* (1702), satirized the extreme religious prejudice of the age:

> Both [Dissenters and Catholics] are Enemies of our Church, and of our Peace, and why shou'd it not be as criminal to admit an Enthusiast as a Jesuit? Why shou'd the *Papist* with his Seven Sacraments be worse than the *Quaker* with no Sacraments at all? [. . .] *Alas, the Church of England!* What with Popery on one Hand, and Schismaticks on the other; how has She been Crucify'd between two Thieves.
>   Now *let us Crucifie The Thieves*. (p. 99)

The death of Charles, in February 1685, focused concern about the future of the throne. Though there was general consent to the succession of James II, two linked rebellions immediately threatened, an ineffectual one in Scotland, and a more dangerous one in England, led by the Duke of Monmouth. James survived both, but he was soon overplaying his political hand, placing Catholics in important roles, and flouting the Test Acts of 1673 and 1678 (which excluded non-Anglicans from positions of political power). He then issued two Declarations of Indulgence, ostensibly to end the political persecution of Dissenters and Catholics alike, but primarily to legitimize further Catholic appointments. The second was resisted by Archbishop Sancroft and six bishops, who were consequently arrested for 'seditious libel'. They were found not guilty, to widespread celebrations.

On 10 June 1688, James II became father to a legitimate heir: James Francis Edward (who would come to be known as the 'Old Pretender'). Now the Catholic line seemed 'assured', but, within only three weeks, a group of key figures in the state, church and military had written to William of Orange, husband to James II's Protestant daughter Mary, ruler of the United Provinces (now, loosely, the Netherlands), effectively inviting him to invade. So began the period of the 'Glorious Revolution', not glorious at all for Catholics (especially Irish Catholics) and not much of a revolution in the military sense (the major armies did not seriously engage), but politically an event that would shape the destiny of modern Britain. James fled to France in December 1688; a 'Declaration of Rights' stated that he had attempted to subvert the 'Protestant Religion'; and the throne was offered jointly to William and Mary. James soon returned to join the Irish in Catholic rebellion against the Crown, but lost the key Battle of the Boyne on 1 July 1690, a famous Protestant victory still celebrated by 'Orangemen' today.

And so James went into permanent exile, near Paris, and the expectation of possible Jacobite invasion (after the Latin Jacobus for 'James') would persist until the middle of the next century, and often colour the literature of the period.

The rest of our period was dominated by war against France, first under William and Mary (the 'Nine Years War'), and then (the 'War of Spanish Succession') under Queen Anne, the second of James' Protestant daughters, who succeeded to the throne in 1702. This second war saw the Grand Alliance of Britain, Austria, Prussia and the United Provinces challenge the French domination of Europe. Under the military leadership of the brilliant Duke of Marlborough there was a series of spectacular successes at Bleinheim (1704), Ramillies (1706), Oudenarde (1708), and Malplaquet (1709).

At home two key developments had prepared the way for a new geo-political future. After much unrest (including, in 1692, the massacre of the MacDonalds in Glencoe), the Act of Union with Scotland of 1707 was passed, creating a new Great Britain. Also secured was the succession after Anne. When she had lost her only son, William had passed the Act of Settlement (1701), settling the British crown on the House of Hanover, preparing the way for George I.

So, at the end of our period, with the 1713 signing of the Treaty of Utrecht ending the war with France and the Protestant succession assured, the country could look forward to a period of peace and prosperity that would make it the leading world power. Alexander Pope's celebration in *Windsor Forest* (1713) expresses the sense of relief: after war and revolution, death by fire, plague and cannon, Britain could look forward to a new age:

> What Tears has *Albion* shed,
> Heav'ns! what new Wounds, and how her old have bled?
> She saw her Sons with purple Deaths expire,
> Her sacred Domes involv'd in rolling Fire,
> A dreadful Series of Intestine Wars,
> Inglorious Triumphs, and dishonest Scars.

At length great *ANNA* said – Let Discord cease!
She said, the World obey'd, and all was *Peace*! (p. 206, ll. 321–28)

Key Authors and Texts

It seems implausible, in an age notorious for its licentiousness and libertinism, to think of John Milton as a Restoration writer, but *Paradise Lost* was published in 1667 (see the 'Literature 1600–1660' chapter). Here is the opening of Book II of the greatest epic* poem in English:

High on a throne of royal state, which far
Outshone the wealth of Ormus and of Ind,
Or where the gorgeous East with richest hand
Showers on her kings barbaric pearl and gold,
Satan exalted sat (pp. 90–91, ll.1–5)

All the features we think of as typical of Milton's 'grand style' are here: the syntactic inversion* affecting expressions (they are not 'barbaric kings' but 'kings barbaric') and whole structures ('Satan sat high on a throne' is hardly impressive by comparison); the exotic place-names; and the elevated diction. Of course, Satan is neither really 'High' nor 'exalted': he has been hurled by God into the 'great deep'. The grandeur suggests not only Satan's threat, but his vanity: his 'rule' is threatened by bathos* – the fall from the sublime 'empyreal heaven' of God to the debased fiery home which he now calls his own.

Milton's description obviously impressed the age. John Dryden could soon expect his readers to pick up on an allusion* to the passage in his poem *MacFlecknoe* (1684):

The hoary prince in majesty appeared,
High on a throne of his own labours reared.
At his right hand our young Ascanius sate,
[. . .]
As Hannibal did to the altars come,
Sworn by his sire a mortal foe to Rome;
So Shadwell swore, nor should his vow be vain,
That he till death true dullness would maintain (p. 145, ll. 106–08, 112–15)

Dryden's poem is an important early example, for the following century, of the 'mock-heroic*' or 'mock-epic*' style that deals with what was perceived as the advance of ignorance. Here, the 'King' is no Satan, but one Richard Flecknoe, the writer of poetry generally agreed to be very bad. He is ready to hand over his crown of 'Dullness' to his protegé Thomas Shadwell, a poet and dramatist with whom Dryden had fallen out. The passage alludes not only to Milton but also to Virgil (Ascanius is the son of Aeneas in Virgil's *Aeneid* (19 BC), a work Dryden would later famously translate). Dryden wants to use the grandeur of the classical and modern epic* to ridicule his own decidedly un-epic subject by comparison.

In *Paradise Lost* the early years of the Restoration produced a poem of unequalled weighty seriousness. But the spirit of *MacFlecknoe*, with its clever, dismissive, mockery of idiocy, would be even more important for the following age and its development of the most successful period of satire* in English literature.

In Dryden's work we can see the beginnings of what has come to be known as the Augustan age of English literature, an age inspired by classical models generally, and by the writings of Horace and Virgil particularly (both poets were contemporaries of the Emperor Augustus (63 BC – AD 14)). Later, King George II's name ('George Augustus') would provide opportunities for the connection between ancient Rome and modern Britain, but the Restoration had already often drawn the parallel. Here is Aphra Behn's elegy* 'On the Death of the Late Earl of Rochester' (written 1680):

> Had he been to the *Roman* Empire known;
> When great *Augustus* fill'd the peaceful Throne;
> Had he the nobel wond'rous Poet seen,
> And known his Genius, and survey'd his Meen,
> (When Wits, and Heroes grac'd Divine abodes,)
> He had increas'd the number of their Gods (1972, p. 103, ll. 74–79)

The homage is not, perhaps, as overblown as it appears. Bishop Burnet, who took Rochester's last confession, noted that he 'was exactly versed in the incomparable Authors that writ about *Augustus*'s time' (Farley-Hills, p. 48). His 'Allusion to Horace' (written 1675–76) is the first poem of its type in English: a formal verse imitation of the tenth of Horace's *Satires* (35 BC). The 'imitation' adapts its model closely to suit new satiric subjects. So where Horace opens with a criticism of the poetry of Lucilius, Rochester begins with an attack against Dryden, who had himself already cited the Horace source in one of his essays. But the poem is more important for its contribution to literary history than for the details of its attack. It established a method and form that would influence all the important English Augustans: Jonathan Swift would follow, as would Alexander Pope, who perfected the form in his celebrated *Imitations of Horace* (1733–38). Samuel Johnson would make his first literary mark with *London* (1738), an imitation of one of Juvenal's satires*.

The Restoration, then, was establishing the ideas, forms, and methods that would dominate the literary establishment for the next eighty years or so: the importance of satire*; the use of the mock-heroic* and mock-epic* to debunk the ignorance of the age; and the acknowledgement, through forms such as the imitation, of the formative role of the 'ancients'. This Augustan agenda continued to be refined. In his 1693 *Discourse Concerning the Original and Progress of Satire* Dryden drew together all the learning of the age to debate the history and the varieties of satire*. The work, as a compendium of arguments, precedents, definitions, and models, would shape the way satirists would think about their enterprise for decades. Later still, the young Alexander Pope would try to establish, in his *Essay on Criticism* (1711), the key literary principles of the period:

> *True Wit* is *Nature* to Advantage drest,
> What oft was *Thought*, but ne'er so well *Exprest*,
> *Something*, whose Truth convinc'd at Sight we find,
> That gives us back the Image of our Mind (p. 153, ll. 297–300)

It is a brilliant idea that enacts itself as we read. But the thought itself – that skill in writing depends on capturing something already well-known – is foundational. What Virgil, Horace, and the rest had already known and 'so well' expressed would be of relevance to the here and now. Art does not deal with new things; it deals with old things anew.

If this seems a slightly alien perspective to a twenty-first-century reader (whose culture places an unprecedented emphasis on originality) another very different literary development was beginning in this period that would lead to the literary embodiment of newness itself: the English novel. Though the novel would flourish in the eighteenth century (and for many years Daniel Defoe's *Robinson Crusoe* (1719) was thought to be a good candidate for the first English novel), it is important to note that there were a number of earlier and influential prose initiatives. Aphra Behn's *Oroonoko, or The Royal Slave: A True History* (1688) tells the story of a black African Royal Prince and his love Imoinda, tricked and sold into slavery, transported to the plantations of Surinam:

> I was my self an Eye-Witness to a great part, of what you will find here set down; and what I could not be Witness of, I receiv'd from the Mouth of the chief Actor in this History, the *Hero* himself [. . .] though I shall omit [. . .] a thousand little Accidents of his Life, which [. . .] might prove tedious and heavy to my Reader, in a World where he finds Diversions for every Minute, new and strange [. . .].
>
> The Scene of the last part of his Adventures lies in a Colony in *America*, called *Surinam*, in the *West-Indies*. (p. 8)

The emphasis on the 'Eye-Witness' authenticity of the account, the insistence that this is 'History' rather than fiction, together with the acknowledgement of a reader who expects adventure, diversion, the new and the strange, locates the narrative between fact and entertainment, in a way that precisely anticipates Defoe's method. The exotic, colonial geography, with its attendant political content, equally anticipates Defoe's settings (Crusoe stranded on an island with a virtuous heathen; Moll Flanders transported to Virginia for her crimes). Other themes will influence the rise of the novel: John Bunyan's *Pilgrim's Progress* (1678), for instance, integrates Puritan spiritual autobiography within a symbolic* narrative framework in a way that also anticipates *Robinson Crusoe*, but perhaps in Behn's work we have the first evidence of a wonderful new world of English fiction.

We have touched on the publication of the greatest epic* in English, the establishment of a new Augustan aesthetic, and the beginnings of the English novel. But despite these achievements, the period is still known primarily for its drama. John Dryden is a key figure, here, particularly for his heroic plays (such as *The Conquest of Granada* (1670–71)), and his tragedies (*All for Love; or, The World Well Lost* (1677), based on the story of Antony and Cleopatra, is often regarded as the greatest tragedy of the period). But Dryden was also one of those dozens writing what we now know as Restoration comedy.

There are too many important comedies in the period for any exhaustive list, but those most studied include: William Wycherley's *The Country Wife* (1675) and *The Plain Dealer* (1676); John Vanbrugh's *The Relapse* (1696) and *The Provoked Wife* (1697); George Farquhar's *The Recruiting Officer* (1706) and *The Beaux' Stratagem* (1707); and the plays of Aphra Behn, George Etherege, and William Congreve. We will explore Behn's *The Rover* (1677) in detail in the 'Case Study' below, so here we can take two plays by other great exponents of the genre to characterize the whole: *The Man of Mode* (1676) by Etherege (also author of *The Comical Revenge* (1664) and *She Wou'd If She Cou'd* (1668)); and *The Way of the World* (1700) by Congreve (who also wrote *The Double Dealer* (1693) and *Love for Love* (1695)).

Typical is the central figure of the rake, a witty, irresistible libertine*, whose past affairs threaten his present designs. Dorimant, in *The Man of Mode* (known to be modelled on Rochester), has toyed with the formidable Mrs Loveit, who swears revenge, breaks her fans in a rage, but remains infatuated: 'I must love him, be he never so wicked' (Etherege, 2.2.16). Mirabell, in *The Way of the World*, has toyed with the formidable Lady Wishfort, who swears revenge, curses her ruined looks – 'I look like an old peeled wall!' (Congreve, 3.1.131) – but also remains infatuated: 'Oh he has witchcraft in his eyes and tongue!' (5.1.371).

The hero, against his better nature, finds himself in love, though he tries to resist it. When Dorimant falls for Harriet Woodvill, for example, he comments on the image she has left in his soul, but determines 'It must not settle there' (Etherege, 3.3.128–29). It does. Congreve's Mirabell is in love with Millamant, and has tried to catalogue her faults and errors to protect himself from her charms, but to no avail. The heroines, for their part, are the wittiest of women, who know their men thoroughly.

The plays offer unrelenting criticism of human relationships. There is general cynicism about women (often to the point of misogyny), men, and marriage (though the plays end in betrothal). At one point in *The Man of Mode* there is even an anti-marriage ceremony, where Harriet and Bellair join hands and 'solemnly' vow never to marry (3.1.70–78). Similarly, in *The Way of the World* the two lovers enter into a long parody* of a marriage contract, where, with 'conditions', 'provisos', and a number of legal 'items', they ridicule the codes of expected and fashionable behaviour that generally go with marriage (Congreve, 4.1.169–252).

The town in Restoration comedy is full of ludicrous 'modishness' and vanity, personified in *The Man of Mode* by the hilarious Sir Fopling Flutter (the 'Man of Mode' himself) or the ridiculous Petulant in *The Way of the World* who so wants a reputation for being in demand by society that he is known to 'call for himself, wait for himself, nay and what's more, not finding himself, sometimes leave a letter for himself' (Congreve, 1.1.330–32).

The emphasis is on wit, quickness of plotting, sharpness of tongue, attack, parry, and riposte. The dominant themes are sexual intrigue and inheritance. Everyone is out for what they can get, and the best deal is usually either sexual revenge with a legacy or the attainment of the beautiful (or handsome) object of desire, also with a legacy. The plays are some of the funniest in the language; the twists and turns of plot are sometimes fiendishly complex; the contests of wit reveal an exuberant love of language. The main critical issue, perhaps, depends on the satire*. Clearly the 'way of the world' is held up to view in all its colours, but it is often simultaneously deplorable and appealing. In this sense the plays are like their naughty heroes. Bad as the behaviour is, we cannot help liking them. Ultimately, the plays tell us, with comic exaggeration, about a worldly world with its dubious motives and selfish designs, but if they are cynical about London life they are entertainingly so, and we would surely prefer to be there than anywhere else.

Criticism and Literary Theory

One of the functions of criticism is the establishing of the canon* of works that together constitute what our culture calls 'literature'. The period of the Restoration is particularly interesting in this respect, as a number of its important figures were relatively neglected until the 1970s and 80s.

When I was at university, in the 1970s, both Rochester and Behn were of marginal importance. There was hardly any published critical material on their works, and even reliable editions were hard to find. Now, forty years later, both are major figures you are likely to study. The reasons they were previously neglected show that a piece of criticism is a product of its time. Here is Nicholas Fisher, in 2000, opening a collection of essays on Rochester:

'No one doubts now the importance of Rochester's poetry.' Graham Greene's confident assertion conceals a heavy irony: it forms part of a preface to *Lord Rochester's Monkey*, a book he had written around 1931 to 1934, but which, in consequence of 'the almost Victorian atmosphere of the time', did not achieve publication [. . .] until 1974. (p. 1)

Considering its often shocking sexual explicitness, 'the importance of Rochester's poetry' could only be properly assessed in a climate of sexual toleration. It is interesting that what we could call a complete, accurate, modern edition of Rochester's poetry was not published until 1968, when David M. Vieth's pioneering work on attribution led to his *Complete Poems*. Perhaps the rise of Rochester owes something to the connection between one period of sexual revolution (the 1660s) and another (the 1960s). Looking back, James William Johnson, in a 2004 biography of Rochester, acknowledges the change: 'Only in the past few decades have scholars been free to discuss openly the previously tabooed, sexual dimensions of English life' (p. 3). Now there is a wealth of Rochester criticism, and it reveals not only our own period's interest in 'transgressive' sexuality, but also a range of other twenty-first-century obsessions. Here, by way of example, is an excerpt from my review of Fisher's essay collection:

Warren Chernaik [. . .] notes that Rochester's poetry tends to exclude 'the possibility of transcendent ideals' and never gives us 'the sense [. . .] of a secure ethical perspective'. Marianne Thormählen [. . .] acknowledges that the 'classic critical turbulence around the notion of authorial intention' applies to attempts to categorize Rochester, who is, at least partly, an 'out-and-out' sceptic and for whom 'true and false are "the subject of debate" '. Howard Erskine-Hill [. . .] notes [. . .] that *Love and Life* 'questions the continuity of the self'. Paul Hammond, in a complex analysis of the role of the homoerotic, warns against seeking in the verse 'a coherent mode of subjectivity', finding 'a desire to lose selfhood in a series of roles and masks and voices', and David Farley-Hills, in a brilliant chapter on satire and the theatre, sees Rochester's affinity with the stage as part of a preoccupation with 'the constant re-inventing of the self', with 'the shadows of our shadows' and 'infinitely postponed' truths. (Alsop, pp. 174–75)

All the uncertainties here—about morality, truth, authorial intention, identity, and selfhood—tell us about our own times, and the themes of twenty-first-century thinking.

The act of reviewing reminds us that reading criticism is itself a critical activity. It is certainly not an 'easy' activity: all our critics above are putting forward complex arguments about Rochester's writing. As I read I am trying to grasp the main theme, selecting a key idea or argument that characterizes each essay, making connections. Here, it is clear that one connection is uncertainty. If I find that critic after critic touches on some aspect of uncertainty in Rochester's writing, then this might lead me to my own insights. It also might confirm something I had already sensed.

Of course, the more criticism you read the better you are in a position to judge the best, but you do not have the time to read all the important books on Rochester, so you need to depend on your tutors and their bibliographies. If your tutor says that Marianne Thormählen's book, *Rochester: The Poems in Context* (1993), is the best, most comprehensive, survey of Rochester's poetry, full of detailed and sensitive readings and a wealth of contextual information and insights, then it makes sense to start there.

If Rochester's status was in need of one kind of 'sexual revolution', then Aphra Behn's was in need of another. For those interested in women's writing particularly, the omission of Behn from the canon* of Restoration literature for most of the twentieth century had been a scandal. Here is Cynthia Lowenthal:

> In a moment I will never forget, back in the dark ages of the early 1970s, a
> scholar of Restoration literature was asked by a member of an audience
> to say a few words by way of introduction about 'this Aphra Behn person'
> to whom so many male writers refer in their works. With an airy and
> dismissive wave of his hand, the scholar said, 'Oh, she was a whore . . . and
> a sometime second-rate playwright'. Thus was one of the major writers of
> the Restoration banished that night, as she had been for centuries before,
> from the legitimate realms of scholarly inquiry. (Owen, p. 396)

This anecdote is hard to believe in 2009 (where, even if sexism still exists, political correctness forbids its public expression). There is an emotional force behind the story, of course, reminding us that criticism is personal. Literary theory of the past thirty years has often challenged (and rejected) the idea that criticism is about value judgements, but such values persist. It *matters* to Lowenthal that Behn is a major writer, neglected by male critics. Immediately we look into the developments that led to Behn's reassessment, though, we find that the issues are more complicated than they might at first seem.

Janet Todd's *The Critical Fortunes of Aphra Behn* (1998) explores in great detail the slow progress towards Behn's critical 'Fame at Last' in the 1980s. She cites one critical essay in particular as having a crucial influence on recent scholarship: Catherine Gallagher's 'Who was That Masked Woman? The Prostitute and the Playwright in the Comedies of Aphra Behn' (1988). All students need guidance, so the recommendation of perhaps the leading Behn scholar of her age might seem a good starting point. But, following her lead and turning to Gallagher's essay, the student will not have an easy time. Students often turn to criticism hoping that it will help them, simply, to understand a text, only to find that critics make things harder. A synopsis of some of the ideas in this essay will prove the point.

Behn, argues Gallagher, as the 'first professional female author' 'was a colossal and enduring embarrassment to the generations of women who followed her into the literary marketplace' (p. 12), because of her bawdy and dangerous reputation. But Gallagher thinks her real scandal was to introduce 'to the world of English letters the professional woman writer as a new-fangled whore' (p. 13). Our first critic, Lowenthal, had rightly rejected the outrageous dismissal of Behn as a 'whore', but now we find that Behn herself presents the woman author (even herself) *as* a whore. Gallagher draws on the real and repeated association in Restoration discourse between 'poetess' and 'punk' (or prostitute). A woman's writings – her publications – make her 'public' property. In that a woman is supposed to give herself wholly – mind and body – to her husband, a woman writer is prostituting a part of herself that should belong to him. But Behn sacrifices this notion of a 'totalised woman' (a woman '*wholly* given away'), creating instead a 'multiple' image of woman. Gallagher discusses Wycherley's poem on Behn, 'To the Sappho of the Age' (first published 1704), which explicitly links her status as writer and whore (pp. 18–19). The poem argues that Behn is now more desired the more she is 'clapped' (with a pun on venereal disease); men can now 'enjoy your Parts for Half a Crown' whereas her parts would have cost a hundred pounds before being made 'public'. Gallagher's essay sees Behn selling herself off piecemeal in her works, and therefore escaping the idea that anyone can truly, wholly, possess her. In the process the idea of a true, whole female self is sacrificed and a woman becomes everything and nothing.

This is clearly a controversial essay, and it is right that we should read it. It shows that easy assumptions about the impact of patriarchal* power can be misleading. But the real experience of reading this essay is one of difficulty. It is a highly complex piece of argument, drawing on a range of historical and theoretical ideas; its aim is certainly not to simplify. To read criticism is often to face new challenges of interpretation and understanding. We might not agree with Gallagher's argument, but before we make a judgement about this we have several hours of reading, thinking, and re-reading to do.

Rochester's Poetry

Rochester, in his short, busy life, was not a prolific poet, but he was certainly versatile. A writer of clever, witty, lyric* poems, he was also a scathing satirist (by turns apparently misogynist and misanthropic). Superficially, the outcomes can seem irreconcilable: how can the author of the most infamously obscene poetry in the history of English literature also write some of the most beautiful love songs? Actually, there is a consistency of theme and subject that unifies the body of work. Rochester is interested in failure and impotence. This study will concentrate on 'The Imperfect Enjoyment' (first published 1680), a poem which is conveniently both about love and abuse.

Impotence, in Rochester's verse, expresses itself literally. Penises generally do not work properly. From poem to poem we can follow the demise of the male organ from the Fall of Man (the joke is Rochester's own), through boastful but failing adulthood to frigid old age. In Eden, Adam and Eve have no sexual problems: 'Each member did their wills obey, / Nor could a wish set pleasure higher'. After Eden none but 'dull delights endure' ('The Fall', p. 86, ll. 7–8, 12). This is an interesting oxymoron*. Whatever 'delights' we want, we will not be satisfied when we get them, and experience teaches us to anticipate our dissatisfaction even as the deluding promise of fulfilment approaches. But Rochester's women all too often do not even get to the point of sexual delight, because their men cannot get it up (or in, or keep it there). Here is the great French essayist Montaigne (1533–92), in a wonderfully colourful Restoration translation:

> The indocile and rude Liberty of this scurvy Member, is sufficiently remarkable, by its importunate, unruly, and unseasonable Tumidity and Impatience, at such Times as we have nothing for it to do, and by its more unseasonable Stupidity and Disobedience, when we stand most in need of his Vigour, so imperiously contesting the Authority of the Will, and with so much Obstinacy denying all Sollicitation both of Hand and Fancy. (vol. 1, p. 102)

Here is Rochester's speaker, in 'The Imperfect Enjoyment', experiencing exactly Montaigne's lack of control:

> But I, the most forlorn, lost man alive,
> To show my wished obedience vainly strive:
> I sigh, alas! and kiss, but cannot swive.

Eager desires confound my first intent,
Succeeding shame does more success prevent,
And rage at last confirms me impotent.
Ev'n her fair hand, which might bid heat return
To frozen age, and make cold hermits burn,
Applied to my dead cinder, warms no more
Than fire to ashes could past flames restore.
Trembling, confused, despairing, limber, dry,
A wishing, weak, unmoving lump I lie. (p. 38, ll. 25–36)

I want to use this poem to illustrate the importance of tone, because its sexual failure is by turns comic and pathetic*, heroic and absurd, and we have to step carefully. Our speaker is 'forlorn' and wishes to show 'obedience', but 'alas' he cannot, the language implying a courtly formality. He wants to satisfy his mistress as a *gentleman* should. But this decency is rather at odds with the physicality of the subject. He is trying to 'swive', an earthy old word for the sexual act. His 'shame' is the key: the euphemisms and metaphors are not only signs of delicate censorship, but an indication of embarrassment. It is mortifying that to show his passionate love he has to do the thing he cannot do, and she has to become a kind of mechanic, lending a helping hand. Noble and elevated ideas of love soon seem ridiculous in such circumstances and end in the ordinary, ignoble, 'lump' he has become.

The failure is particularly disappointing, as the speaker had opened in full loving passion, she beautifully 'naked' in his arms; both lovers 'melting' into one. Their union has full physical force:

With arms, legs, lips close clinging to embrace,
She clips me to her breast, and sucks me to her face.
Her nimble tongue, Love's lesser lightning, played
Within my mouth, and to my thoughts conveyed
Swift orders that I should prepare to throw
The all-dissolving thunderbolt below. (ll. 5–10)

Rochester finds a vocabulary for the details of real passion. The urgency of those 'arms, legs, lips' and breasts trying (with the simplest of alliterative devices) to 'close cling' and 'clip' the two together suggests the normal desperation of physical love. The description of the tongue in the mouth is daring, but Rochester succeeds in making it erotic. It is a 'nimble' tongue, suggesting the liveliness of the love-making, and its 'lightning' suggests electric intensity. But the hint of the heroic (Zeus controls lightning darts) shifts the passage into a different tone: the mock-heroic*. Her tongue makes our speaker suddenly self-conscious, as he prepares to do the deed. The military instruction ('swift orders') suggests Montaigne's divorce between his will and his body. The speaker's body wants to melt, but he cannot allow that: he must make *her* melt with his 'all-dissolving thunderbolt'. But he cannot control himself and has a premature ejaculation, ironically 'melt[ing] into sperm': 'A touch from any part of her had done't: / Her hand, her foot, her very look's a cunt' (ll. 17–18). We have to be *particularly* careful about the tone of this 'cunt', the most shocking word in our language. Rochester himself often uses it with violent offensiveness (read 'A Ramble in St. James's Park' (disseminated 1672–73; first published 1680), for many instances), but I want to suggest that in this instance 'cunt' evokes intensity, passion, love, and beauty. *So* erotic is the experience, *so* thrilling her every touch that she is all cunt. Her 'very look' threatens his self-control; he is so excited that everything about her pushes him to the limit – and over it. Her response is a good answer to those who argue that Rochester is genuinely a misogynist:

> Smiling, she chides in a kind, murmuring noise,
> And from her body wipes the clammy joys,
> When, with a thousand kisses wandering o'er
> My panting bosom, 'Is there then no more?'
> She cries. 'All this to love and rapture's due;
> Must we not pay a debt to pleasure too?' (ll. 19–24)

This is a genuinely tender, playful moment, strangely touching in the detail of the mopping up. She asks the question that many disappointed women would like to ask: what about me? The 'happy' or 'lucky minute', Rochester's regular euphemism for the male orgasm, is often too sudden and too quick to be either 'lucky' or 'happy' for the woman. But many men will be able to identify with the post-orgasmic reaction. In a typically phallocentric* way our embarrassed speaker cannot enter into the spirit of further (perhaps manual) love-play, and resorts instead to abusing his penis:

> Mayst thou to ravenous chancres be a prey,
> Or in consuming weepings waste away;
> May strangury and stone thy days attend;
> May'st thou ne'er piss, who didst refuse to spend
> When all my joys did on false thee depend.
> And may ten thousand abler pricks agree
> To do the wronged Corinna right for thee. (ll. 66–72)

As is often the case in Rochester's verse, the poem moves from the comedy of sexual bungling to the satire* of violent, mock-heroic* cursing: the penis is a 'base deserter' of his 'flame' and 'fatal' to his 'fame' (ll. 46–47). But there is also a tragic edge to this fiasco. Both man and woman agree that the failure is the result of 'love': if he loved her less he could 'fuck' her better. Indeed he goes on to boast bitterly about his former success, claiming 'ten thousand' virgins have been 'pierced' on his 'point' (ll. 37–38), but male bravado (and humiliation) explain the hyperbole*. Montaigne's point (excuse the pun) is that the more you want your penis to do its job the less likely it is to respond. The failure of the penis, in Rochester, is the paradigm* for the failure of all ideals and hopes and aspirations.

And what about that offer? Our speaker hopes that poor, disappointed Corinna will be satisfied by 'ten thousand abler pricks'. This is generous and equitable libertinism*: ten thousand virgins for him; ten thousand pricks for her. If partners loved with disinterested unselfish love then why would they deny each other the pleasure of different sexual encounters? But we do not believe the speaker. Not only are we beset with failure, but the consequent feeling of inadequacy makes jealousy, not generosity, the common emotion. The anger may not be directed at Corinna, but it *is* directed at women. Sex is always at least partly a performance, and heterosexual men depend on women for their sense of sexual prowess. When our speaker fails in his performance, the response is misogynistic, and 'cunt' becomes an obscenity again. His penis is, normally: 'a common fucking post, / On whom each whore relieves her tingling cunt / As hogs on gates do rub themselves and grunt' (ll. 63–65). The spirit of this poem finally belongs with the rest of Rochester's verse. We are cast out of Eden, and cock everything up.

To get the most out of this poem, we have to read very carefully: even the same word, in different contexts, can create completely contradictory effects, and the tone ranges and shifts from coy to obscene, from touching to offensive. We also have to keep the idea of Rochester, behind the verse, separate from our idea of the speaker. Critics of Rochester have themselves often made the mistake of conflating the two. After all, Rochester was a notorious rake and sexual libertine*, so he must be using his own voice. This does not follow, and it is often more revealing to imagine a detachment between author and voice.

 ## Aphra Behn's *The Rover*

It is always important when reading a play (rather than watching a performance) to attend to the stage directions and try to imagine what is happening on stage and in the wings. If we do so with *The Rover*, one of the main themes of the play becomes immediately obvious. Many stage comedies link masquerade with incidents of mistaken identity, but in *The Rover* the ploy threatens universal chaos. The stage directions alone give over thirty instances of miscellaneous '*masqueraders*', or characters in '*masquing habits*' or '*vizards*' (variously whipped on and off). The leading women are first dressed '*like gypsies*'; later '*in antic different dresses*'; and later still '*in habits different from what they have been seen in*'. In addition to these various outfits, we have Belvile dressed as Antonio, Hellena dressed as a boy, Blunt dressed '*in a Spanish habit*', and Florinda '*in an undress*' (which proves to disguise her as effectively as any other costume). What must it be like back-stage? I imagine an actress wondering what dress she is to appear in next: this one, the different one, or the different different one. On stage, more or less everyone is baffled most of the time. Lovers find the objects of their desire indistinctly obscure: any mask and costume will do to completely disguise those you profess to love. Belvile, for instance, does not recognize his lover Florinda whether she is in her gypsy costume *or* her 'antic' dress, and when *he* walks on stage in Antonio's clothes, she immediately exclaims: ' 'Tis not Belvile' (4.2.24).

These disguises and masks, the dressing and cross-dressing are, on one level, typical devices. They contribute to an entertaining spectacle, and enable the twists and turns of plot. The resulting confusion and misunderstanding bring the normal pleasures of comedy. But are they more important than this? Can we look beyond the facts of stage costume to the *significance* of dress? In interesting plays, 'appearances' relate to deeper 'realities'.

If we look closely at the opening scene, we immediately find that clothes and disguise are linked with freedom and independence. The play opens with an emphasis on sexual politics, as Florinda and Hellena assert their right to love whom they will. When their brother Don Pedro enters, the first thing he does is to put on a 'masquing habit' in front of them. He is off to the carnival for sexual adventure, but wants to lay down some rules before he goes. He intends Florinda to marry Antonio, but toys with the prospect of her marrying the old, rich Don Vincentio. Hellena defends her sister with a satire* on the fate of such a young wife. Her bridal bedchamber will become the husband's dressing room, 'and being a frugal and jealous coxcomb, instead of a valet to uncase his feeble carcass, he desires you to do that office' (1.1.106–08). The Don's first action and Hellena's image of grotesque marriage show that dressing and undressing are signs of male control. Not only do men dress and undress as they wish, but women are supposed to look on passively or serve submissively. The women's clothes are chosen for them. Don Pedro will have Florinda in her wedding dress 'tomorrow' and will send Hellena to the nunnery, the costumes of bride and nun suggesting his right to control the sexual destiny of his sisters. He will lock Hellena up 'all this Carnival' (1.1.134) for good reason. If for the men masquerade is an occasion for adventure and entertainment, for the women it is also an opportunity to find relief from the constraints of patriarchal* rule. Don Pedro leaves both sisters, he thinks, safe under the watch of their governess:

> Callis: I must obey the commands I have – besides, do you consider what a life you are going to lead?
>
> Hellena: Yes, Callis, that of a nun; and till then I'll be indebted a world of prayers to you if you'll let me now see what I never did, the divertisements of a carnival.
>
> Callis: What, go in masquerade? 'Twill be a fine farewell to the world, I take it – pray, what would you do there?
>
> Hellena: That which all the world does, as I am told – be as mad as the rest and take all innocent freedoms. Sister, you'll go too, will you not? Come, prithee be not sad. We'll outwit twenty brothers if you'll be ruled by me – come, put off this dull humour with your clothes, and assume one as gay, and as fantastic, as the dress my cousin Valeria and I have provided, and let's ramble. (1.1.164–76)

Hellena's last idea is revealing. You can be a miserable bride-to-be or an incarcerated nun, or you can oppose brotherly rule, strip off, put on your carnival dress and be free. Of course, such a suggestion raises deeper questions about identity. Are you really what you wear?

Hellena's use of the word 'ramble' is interesting. It is important to remember that familiar words may have different associations in earlier literature. The more you read, the more you pick up on these associations, and Rochester's 'A Ramble in St. James's Park' reminds us that the word has sexual connotation: in the seventeenth century, you 'ramble' in search of sex.

So, just by thinking about this idea of clothing in the opening scene of the play and putting together the references, images, and symbolism* associated with different kinds of 'dress', we can see that the whole stage business of the play's many costumes links with the place of women in a patriarchal* system, and their attempts to free themselves and chose their own sexual destinies.

Through Hellena, particularly, the play goes on to challenge the dominance of the men. But women are still allowed few roles. The threat of enslavement (to father, brother, husband) is countered by masquerade, which then exposes women to other forms of abuse (Florinda is threatened with rape more than once in the play). The best you can do is to embrace the spirit (and the costumes) of the carnival, and hope you end up with a tolerable partner.

But there are two characters who seem to be playing by different rules, and it is always worth exploring such 'exceptions' when you find them. Themes usually have counter-themes. In a sense both Angellica Bianca and Willmore reveal themselves for who they really are. Angellica, at first, seems to offer a satire* on the way of the world. Far from being simply 'masked', her face itself is part of an advertising campaign, as she offers herself up for the thousand crowns a month that her reputation as famous courtesan merits. But she falls in love with Willmore, and seems, then, to belong to a rather different play. Her speeches become confessional, open-hearted, and passionate. She has discovered a self *behind* the 'face'. She talks, now, of offering her 'soul', her 'life', her 'love', even her 'virgin heart' (4.2.151). Her language has an intensity lacking elsewhere in lovers' speeches. While everyone else is running around the stage giddy with their designs, she has a soliloquy of self-reflecting despair: 'I had forgot my name, my infamy, / And the reproach that honour lays on those / That dare pretend a sober passion here' (4.2.400–02). Her presence gives the play another dimension. Women are there to be prostituted, sold into marriage, as Angellica explicitly argues to Willmore (2.2.85–89). Whether in or out of vizards or portraits, their faces are up for sale. Literal prostitution is an alternative, and brings a kind of independence. But when Angellica gives up this role she realizes she has lost the right to another (she has nothing 'for sale' any more). (For a more complicated feminist* reading, see Catherine Gallagher, discussed in 'Criticism and Literary Theory', above.)

But why does she fall for Willmore, of all people? This is a man who no sooner looks at a woman but wants her (and will have her if he can). He lusts after, in sequence: a group of masquerading women; Hellena as gypsy; Angellica's picture; Angellica in person; Florinda's picture; Florinda, again (whom he does not recognize); an unknown, unseen lady described as his admirer; Valeria in masquerade; whichever unseen woman Blunt has captured; Florinda again (finally fully dressed as herself), and Angellica again, in disguise. He settles, finally, for the woman who most understands him, but 'settles' seems the wrong word.

Of all men to pledge your heart to! Of course, Behn too has a soft spot for him; it was widely recognized that *Willmore* was modelled on John *Wilmot*, the Earl of Rochester, with the additional frisson that Hellena was first played by Elizabeth Barry, Rochester's mistress. (You probably need the notes of a good edition for this kind of contextual information.) Perhaps, besides his evidently good looks, what appeals in Willmore is his transparency: what you see is what you get. In a world where usually you do not know what you see because everyone is disguised, this is no mean virtue. The two most interesting women in this world of exhausting, unrelenting masquerade fall for the one man who never wears a mask. In this sense, perhaps the most revealing stage direction, of all those many directions relating to disguise, is given at the opening of Act 2, Scene 1: '*Enter Belvile and Frederick in masquing habits, and Willmore in his own clothes, with a vizard in his hand.*' Better the devil you know!

Further Reading

Chernaik, Warren (1995), *Sexual Freedom in Restoration Literature*. Cambridge: Cambridge University Press. An insightful and enjoyable study that is worth reading from cover to cover; includes two single-author chapters: 'The Tyranny of Desire: Sex and Politics in Rochester'; 'My Masculine Part: Aphra Behn and the Androgynous Imagination'.

Hammond, Paul (2006), *The Making of Restoration Poetry*. Cambridge: D. S. Brewer. A detailed consideration of 'the complex ways in which authors, publishers, and readers contributed to the making of Restoration poetry'; includes chapters on: 'The Restoration Poetic Canon'; 'Anonymity in Restoration Poetry'; 'Intertextuality in Restoration Poetry'; 'Rochester and His Editors'; 'Flecknoe and *Mac Flecknoe*'.

Kewes, Paulina (1998), *Authorship and Appropriation: Writing for the Stage in England, 1660–1710*. Oxford: Oxford University Press. This places the work of Dryden, Behn, Congreve, and others in full cultural and historical context, and will help you further consider issues such as authorship, the canon*, intertextuality*, and plagiarism.

Owen, Susan J. (ed.) (2001), *A Companion to Restoration Drama*. Oxford: Blackwell. A comprehensive overview; includes chapters on: 'Libertinism and Sexuality'; 'Masculinity in Restoration Drama'; 'Restoration Drama and Politics: An Overview'; 'Restoration Comedy'.

Quintero, Ruben (ed.) (2007), *A Companion to Satire: Ancient and Modern*. Oxford: Blackwell. A good starting point to help you get to grips with satire; focus on Part II, 'Restoration and Eighteenth-Century England and France'. There are full discussions of Swift and Pope, and Rochester is discussed in the chapter on 'Dryden and Restoration Satire'.

Zwicker, Steven N. (ed.) (2000), *The Cambridge Companion to English Literature, 1650–1740*. Cambridge: Cambridge University Press. A helpful overview, includes chapters on: 'Gender, Literature, and Gendering Literature in the Restoration'; 'Theatrical Culture I: Politics and Theatre'; 'John Wilmot, Earl of Rochester'; 'The Authorial Ciphers of Aphra Behn'.

'Eighteenth-Century Resources': http://andromeda.rutgers.edu/~jlynch/18th/. Click the 'Literature' link to get a list of websites you might find useful.

'Voice of the Shuttle: Restoration & 18th Century': http://vos.ucsb.edu/browse. asp?id=2738. Study the links and see which websites might be useful.

Do not forget to keep a record of *all* the texts and websites you look at when researching for an assignment: you will need to list them in your bibliography.

6 Literature 1714–1789

Derek Alsop

Chapter Overview

Historical Context

The long-awaited peace that ended the discussion of the previous period did not last. The death of Queen Anne on 1 August 1714 and the consequent succession of George I met immediately with Jacobite reaction. Some of those who had planned to recognize the Old Pretender as a new King James fled to France, including Alexander Pope's friend, Bolingbroke. The culmination of a series of disturbances was the Earl of Mar's open rebellion of raising the Stuart flag at Braemar on 6 September 1715. Perth was taken by the rebels, and then the whole of the north of Scotland. A formidable army, gradually swelling to 10,000, was established in the next month. But there was a crucial delay, and an expected rising in England was disappointing; the Scottish conflict stagnated after the Battle of Sheriffmuir, and the advance south into England got as far as Preston before meeting superior forces and surrendering. The Old Pretender finally landed at Peterhead on 22 December to support a rebellion that had already floundered, and returned to France in early February 1716.

In the aftermath of 'the 15', as this conflict came to be known, the Whigs gradually secured a formidable political ascendancy. But one Whig, in particular, was to dominate British politics for the next twenty-five years, and inspire, in opposition, some of the greatest satire* of the period:

I was diverted with none so much as that of the Rope-Dancers [. . .].

This Diversion is only practised by those Persons, who are Candidates for great Employments, and high Favour, at Court [. . .]. When a great Office is vacant, either by Death or Disgrace, (which often happens) five or six of those Candidates petition the Emperor to entertain his Majesty and the Court with a Dance on the Rope; and whoever jumps the highest without falling, succeeds in the Office. Very often the chief Ministers themselves are commanded to shew their Skill, and to convince the Emperor that they have not lost their Faculty. *Flimnap*, the Treasurer, is allowed to cut a Caper on the strait Rope, at least an Inch higher than any other Lord in the whole Empire. I have seen him do the Summerset several times together. (*Gulliver's Travels*, p. 33)

This is Jonathan Swift's preposterous traveller Gulliver being entertained by the miniscule rulers of the tiny island of Lilliput. The satire* is general enough to take in any corrupt politician currying favour with any court, but all readers, in 1726, would have thought of Flimnap as Walpole. Though Whiggish through and through, Walpole had a reputation as something of a 'trimmer', shifting allegiances between 'parties' to suit his ends, hence the reference perhaps to the somersaults. Swift's was one of many such literary attacks against Walpole. One historian, listing the figures who joined in opposition to Walpole, notes the particularly *literary* nature of the group:

Most of all, the addition of the names of many of the greatest writers of the age – Arbuthnot, Fielding, Gay, Pope and Swift – ensured that the power of the pen and the influence of the stage were alike turned upon the ministry of Sir Robert Walpole. There can be no question that this was one of the most brilliant, most famous, and most talented but, at the same time, most unsuccessful oppositions in modern British history. (O'Gorman, p. 80)

The attacks were various, but there was a general assumption that the ministry was corrupt and self-serving. A popular satiric theme was the comparison of low-life criminals with Parliament, as in the opening song of John Gay's *The Beggar's Opera* (1728):

Through all the employments of life
  Each neighbour abuses his brother;
Whore and rogue they call husband and wife:
  All professions be-rogue one another.
[. . .]

> *And the statesman, because he's so great,*
>   *Thinks his trade as honest as mine.* (p. 43)

This idea of the 'great' statesman, as Walpole was often considered, was brilliantly satirized by Henry Fielding in his *Jonathan Wild* (1743), where the concept of 'greatness' is reserved for ruthless criminal behaviour (as opposed to 'goodness') and applied both to the notorious criminal Wild and, by hint and allusion*, to Walpole.

Swift had certainly come to see this administration as corrupt early in its tenure. An English scheme to introduce a new coinage into Ireland, William Wood's halfpence, became a scandal when it was revealed that the coin was of a baser metal than its supposed value. In his *Drapier's Letters* (1724–25) Swift adopted the persona and the language of an ordinary tradesman, the draper M. B. Drapier, to warn the Irish about their potential financial losses. Swift, like many a satirist of the period, found himself a wanted man.

But whatever the reputation of Walpole amongst these key literary figures, there can be no doubt that he was one of the most successful politicians of any age. Gathering about himself a powerful group of supporters, deftly alienating the opposition, and making himself indispensable to George II as much as to George I, he oversaw a period of unprecedented peace and prosperity; prosperity despite the early scandal of the South Sea Bubble in 1720, when a dodgy series of stock investments ended in disaster, touching most and ruining some of the most important families in the country (in fact, Walpole turned this fiasco to advantage, gaining a reputation for a calm approach at times of crisis).

The end of Walpole's period of dominance was also the end of twenty-five years of peace. The next forty years would be years of conflict: two major wars in Europe; one major rebellion at home; and a revolution in the colonies.

The War of Austrian Succession (1740–48) saw George II exercising his dynastic interest in the Hanoverian cause; the Battle of Dettingen, in 1743, being the last time a British monarch was to lead his troops into battle in person. At the same time, in an extension of hostilities, the French were preparing to invade Britain, assembling an army at Dunkirk to bring across Charles Edward Stuart (son of the Old Pretender, hence the Young Pretender to the British throne, popularly known as Bonnie Prince Charlie). Bad weather and an English naval blockade prevented the invasion.

It was not until July 1745 that the Prince landed in the Hebrides, and he did so practically alone. But a rising soon furnished him with 2,000 troops, and he marched on Edinburgh, taking it in September. So began what is famously known as 'the '45', the last major Jacobite rising in Britain, and the most dangerous by far. The rebels took Scotland and marched on England, reaching as far south as Derby. Finally, in retreat, the Jacobites were routed in the conclusive Battle of Culloden in April 1746. Though he remained in Scotland for five months, Charles had to return to exile in France, like his father and his grandfather before him.

It is important not to underestimate the impact of this last rebellion. Fielding's comic masterpiece *Tom Jones* (1749) is set at the time of the '45, when rumour of further Jacobite successes is rife, and the crown seems in genuine jeopardy. As far south as Somerset, the prospect of an encounter with Prince Charles is the subject of gossip. Indeed Tom's sweetheart, Sophia Western, taking refuge in an inn, is taken for the romantic Jacobite figure Jenny Cameron, in hiding. And there is a certain hedging of bets. The landlord will wait to see how the rising goes before he thinks of giving her up to the authorities. Tom's own friend and sidekick, Partridge, a closet Jacobite, is rather alarmed to find his 'master' determined to fight and die *against* the rebels rather than *for* them, but keeps his peace to await further eventualities.

In Europe, another major war – the 'Seven Years War' – broke out in 1756 between the seemingly overwhelming alliance of Austria, France, Russia, Sweden, and Saxony against Prussia. Britain, already at war with France at sea and in the colonies, joined Prussia. On land, the conflict was dominated by the brilliant military commander, the King of Prussia, Frederick II (or 'Frederick the Great'). A series of audacious and innovative strategies and tactics resulted in one unlikely Prussian victory after another. At sea the Royal Navy destroyed France as a naval power and emerged to 'rule the waves'.

In America there was revolution, which, after years of complex colonial fighting, saw American Independence from British rule (1775–83). In a sense this British loss – and King George III had made the American war particularly his own, personal war – had greater consequences than any of the battles in Europe. America would emerge not only as a symbol of independence and liberty, but as a major world power.

But another revolution, of more immediate and shocking impact, was waiting in the wings. As we can choose a date in 1789 to end this survey, it should perhaps be 13 July. The following day – though the French King, Louis XVI, would write in his diary 'July 14th; nothing' – would change the shape of European politics forever. The King did not yet know that a mob had stormed a Parisian prison. The prison was, of course, the Bastille.

Key Authors and Texts

It seems fitting to open the discussion of this period, which, like the last, sees a new succession to the English crown, with another enthronement in the Miltonic mock-epic* style:

High on a gorgeous seat, that far outshone
Henley's gilt Tub, or Fleckno's Irish Throne,
Or that, where on her Curlls, the Public pours
All-bounteous, fragrant grains, and golden show'rs;
Great Tibbald sate (Pope, *The Dunciad*, p. 371, Bk 2, ll. 1–5)

Richard Flecknoe, we have already met (see the 'Literature 1660–1714' chapter), and his presence confirms the acknowledgement of Dryden; Edmund Curll is the notoriously shameless bookseller and publisher of anything, including pornography; Henley is the famous preacher known as 'Orator Henley'; Tibbald is Lewis Theobald, a very good editor of Shakespeare's works who made the mistake of criticizing Pope's own work in that field. Topical satire* always needs extensive footnotes and explanations when we are nearly three hundred years ahead of the times; the challenge is to see through the superficial problems of reference and allusion* and to enjoy the wicked fun of a poem like *The Dunciad* (1728 and 1729, revised 1743). Here we have the Prince of Dulness (not Satan, the Prince of Darkness) sitting on a throne that outshines the pillory where Edmund Curll is humiliated, the crowd throwing its rotten eggs and vegetable matter at the place of public humiliation. But there is also a hint of another 'throne' altogether, a euphemistic 'throne' that gives the grains and golden showers a very different association! (There are many visual and literary representations in the period of the regal throne as a toilet.) Later in the poem, in a parody* of epic* games (with javelin- and discus-throwing heroes), we find Curll himself entering a pissing contest: the highest jet wins the prize, and 'shameless Curl' wins the day with his 'impetuous stream' (Bk. II, ll. 149–82). Satire* in the period is often scatological because the easiest way to mock our self-importance is to remind us of our basic, animal functions.

The Dunciad is the development of all the mock-epic* skills Pope first refined in *The Rape of the Lock* (see the 'Case Study', below). Both poems show that perfect combination of classical learning and contemporary satire* that typify what we call the Augustan age.

But this elite art often intersects with a very different kind of writing. Edmund Curll's prize for his urinating exploits is to walk off with one Eliza Haywood – described as a 'Juno of majestic size, / With cow-like-udders' (Bk II, ll. 155–56) – and *her* writing career takes us back to the origins of the English novel.

We can take 1719 as a particularly important date for this altogether more 'popular' literary form. For many years Daniel Defoe was held to be the 'father' of the English novel, and his *Robinson Crusoe* (1719) the first true novel. But more recently, the patriarchal* lineage of the novel has been challenged and Eliza Haywood has emerged as one of its several possible 'mothers'. Haywood's *Love in Excess* was also published in 1719. Defoe's and Haywood's novels were amongst the most popular of our entire period, and we can see in the very different interests of each a sense of what was to follow.

In *Robinson Crusoe* we have the widest of vistas, a world of adventure and danger, of shipwrecks and cannibals. The stranded islander Crusoe is a survivor and craftsman, someone who can turn his hand to anything. With its emphasis on authenticity (Defoe presents Crusoe as the author), the novel gives us a *particularised* reality. Here is an individual striving to master a forbidding environment, and there is a fascination in watching him develop all the specialist skills of hunter, builder, baker, farmer, clothes-maker, barrel-maker, etc. Crusoe civilizes his world, and is, in turn, civilized by his relationship with Friday, whose simple questions about his life, his God and his faith force him to reassess his own values and beliefs. It is a marvellous book and has captured the imaginations of more readers than possibly any novel written since.

But if this novel can be said to represent the adventurous spirit of fiction, its reaching out to create new worlds, an encounter with external difference, Haywood's *Love in Excess* deals with the world of feeling and sensation (actually, sensationally: the novel is full of explicit sexual encounters). Here is the scorned Amena who has been told that her lover D'elmont has married another:

> *Can love like mine so fierce, so passionately tender, e're sink to a calm, cold indifference? Can I behold the fond endearments of your bridal joys (which you'd not be able to restrain, even before me) and not burst with envy? No, the sight would turn me quite distracted, and I should commit some desperate violence that would undoe us all.* (p. 91)

If readers found in *Robinson Crusoe* the glimpse of a whole new world, in *Love in Excess* they found something else that the novel would provide: an account of the *internal* world of our passions and yearnings. The eighteenth-century novel would find new ways of expressing both the inner and the outer worlds of our experience.

Perhaps the greatest of all the novels of feeling and sensation in the century was Samuel Richardson's epistolary* *Clarissa* (1748). It is not surprising that this novel is rarely taught at undergraduate level. The Penguin edition runs to 1,536 pages, the Everyman edition to four volumes and over 2,000 pages, and Samuel Johnson (who much admired it for its moral precepts) admitted that if you read Richardson for the story you would hang yourself. I can do little more here, though, than to urge all readers of this chapter to read it at some point in their lives. It is an utterly compelling masterpiece. Usually Richardson is represented on novel courses by the historically important

Pamela (see the 'Case Study', below, on *Joseph Andrews*). Important though this novel is, its expression of female vulnerability in the face of male sexual aggression pales in comparison with the same theme in *Clarissa*, where we see a beautiful and intelligent young woman tortured by the attempts of those around her – first her family, then the notorious rake Lovelace – to control her destiny, her body, and her soul.

The epistolary* novel is the perfect vehicle for depicting inner worlds. After all, Richardson's heroines cannot be *doing* anything while they are writing their letters. Richardson's women, conveniently, are usually locked up in houses and rooms either by themselves (seeking refuge) or by those who would imprison them, thus allowing them the time to write. Expertly, the epistolary* form expresses and embodies their constraint. Many others – not only in parody*, like Fielding – would use Richardson's technique, including the two greatest women novelists of the following period – Frances Burney and Jane Austen (see the following chapter) – but none would use it as well.

As the epistolary* form develops, there is a complex attempt to move beyond the confines of house and gardens. Tobias Smollett's *The Expedition of Humphry Clinker* (1771) sends a whole household on a series of adventures around Britain, so that we get the fascinating multiple perspectives of master, servant, father, and daughter, all writing to their own confidantes back home. This kind of epistolary* text suggests that the world 'out there' is always mediated. The famous pleasure gardens of London's Vauxhall are absolutely captivating to one young letter-writer and are the embodiment of modern horrors to another. So what is the 'truth' about the pleasure gardens? In Smollett's novel 'reality' is always something *experienced* and formed by that experience.

Frances Burney's *Evelina* (1778) is interesting for other reasons. By now the epistolary* method has become something of a burden (letter after letter is headed 'Evelina in continuation'), but the account it offers, of a young, intelligent but inexperienced woman's entry into society, is fascinating. The novel's interest is partly in 'propriety': Evelina is learning to do and say 'the right thing', and growing in confidence in her judgement of the manners and conduct of others. Of all the novels in the period, Burney's most look forward to the world of Jane Austen.

Of course the epistolary* novel is a relatively minor form now, but in this period all the other narrative methods were also being developed. Defoe followed his *Robinson Crusoe* with other first-person pseudo-autobiographical fictions, notably *Moll Flanders* (1722) and *Roxana* (1724). And Fielding and others were developing the third-person voice, which reaches its omniscient authorial climax in the funniest novel of the century, Fielding's *Tom Jones* (1749).

But along with the new experiments in fiction there are also experiments in what we might call anti-fiction. The most important literary commentator of the period, Samuel Johnson, famously attacked the new novel form in an essay for the periodical *The Rambler*, questioning the moral validity of a genre that describes the world 'promiscuously', *as it is*, 'without discrimination' (p. 177). For Johnson, art should improve the world, not merely describe it. Johnson's own greatest creative works, whether in verse – *The Vanity of Human Wishes* (1749) – or in prose – *Rasselas* (1759) – are all governed by a primarily moral and philosophical (rather than a realist*) agenda.

Satire*, of course, has such an agenda. On a number of levels, Swift's *Gulliver's Travels* (1726) looks rather like *Robinson Crusoe*. Gulliver, like Crusoe, has all the seafaring jargon (taking in sprit-sails, reefing the foresail, scudding and spooning before the sea (pp. 75–76)); and he too becomes a castaway and reflects on 'so desolate a place' (p. 143), 'lamenting' his folly and 'bemoaning' his family at home (p. 78). Most of all, he tells of his adventures in strange and foreign parts, criticizing the 'strange improbable Tales' of other writers of travelogues (p. 272). But this is just part of the satiric fun. *Gulliver's Travels* is neither a travel book nor a novel, but rather a thoroughgoing *satire*, brutally attacking every aspect of the political and cultural England of its day. In Book I, in Lilliput, we find ourselves with all our vanity and importance ridiculed in the form of six-inch despots whose tiny island (like our own) tries to exert its dominion over the 'world'. If we thought, here, that Gulliver was the gentle giant, then in Book II he is decidedly a Lilliputian, and the preposterous giants of Brobdingnag are civilized in comparison. In Book III our vain pretence to learning is ridiculed in parodies of our institutions, and in Book IV we find ourselves to be less rational than a race of talking horses. Swift's masterpiece peels away the layers of our vanity, until Gulliver has nothing left but to go melancholy mad. It is one of the best satires* of this or any other period.

One other very strange 'novel' deserves to end this section. On one level the narrator of Laurence Sterne's *The Life and Opinions of Tristram Shandy, Gentleman* (1759–67) belongs with the mock-editors of the notes to Pope's *Dunciad Variorum* (1729), with Martinus Scriblerus himself or the deranged narrator of Swift's *A Tale of a Tub* (1704). Just as Swift's narrator cannot keep to his tale, but forever digresses (Section VII is even titled *A Digression in Praise of Digressions*), so Tristram finds he cannot tell the story of his life in any straightforward way: 'Digressions, incontestably, are the sun-shine; —— they are the life, the soul of reading; --- take them out of this book for instance, -- you might as well take the book along with them' (p. 58). At one point, hilariously, Tristram finds he is living 364 times faster than he can write (p. 234).

But Sterne has not really created a dunce. This is the first important English novel to question the assumptions behind the novel itself. How can any piece of continuous prose tell us everything about anything? In accounting for himself and his opinions Tristram finds he has to account for others and their opinions. In expressing a life, he finds an explosion of expression that challenges all attempts at representation. The result is typographical and graphological chaos. There are blank pages, a completely black page and even a marbled page; there are line drawings of the story's progress so far, and of the movement of a stick through the air; there are missing pages and misplaced pages; and rows upon rows of asterisks for the unsaid (and the unsayable). Sterne even invents a new form of punctuation —— the Shandean dash as it has come to be known —— as the desperate acknowledgement that everything is connected to everything else. In *Tristram Shandy*, the learned world of the Augustans (the novel has as much reference to learning as any text in the age) meets completely with the world of narrative representation. Our 'opinions' are as important as our 'lives', and there is no end of either, though Sterne does give us the story of someone who dies mid-sentence, to prove the ludicrousness of the autobiographical enterprise. His own story ends, explicitly and literally, as the story of a cock and a bull, and that seems as reasonable a point of ending as any in this impossible synopsis of one of the most fascinating of all periods of literature.

But perhaps not before, in typical Shandean manner, at least trying to tie up some important loose ends. Sterne was associated, particularly through his short, unfinished novel *A Sentimental Journey Through France and Italy* (1768), with one of the many movements towards the end of our period which have been seen as presaging Romanticism. Actually, Sterne's book is more of a satiric comedy than a piece of genuinely 'sentimental' fiction, but there is no doubt that 'sentiment' and 'feeling' were becoming more important in literature as the century progressed. Alongside the satirical, social sweep of the Augustans was a more personal poetry concerned with the self and the landscape that was to influence William Wordsworth, Samuel Taylor Coleridge and the other major poets of the next period (see the following chapter). The work of Thomas Gray, here, is particularly important. More famous for his two brilliant meditative poems, *Ode on a Distant Prospect of Eton College* (1747) and *Elegy Written in a Country Church Yard* (1751), his later works, including *The Bard* (1757), developed his interest in medievalism, the picturesque and the sublime*. James Thomson had already contributed significantly to the period's view of nature in his highly influential sequence of four poems, *The Seasons* (1726–30), later much admired by Wordsworth. Thomson's friend William Collins, the author of *Odes on Several Descriptive and Allegorical Subjects* (1746), brought an intensity of feeling and a sense of the sublime* and the visionary to his subject that also anticipated later developments. There was a growing interest in rural life, whether seemingly idyllic, as in Oliver Goldsmith's *The Deserted Village* (1770), or grimly realistic, as in *The Village* (1783), George Crabbe's response to Goldsmith. William

Cowper's meditation on physical and mental landscapes in his wide-ranging masterpiece, *The Task* (1785), echoes throughout Wordsworth's *The Prelude* (1805).

Romanticism did not just happen; it emerged from existing interests in the medieval and the primitive, in the self's place in the landscape and the exploration of inner states (often intense: Collins and Cowper suffered from severe depression), and in the expression of profound feeling. A period usually characterized by its emphasis on sense (it is often referred to as the 'Age of Reason') was becoming increasingly interested in sensibility*.

Criticism and Literary Theory

As with the study of any period it is important to know what you are going to secondary sources *for*. Often, in reading literature of the eighteenth century the student will be faced with 'superficial' problems, but they can seriously get in the way of understanding. Such problems include simple matters of vocabulary, reference, allusion*, and the history of people and places. Readers today would not normally know what a 'jordan' is when they find the word in one of Pope's poems. The context will help, but you may still have to look up the word (it is a chamber-pot). If you read Swift describing someone in negative terms as an 'enthusiast' you might be confused. You thought you knew the word, but for Swift an enthusiast is a wild, possibly insane, religious fanatic. All the time you will come across people you have never heard of before: who was Richard Bentley, or Colley Cibber, Edmund Curll, John Dennis, Conyers Middleton, Lewis Theobald? And what about historical events? What was the '45 rebellion and why is it important? What was the War of Austrian Succession and who fought it? In themselves none of these issues poses problems of interpretation: we need the facts, and then we can make sense of the text. They are problems only inasmuch as we lack simple knowledge. But even some seemingly complex problems of allusion* and reference are essentially superficial. When Sterne gives as one of his Latin quotations '*non Ego, sed Democritus dixit*' (p. 280) you will need more than a translation: over the next few pages Sterne, attacking plagiarism, apparently *himself* plagiarizes sections of a famous book by Robert Burton called *The Anatomy of Melancholy* (1621), but Burton had called himself 'Democritus Junior', so the Latin 'it is not I, but Democritus who said it' is a devious, funny, acknowledgement. We would not normally 'know' any of this, but when it is explained (and it is the job of criticism to help) we can easily see the joke: Sterne attacks plagiarism by plagiarizing, but avoids really being a plagiarist by giving a clever acknowledgement of his source.

The literature of this period is particularly full of such problems, for a number of simple reasons. The language is 200–300 years old, so there are bound to be words we do not know or senses we have lost. The people and history pose the same kind of problem. And so much of the best writing in the period is satire* which *often* draws on the details of current affairs and personalities for its attacks. If, in 2009, I wanted to satirize Tony Blair and criticize him for his part in the Iraq War, you would not need footnotes explaining who Blair was, or Bush, or the Iraq War, or 9/11. In two hundred years you would need all these things explained. At the time of writing their satires*, Pope and Swift knew their readers already knew what they were writing about. The period was also particularly fond of allusion* and reference because there was a common belief that 'modern' literature should draw on the best examples of literature from the past, so there are likely to be many intertextual* references.

Before moving on, then, to other kinds of secondary sources, make sure you do some basic research to find out the simpler things. As we have seen, literary criticism can *complicate* rather than *clarify* (see 'Criticism and Literary Theory' in the 'Literature 1660–1714' chapter), so you need as clear a sense as you can of what the text is saying. Crucial to this process is getting the best editions, with notes, explanations, and appendices. Your tutors will not always recommend the best editions, as they know you may not be able to afford them, but they will be in the library.

There are other kinds of sources available that supplement this basic work. To take one example: Martin C. Battestin's *A Henry Fielding Companion* (2000) will tell you everything you need to know about the context for a study of Fielding. Returning to my list of unknown people above, all of them are to be found there (as they all relate to Fielding in some way) with perfect, well-written, critically-aware biographies. There are also some excellent general guides and companions. For instance, if I wanted to know about women writers of the period I would go to Lorna Sage's edition of *The Cambridge Guide to Women's Writing in English* (1999). There I will find that the King himself commanded performances of Susanna Centlivre's plays, that Eliza Haywood's novels are said by some to anticipate those of Jane Austen, that Delarivière Manley married her cousin and guardian.

When we have as many of the facts as we can easily gather, and have read the texts as carefully as we can, there will be other reasons for going to criticism. If we are reading Pope's *The Rape of the Lock* (see the 'Case Study', below) we might want some guidance on how this poem fits in with the rest of Pope's work, or with other satire* of the period. Ideal for this (even the title tells us so) would be Brean Hammond's *Pope Amongst the Satirists 1660–1750* (2005). Here we will find all kinds of helpful background information, but also some interesting critical ideas, such as the claim that even Pope's serious verse is 'ambushed', 'surprised' or even 'sabotaged' by satire* (p. 35).

But we might want a broader sense of literary history. We might want to know, for instance, how Richardson's epistolary* novel *Pamela* 'fits in' with the other novels of the period. On every reading list for a course in the eighteenth-century novel there will be Ian Watt's *The Rise of the Novel: Studies in Defoe, Richardson, and Fielding* (1957). That a book as old as this should still appear shows that it has particular importance. Watt helped to establish the twentieth-century version of the canon* for the early novel: the key authors were identified as Defoe, Richardson, Fielding, Sterne, and Smollett. Soon we will find, as we read further, that this idea of what one critic calls ironically 'the dream team' has become controversial, that it is part of a debate. Feminist* critics, for instance, have rejected the marginalizing of women's writing in the period. Jane Spencer, in a title that directly challenges Watt, re-writes the canon* as *The Rise of the Woman Novelist: From Aphra Behn to Jane Austen* (1986).

Imagine we become interested in this question of the canon* and its possible feminist* revision, but we are studying Fielding's *Joseph Andrews* (see the 'Case Study', below). Then we might turn to Angela J. Smallwood's *Fielding and the Woman Question: The Novels of Henry Fielding and Feminist Debate 1700–1750* (1989), where we find that: 'significant areas of the content of [Fielding's] novels are informed by relatively enlightened, liberal views on the woman question as it was articulated in his time' (p. 173).

Further research will take us, perhaps, to Rachel Carnell's *Partisan Politics, Narrative Realism, and the Rise of the British Novel* (2006), which will show how far the critical climate has changed since Watt: 'To scholars of the eighteenth-century novel, it may seem "a truth universally acknowledged" that "narrative realism" and "the rise of the novel" are outmoded categories. We are now cautious about focusing on formalist* conventions that have been used to distinguish "great" from "lesser" works of literature' (p. 1). But Carnell – as her reference to the famous ironic opening of *Pride and Prejudice* implies – will also want to challenge this new assumption.

Just by following a trail of critical interest like this we not only learn about the text we are reading but about the nature of criticism itself. Watt writes an important book; gradually, over time, the assumptions of that book are questioned and challenged; one of the challenges is political and theoretical, and a new view of the rise of the novel becomes possible; a new canon* emerges, but then the old canon* is reassessed in the light of the new approach. Watt was right; then he was wrong; and finally he was neither exactly right nor completely wrong.

But how does this sense of literary history help us? It should, actually, liberate us. At this level, criticism is about opinion and debate, the cut and thrust of argument. And there are many possible tenable arguments. My suggestion is that you do not read this kind of criticism simply to find out about the text. Read it because you are interested in the debate.

Does this variety of arguments mean that 'anything goes'? Not in practice. We are always reading and interpreting texts with others in mind. Whatever we think a primary text shows, we will have to persuade others that this reading is a possibility. In the end, whatever our position, whatever surveys, guides, theories, or criticisms we read to support us, it is to the primary text we turn for the crucial evidence. But the evidence is not just 'there'; it needs interpreting.

Some criticism your tutors may recommend is very difficult. Every now and then, though, you will come across a book that throws light on everything, a book that is beautifully written, and takes you into the world of texts in new and refreshing ways. Just such a book is David Fairer's *English Poetry of the Eighteenth Century 1700–1789* (2003). Here is how it opens:

> The manuscript* looks like a printed book. Its nineteen leaves are written with meticulous care in a small italic hand that mimics type. The lines are neatly spaced just as on a printed page, including even the 'catchwords' (the first word of the next page set in each right-hand corner). There are running headlines, and in the titles of the four poems each large individual capital letter is elegantly shaped. It seems newly delivered from the printing house. (p. 1)

Fairer is describing the beginning of Alexander Pope's literary career. The careful description of the look of this manuscript* immediately takes us into a world where 'the cultures of manuscript* and print overlapped and engaged with each other as never before' (p. 1). But also, imaginatively, it captures the sense of a young writer confident in his abilities, proud of his work, knowing he is on the verge of something important. The meticulousness of the manuscript* suggests something about Pope's whole attitude to poetry, as a craft which requires the greatest care and accuracy. At its best, critical writing is inseparable from creative writing: its appeal is essentially imaginative. When I read Fairer's words, I feel I can see Pope at his desk, working away. In an age of e-books and e-mail it is also pleasing to be reminded that our love of literature is also a love of books – real books – and that the creation of the text itself, line by line, page by page, is the source of our excitement.

 **Alexander Pope's Poetry**

Here is Pope in philosophical mood in *An Essay on Man* (1733–34), explaining that everything is governed by a divine order we are not always aware of:

All Nature is but Art, unknown to thee;
All Chance, Direction, which thou canst not see;
All Discord, Harmony, not understood;
All partial Evil, universal Good:
And spite of Pride, in erring Reason's spite,
One truth is clear, 'Whatever IS, is RIGHT.' (p. 515, II, ll. 289–94)

My students, when they arrive at university, are generally uneasy when it comes to the close analysis of poetry. Some have heard of iambic pentameter*, but they do not really know why they know this, or why it matters. As soon as we start analysing passages like the one above, a range of other technical terms looms. But they are there to help, not hinder. Take the example of caesura*. A caesura* is a pause around the middle of a line of poetry, often marked by punctuation. In each of the lines above there is a caesura* between 'Art' and 'unknown'; 'Direction' and 'which'; 'Harmony' and 'not'; 'Evil' and 'universal'; 'Pride' and 'in'; and 'clear' and 'Whatever'. It is clearly much easier to refer to this pause as a caesura* rather than as 'a pause around the middle of the line'. But why would we want to refer to it at all?

This is a crucial question. There is absolutely no point in using terms if you have nothing to say about their *significance*. Poetic analysis is not a matter of spotting devices, but of showing how poetry achieves its effects. The caesuras contribute significantly to the effect of the lines above. They create, literally, a 'pause for thought'. Look at the content and structure of the first three lines: each line says 'this is that, but you do not know it'. The caesura* divides the truth (for instance, that 'nature' is actually God's 'art') from our ignorance ('unknown to thee'), and the combination of caesuras reinforces the pattern affecting all such truth and ignorance. Each caesura* creates a moment of revelation.

Notice also the intense contraction. Having created the grammatical structure of 'All Nature is but [meaning "only"] Art', Pope then uses ellipsis* for all the other similar expressions. Ellipsis* describes the omission of certain words, which are taken to be 'understood'. So 'All Discord, Harmony' means 'all discord is only harmony'. Again you might feel, so what? Well, not only does this technique create conciseness and density, but it serves to stress the combination of opposites. Nothing exists between 'Discord' and 'Harmony' but the surprise that confirms they are one and the same thing. And the idea that discord is harmony suggests oxymoron* or verbal paradox*. Indeed, elsewhere Pope uses the oxymoronic* construction 'harmoniously confus'd' (*Windsor Forest* (1713), p. 195, l. 14), drawing on one of his favourite classical poets, Horace, whose 'concordia discors' means 'discordant harmony' or 'harmonious discord' (p. 328, I, xii, l. 19). Again, though, we have to feel that the device is significant before referring to it. Here, of course, it is significant.

Pope is arguing that God resolves all things; that what seems discordant to us is actually part of a harmony we cannot properly hear. God puts opposites beautifully together, so Pope uses oxymoron*. The musical metaphor of 'harmony' to describe the divine order is particularly apt in poetry, which depends on rhythm and sound. So, let us turn to the subject that most unnerves my students: metre*.

It is no accident that you may have heard of iambic pentameter* as it is the most important rhythm in English poetry. The expression means that there are five patterns of (broadly) iambic* rhythm in each line. The basic pattern gives a relatively unstressed syllable followed by a relatively stressed one (an X marks the weaker stress and a forward slash the stronger):

> X / X / X / X   / X /
> All Na ture is but Art, un known to thee

But again, *why* would we want to discuss the metre* of the passage? Because Pope is doing everything possible to convince us of the truth of his message and the rhythm helps: 'one *truth* is *clear*' it keeps saying. The rhythm contributes to the sense of argument. The simple use of rhyme (in what we call, here, heroic couplets*) also reinforces the harmony, balancing one line against another. But there are more complex devices, too. The structures 'spite of Pride, in erring Reason's spite' and 'Whatever IS, is RIGHT' are forms of chiasmus*. Chiasmus* creates a special kind of symmetry that goes A then B / B then A, and the repetition of words in these two expressions hint at this pattern.

The point of this kind of analysis is not to show off the terms, but to understand all the different things Pope does with his lines to express the force of his idea that everything in the universe is perfectly, harmoniously, beautifully, and rightly *ordered* by God.

So, now we have a kind of formula for the relationship between form and subject in Pope's work. When he is *not* being satirical, all the devices of order and balance will perfectly *complement* the subject, whether that subject is God's universal design, a view of a landscape (see *Windsor Forest*) or the qualities of the perfect critic (see *An Essay on Criticism* (1711)). But when he *is* being satiric, then the order and balance of the verse will perfectly *contradict* its unbalanced subject.

Here, in his first great mock-epic* poem, *The Rape of the Lock* (the revised version of 1714), we have Ariel (the leader of an imaginary race of tiny supernatural 'sylphs' whose job is to guard the honour and reputation of their human mistress Belinda) urging his fellow sylphs to be on their guard, as something fateful seems about to happen (Belinda will have a lock of her hair forcibly cut off by an admirer, the 'rape' that the poem advertises):

This Day, black Omens threat the brightest Fair
[. . .]
Whether the Nymph shall break *Diana*'s Law,
Or some frail *China* Jar receive a Flaw,
Or stain her Honour, or her new Brocade,
Forget her Pray'rs, or miss a Masquerade,
Or lose her Heart, or Necklace, at a Ball (p. 255, II, ll. 101, 105–09)

Here are all the devices of harmony, but in an unharmonious world. The couplet* form suggests that the losing of your virginity is exactly as important as cracking a vase. The use of the caesura* implies an equivalence between staining your dress (or 'Brocade') and your honour, or between losing your necklace or your heart. This idea is reinforced by a variety of zeugma* where one verb applies (with ellipsis*) to two different nouns, one literally and one metaphorically: (will the nymph) stain her honour, or (will she stain) her new brocade (?); (will the nymph) lose her heart, or (will she lose her) necklace (?). The rhythmic and syntactic devices (note the parallels again) all contribute to the sense of fluent harmony and balance. But the balance is all wrong. Belinda lives in a world of twisted, topsy-turvy values. In terms of *meaning* everything is discordant, and the untroubled harmony of the verse creates a formal irony (the balanced form is ironically ill-suited to the lack of balance in the subject).

Pope's *The Rape of the Lock* is the most famous mock-epic* poem in the language, and the mock-epic* thrives on disproportion and disharmony. It treats ordinary subjects as if they were of epic* significance. The poem has everything we expect of the epic*: an invocation to the muse (I, ll. 3–6); a direful prophecy (II, ll. 101–04); a tremendous battle or two (one actually a game of cards; III, ll. 25–100); and a visit to the underworld, the 'cave of spleen' (IV, ll. 11–88). The scale reduction that replaces the great Gods of the classical epics (Zeus, Poseidon, Hermes, and the rest) with Pope's sylphs is an inspired idea. In Homer's *Iliad*, Zeus warns his Gods not to take sides in the great Trojan War. Any God who disobeys will be thrashed and hurled into the gloom of Tartarus (the lowest region of earth, below even Hades). Pope's Ariel warns *his* spirits to make sure they look after Belinda's fan, her earrings, her watch, her pet dog, and her precious lock of hair. If *they* fail in their tasks they will be stoppered up in perfume bottles, 'transfixt with *Pins*', wedged in the eyes of needles, clogged up with make-up, or torn apart by the centrifugal force of a whirling cup of hot chocolate (II, ll. 123–36). Though not exactly off to Troy, Belinda is indeed off to war in the battle of the sexes. But neither the protection of her 'cosmetic powers' (we see her making-up and getting dressed; II, ll. 121–48) or her army of invisible protectors can save her from the fatal snip. The sacred lock finally rises, preposterously, to the heavens to form a new constellation, but at this moment of greatest disproportion, Pope uses the same verse skills we have already seen at work to create a remarkable shift to something actually serious:

> For, after all the Murders of your Eye,
> When, after Millions slain, your self shall die;
> When those fair Suns shall sett, as sett they must,
> And all those Tresses shall be laid in Dust;
> *This Lock*, the Muse shall consecrate to Fame,
> And mid'st the Stars inscribe *Belinda*'s Name! (V, ll. 145–50)

Just look at the use of the caesura* here! It moves us from the ludicrous millions of Belinda's conquests to the fact of her death, all in the space of *one* line; from the ridiculous cliché of her eyes as suns to the fact that the light of her real eyes will die, in another *one* line. I know of no other poet who could achieve such an astonishing effect. Pope's satire* is about the need to achieve a sense of balance and proportion: let us not be so vain, because there are more important things. A very funny poem about a silly lock of hair ends with a reminder of our mortality. And those caesuras have their part to play. To examine a comma might seem trivial, but that comma might well open out into the whole meaning and purpose of Pope's poetry.

 ## Henry Fielding's *Joseph Andrews*

Joseph Andrews (1742) takes us to a crucial moment in the history of the novel, a point of intersection between the works of perhaps the two most influential novelists of the period: Henry Fielding and Samuel Richardson. Fielding's novel is the continuation of a literary quarrel, and for its origin we need to look a couple of years back to one of the most remarkable 'media events' in the eighteenth century (Warner, p. 178). Before university, texts are often studied in isolation, but usually to fully understand the importance of one text we have to consider the literary history that led to it, especially because there is always an implicit or (as is the case here) explicit intertextuality*.

Fielding's *Shamela* (1741) is the wittiest of the many immediate responses to Richardson's *Pamela*, the publication of which, in November 1740, produced, within a year, 'nearly two-dozen pamphlets, continuations, translations and parodies' (Ingrassia, p. 13). *Pamela* is the story in letters of a chaste and intelligent lady's maid who resists all the attempts of her master, the cryptically named Mr B., to compromise her 'virtue' and have his way with her, until the power of her example reforms him and he offers his hand in marriage (*Virtue*

Rewarded is the novel's sub-title). This archetypal* romance* certainly captured the public imagination, and the novel became an immediate best-seller. There were pro-Pamelists who applauded the heroine's model conduct and anti-Pamelists who either rejected the plausibility of Pamela's moral stand or (reading 'against the grain') saw her as a 'sham' (or both). Fielding's parody*, in April 1741, was soon followed, in June, by Eliza Haywood's *Anti-Pamela; or, Feign'd Innocence Detected*. In fact, the idea that Pamela is 'feigning' or 'shamming' virtue in order to drive Mr B. to marriage is explicitly the theme of what we could call the anti-Pamelists in Richardson's own novel. Mrs Jewkes, who aids and abets Mr B., says at one point to Pamela: 'Come, come, no more of these shams with me!' and B. calls her a 'holy hypocrite' a 'saucy designer' and a 'plotting little villain of a girl' (pp. 193, 201). A travesty of Richardson's intentions though it may be, Fielding's *Shamela* is a masterful and very funny parody*. His 'Pamela' is now only the 'real' Shamela's assumed name, and she honestly exposes her own designs on Squire Booby (Fielding helpfully giving Mr B. a fuller identity) in a style recalling Richardson's original in form and subject.

Fielding was not attacking Richardson personally, not knowing the true author of *Pamela* at the time. But he did not let it lie there, and within a year he had invented for Pamela Andrews a brother: Joseph. In this new book – a proper novel in the sense that *Shamela* never was – Pamela makes a guest appearance. She has been re-designed again: no longer a colourful and exuberant wench like Shamela; now a fine lady, but still an arrant hypocrite.

Fielding had one inspired comic idea for the development of the anti-Pamela theme in this novel. What if you dislocate all the ideas associated with virgin chastity by creating a pure innocent *hero* rather than *heroine*? Lady Booby develops a passion for her servant Joseph in the first few pages of the novel (as do most other women, from the hilarious Mrs Slipslop to Betty, the chamber maid). Much of the early fun of Fielding's novel depends on the comic inversions that go with the revised formula for 'virtue'. 'Chastity', as Joseph says, may be 'as great a Virtue in a Man as in a Woman' (p. 41), but it has much more comic potential in a man. When Lady Booby attempts to seduce Joseph he makes the mistake of citing his sister's favourite quality. Lady Booby asks him how he could possibly control himself if she allowed him the freedom of a kiss; he says he hopes he wouldn't allow any natural inclinations 'to get the better of my Virtue' (p. 35). And now, before Lady Booby's spoken response, we see something very different in Fielding's prose, something much more important to his development as a novelist than his mere engagement with the themes of *Pamela*; now we have a narrative voice, a learned and witty narrative voice that engages us, explicitly as readers, directly in the narrative experience:

> You have heard, Reader, Poets talk of the *Statue of Surprize*; you have
> heard likewise, or else you have heard very little, how Surprize made
> one of the Sons of *Crœsus* speak tho' he was dumb. You have seen the
> Faces, in the Eighteen-penny Gallery, when through the Trap-Door, to
> soft or no Musick, Mr *Bridgewater*, Mr *William Mills*, or some other of
> ghostly Appearance, hath ascended with a Face all pale with Powder,
> and a Shirt all bloody with Ribbons; but from none of these, nor from
> *Phidias* or *Praxiteles*, if they should return to Life – no, not from the
> inimitable Pencil of my Friend *Hogarth*, could you receive such an Idea
> of Surprize, as would have entered in at your Eyes, had they beheld the
> Lady *Booby*, when those last Words issued out from the Lips of *Joseph*. –
> 'Your Virtue! (said the Lady recovering after a Silence of two Minutes)
> I shall never survive it. (p. 35)

It seems, here, as if Fielding the man is actually speaking to us (though we
should still insist on the difference between author and narrator even in a case
like this: this is Fielding in 'Fielding the narrator' mode). The voice certainly
draws on Fielding's own past. Evident here, for instance, is the lasting influence of his earlier literary career as a dramatist (Bridgewater and Mills performed in his own plays): the audience; the stage with all its machinery and
business; the performances of the actors; the music; and the spectacle. (All will
feature throughout Fielding's novel-writing career.) And the artist Hogarth
was indeed Fielding's friend. But mixed with the personal, conversational
tone, in the references to Crœsus and the Athenian sculptors Phidias and
Praxiteles, is classical learning. In this sense, Fielding's novels position themselves in the Augustan mainstream. Most important of all, though, in the
space of Lady Booby's two-minute silence, is the sense of a narrator controlling the telling of an entertaining tale, directing (and delaying) the action, and
invoking our imaginative involvement. Here, then, is Fielding's greatest contribution to the history of the English novel: the development of a compelling
omniscient narrator who explicitly guides every aspect of the reading experience *as* an experience of reading (rather than as the revelation of a real world
glimpsed by an editor of letters, or presented as the protagonists'* true life
accounts). When studying novels, the narrative voice is always crucial, and
we need to ask a range of questions about it. Is it in the third- or first-person
(in first-person narratives there is often a question of the reliability of the
account or the trustworthiness of the narrator)? If it is a third-person voice,
does it share the perspective of one or more of the characters it describes, or is
it mainly 'outside' the action, looking on. Does it see and know everything?
Does the narrator acknowledge that a story is being told? Is the narrator
telling the tale directly, or is there someone else's story embedded (in Fielding,
for instance, a number of characters tell their own stories *within* the main

story). Historically speaking, Fielding was one of those key figures who helped develop the models of possible narrative roles. In *Joseph Andrews* the narrator clearly enjoys his role. He is a self-conscious stylist; the inventor, he claims, of the 'comic Epic-Poem in Prose' (p. 4). The novel is obviously comic, but it is mainly epic* in the sense that *The Rape of the Lock* is epic*. It is hardly surprising that Fielding, the author of the mock-heroic* *Tom Thumb the Great; or The Tragedy of Tragedies* (1730), is a more than capable exponent of the mock-epic*. Take, for instance, the magnificent episode of the 'battle of the dogs' (pp. 212–16) when Joseph and Adams take on their assailants' hounds. After introductory references to Homer and Virgil, and an invocation to the muse of biography (there is no such classical entity, so Fielding adds 'or by what other Name soever thou chusest to be called' (p. 212)), we see Joseph, 'swift of Foot' (p. 213), an expression always associated with Achilles, grab his cudgel and lay all about him (though not before a lengthy description of the history and design of the cudgel which makes it the equivalent of the famous shield of Achilles in the *Iliad* (p. 213)). We even have an elegy* for one of the hounds: 'O *Ringwood. Ringwood* the best Hound that ever pursued a Hare, who never threw his Tongue but where the Scent was undoubtedly true' (p. 214; we later find that Ringwood is not even dead, just stunned). And at the end of this long passage of what Fielding generally likes to call 'fine writing' we find that same distinctive voice, simultaneously condescending (there is a hint of royalty about its 'we') and self-mocking, explicitly referring to the act of storytelling, itself:

> Thus far the Muse hath with her usual Dignity related this prodigious Battle, a Battle we apprehend never equalled by any Poet, Romance or Life-writer whatever, and having brought it to a Conclusion she ceased; we shall therefore proceed in our ordinary Style with the Continuation of this History. (pp. 214–15)

Notice the range of contextual and intertextual* information that can help us get the most out of Fielding's novel. We need to look into the history of its creation, and bring some knowledge of at least *Pamela* and *Shamela* to bear. Our sense of the importance of Fielding's narrative voice draws on a knowledge of the various voices of other early novelists. The characterization of the narrator takes us into biographical details. Our understanding of the mock-epic* depends on some knowledge of epic* literature, and benefits from our familiarity with other contemporary mock-epics*, and with the author's own earlier works. When you choose to study literature at university, the excitement of discovery is not only in reading another new text but in relating one text to another. University lecturers of English are fond of quoting E. M. Forster's *Howard's End* (1910) for good reason: 'Only connect . . .'.

Further Reading

Battestin, Martin C. (1974), *The Providence of Wit: Aspects of Form in Augustan Literature and the Arts*. Oxford: Clarendon Press. A seminal discussion of various canonical* authors (including Fielding, Goldsmith, Pope, Sterne, and Swift) and issues such as form, artificiality, aesthetics, and 'Nature'.

Doody, Margaret (1985), *The Daring Muse: Augustan Poetry Reconsidered*. Cambridge: Cambridge University Press. An insightful consideration of the 'peculiar complexity and richness' of the poetry of the period.

Richetti, John (ed.) (2008), *The Cambridge Companion to the Eighteenth-Century Novel*. Cambridge: Cambridge University Press. A decent overview; includes chapters on: 'The Novel and Social/Cultural History'; 'Samuel Richardson: Fiction and Knowledge'; 'Henry Fielding'; 'Women Writers and the Eighteenth-Century Novel'.

Rogers, Pat (1974), *The Augustan Vision*. London: Methuen. An accessible and wide-ranging study that will help further your understanding of the period and various canonical* authors, from Swift and Pope (in Part III, 'Parables of Society: Satire and the Moral Essay') to Defoe, Richardson, Fielding and Sterne (in Part IV, 'Tales and Confessions: The Novel').

Sitter, John (ed.) (2008), *The Cambridge Companion to Eighteenth-Century Poetry*. Cambridge: Cambridge University Press. A good overview; includes chapters on: 'Publishing and Reading Poetry'; 'The City in Eighteenth-Century Poetry'; ' "Nature" Poetry'; ' "Pre-Romanticism" and the Ends of Eighteenth-Century Poetry'.

Woodman, Thomas (ed.) (1998), *Early Romantics: Perspectives in British Poetry from Pope to Wordsworth*. Basingstoke: Macmillan. Contains essays on a range of both canonical* and often overlooked poets; includes chapters on: 'Autobiography and Elegy: The Early Romantic Poetics of Thomas Gray and Charlotte Smith'; 'The Eighteenth-Century Collins'; 'Goldsmith's "Pensive Plain": Reviewing *The Deserted Village*'; ' "Still at Home": Cowper's Domestic Empires'.

'Eighteenth-Century Resources': *http://andromeda.rutgers.edu/~jlynch/18th/*. Click the 'Literature' link to get a list of websites you might find useful.

'Voice of the Shuttle: Restoration & 18th Century': http://vos.ucsb.edu/browse. asp?id=2738. Study the links and see which websites might be useful.

Do not forget to keep a record of *all* the texts and websites you look at when researching for an assignment: you will need to list them in your bibliography.

Part III
Studying Romantic and Victorian Literature (1789–1901)

The Romantic Period

David Higgins

Chapter Overview

Historical Context

The 'Romantic Period' is tricky to pin down. It generally refers a period from about 1780 to about 1830, but there is no consensus over precise start or end dates. The problem is that the adjective 'Romantic' and its associated noun 'Romanticism' are used to describe a diverse set of responses to complex socio-cultural changes that took place in western Europe during about a century. Critics and historians have struggled over the years to define Romanticism and A. O. Lovejoy famously argued in 'On the Discrimination of Romanticisms' (1924) that the term was used so broadly that it had become effectively meaningless. Romanticism has tended to be associated with certain concepts and areas of human experience: for example, feeling, revolution, the imagination, nature, and introspection. It has often been contrasted with eighteenth-century literature's emphasis on reason, order, imitation, urban life, and sociability. However, once you start to unpack these grand generalizations, they become increasingly hard to sustain. For example, plenty of eighteenth-century literature is introspective, and plenty of Romantic literature is interested in sociability (see Cox; James; and Russell and Tuite). And, as discussed in the previous chapter, the focus on the relationship between self and landscape that you see in many Romantic-period texts has its roots in the work of eighteenth-century poets such as Collins, Cowper, Gray, and Thomson. I am not suggesting that the terms 'Romantic' or 'Romanticism' are useless, except in so far as they designate a period of time, but they certainly need to be handled with care. Useful discussions can be found in some of the critical works listed in the 'References' section (see Butler 1982; Day; Ferber; Lovejoy; Ruston; Wellek). My own view is that, at least initially, it is best to take each primary text on its own merits, and to think about its relationship to the period and to other texts, without being overly troubled by whether it is 'Romantic' or not.

The defining 'event' of the period was the French Revolution, which reverberated throughout Europe and had a profound impact on British culture. Many of the writers that you will study addressed ideas of revolution and progress in their works. Although popularly associated with the storming of the notorious political prison, The Bastille, on 14 July 1789, the Revolution was actually a complex set of events and processes that began in the 1780s and ended around 1800. Over the next fifteen years, Napoleon Bonaparte would dominate Europe as Emperor of an expansionist France, finally defeated by the allied powers of Britain and Prussia at the battle of Waterloo on 18 June 1815. The greatest celebrity of the age, Napoleon loomed large in the imaginations of many Romantic authors. Byron, for example, described himself in *Don Juan* as the 'grand Napoleon of the realms of rhyme' (p. 410), and meditated on the French Emperor's 'fall' in several other works (see Bainbridge).

The Revolution began as a movement to limit the power of the monarchy and the aristocracy. It was initially welcomed by many British writers, but various voices soon emerged to criticize its principles. The most powerful of these was Edmund Burke, whose *Reflections on the Revolution in France* (1790) argued strongly for the importance of tradition, hierarchy, and sentiment in the smooth functioning of human society, and attacked the French attempt to create a new order based on reason and 'abstract rights'. Burke predicted that this would lead to anarchy and bloodshed; his conservative position gained authority as the Revolution became increasingly violent, culminating in the Terror of 1793–94, when the revolutionary government under Robespierre executed thousands of people.

Burke was opposed by intellectuals who endorsed the principles of the Revolution – social equality, republicanism, reason – much as they tended to deplore its violence. The most influential was Thomas Paine, who argued in *Rights of Man* (1791) that all human beings had natural rights, which included the right to decide how they should be governed. Another important figure was William Godwin, whose *Enquiry Concerning Political Justice, and Its Influence on Morals and Happiness* (1793) imagined a perfect society in which there would be no need of government because every human being would behave on rational principles. Godwin also wrote a political novel, *Caleb Williams* (1794), which attacked Burke's paternalism. The 'Revolution Controversy' (Butler 1984) impacted virtually on all British authors of the period. William Wordsworth, for example, criticized Burke in a pamphlet of 1793, suggesting that his love of the past and resistance to political change was akin to necrophilia: 'he strove to persuade us that we and our posterity [. . .] were bound to cherish a corse at the bosom, when reason might call aloud that it should be entombed' (Wordsworth, p. 158). And yet, by the end of decade, Wordsworth's poetry was increasingly suspicious of 'reason' and followed Burke in celebrating the importance of custom and memory to human society.

Some Romantic texts that you will study are explicitly political; others may more subtly encode political assumptions. Jane Austen, for example, is still sometimes represented as having little interest in the great issues of the day; a careful analysis of any of her novels in context, though, reveals all kinds of links to the socio-political debates and events of the Romantic period (see Butler 1975; Duckworth; Johnson; Roberts).

Paine's success, and the increasing popularity of radical organizations, led to government repression of British writers and activists who were believed to be threatening the country from within. By the late 1790s, reformers were in disarray. Britain and France were at war between 1793 and 1815 and this made it difficult to criticize the government without seeming unpatriotic. However, after Napoleon's defeat, arguments about the need for political change in order to ensure individual liberty once again came to prominence. This was partly because of the so-called 'distresses' of the period: high taxation; the collapse of manufacturing industries; agricultural foreclosures; and poor harvests. Many people suffered severely and there was genuine starvation. In a number of public meetings, radical demagogues addressed exceptionally large crowds about the need for political change. One of the principal demands was that all men should have the right to vote. This popular radicalism was an important part of what the historian E. P. Thompson identified as the 'making' of working-class consciousness.

The most infamous event of this period was the 'Peterloo Massacre' of 16 August 1819. A very large crowd (perhaps 100,000) met at St Peter's Field in Manchester in support of radical reform. Local authorities tried to arrest the speakers, a riot ensued, and cavalry charged the crowd, causing 11 deaths and hundreds of injuries. This was blamed on the government and became a radical *cause célèbre*; among other responses, it prompted the poet Percy Bysshe Shelley to write his political ballad* *The Masque of Anarchy* (composed 1819). Although the political situation settled down somewhat in the 1820s, in 1832 Parliament passed the Reform Act, which gave more *men* the right to vote and reduced the excessive power of rural landowners. This was hardly a democratic victory, though, given that over ninety percent of the adult population still had no voting rights.

Although there was no substantial movement in support of female suffrage, the Romantic period arguably saw the birth of feminism*. The key figure here is Mary Wollstonecraft, who in *A Vindication of the Rights of Woman* (1792) argued that as women were rational beings, society needed to rethink how they were educated and allowed to behave. Wollstonecraft was not a feminist* in the modern sense of the word, for ultimately she saw a woman's primary duties to lie in motherhood and the home; but her emphasis on the importance of domestic affections for men as well as women, on the intellectual potential of women, and on the dangers of a disjunction between male and female spheres, had a profound impact on later women writers (see, for example, Mary Shelley's *Frankenstein* (1818)). Barbara Caine notes that, while neglected by Wollstonecraft, 'the question of women's political representation' became important in the 1820s and 1830s (McCalman, p. 47). However, it was during the Romantic period that the idea of the middle-class women as the 'angel in the house' – subservient to men but also the moral guardian of society – consolidated its hold on British culture, partly due to the growing social influence of Evangelical Christianity. Having some understanding of the construction of gender roles in the period is important if we are to understand its texts: for example, the powerful pressures on Austen's heroines, and their very limited options.

Scholars have recently become interested in the relationship between Romantic literature and imperialism*. The British Empire expanded markedly over the course of the period. Having lost the American colonies following the American War of Independence (1775–83), Britain turned its attention to other parts of the world. It consolidated its hold over India, and began colonial development in Australia, South Africa, Ceylon, and Java. It also seized more territory in the Caribbean, where the so-called 'sugar islands' were worked by slaves transported from Africa. This imperial expansion, including the war with France, was accompanied and underpinned by emerging discourses of race and nationalism (see Colley; Fulford and Kitson; Kitson; Leask). However, despite the prevalence of patriotic rhetoric, and Britain's increasing commercial prosperity, there were also anxieties about the morality of imperialism* and its effect on the nation. The campaign for the abolition of the slave trade began in the 1780s, but it was not until 1807 that Britain abolished the trade in slaves. The controversy surrounding slavery, and the popularity of narratives of exploration and travel, meant that British writers were more aware than ever before of the cultural diversity of humanity, an awareness that was often marked by xenophobia: for example, the 'Opium-Eater', in Thomas De Quincey's autobiographical *Confessions of an English Opium-Eater* (1822), writes of the Chinese: 'I am terrified by the modes of life, by the manners, and the barrier of utter abhorrence and want of sympathy, placed between us [. . .]. I could sooner live with lunatics, or brute animals' (Wu, p. 817).

This 'want of sympathy' between the British elite and their various 'Others', however disturbing, was also enabling, contributing as it did to the various forms of exploitation, imperial and local, that in combination with a certain industrial ingenuity was to make Britain the most powerful nation in the world. However 'Other' the Romantic period may seem to us, its legacy is apparent in Britain's parliamentary political system and the contours of its landscapes (rural and urban), in many postcolonial* nations, and in contemporary global debates surrounding politics, national identity, the environment, and other aspects of modernity. If we are to understand Romantic literature, we need to reflect on its historical context, which may also help us to reflect on our own period.

Key Authors and Texts

There was a time when to study British Romanticism meant little more than to study the so-called 'Big Six' poets – Blake, Byron, Coleridge, Keats, Shelley, and Wordsworth – with maybe a few supporting characters, like Austen. In the last thirty years, though, this canon* has been questioned and expanded, so that now you might well find yourself studying these authors alongside many others: women poets such as Charlotte Smith and Felicia Hemans; labouring-class poets such as John Clare and James Hogg; dramatists such as Elizabeth Inchbald and Joanna Baillie; and novelists such as Maria Edgeworth and Walter Scott. Furthermore, the barriers between 'literary' and 'non-literary' texts have broken down to the extent that you might also study (for example) travel writing, autobiography, political tracts, and conduct books, as well as poetry and fiction.

William Blake is simultaneously the easiest and the most difficult of Romantic poets. An engraver and artist, he self-published his work in the form of illuminated books. Blake developed a complex private mythos, which makes his later 'prophetic books', such as *Milton* (1804) and *Jerusalem* (1820), extremely challenging. Many of his key ideas, however, are to be found in the more accessible *Songs of Innocence and of Experience* (1794). Responding in part to the moralistic Christian children's verse of the eighteenth century, Blake's songs emphasize imagination rather than reason, freedom rather than restraint, and are fiercely anti-authoritarian. They particularly target an oppressive alliance of Church and State; thus, the suffering child in 'The Chimney Sweeper' from *Songs of Experience* laments that his parents have gone to church 'to praise God and his priest and king, who make up a heaven of our misery' (Wu, p. 196, l. 12). As in *The Marriage of Heaven and Hell* (1790), Blake here inverts conventional Christian imagery to suggest that organized religion is the source of human suffering, rather than its cure.

This emphasis on childhood and the imagination is also intrinsic to the poetry of William Wordsworth and Samuel Taylor Coleridge, who shared Blake's radicalism as young men but became increasingly conservative in middle age. Wordsworth and Coleridge collaborated on *Lyrical Ballads* (1798), a foundational Romantic text that claimed to be trying to write a new type of poetry that avoided the neoclassical conventions of much eighteenth-century verse (see the previous chapter) in favour of accounts of rural life in 'a selection of the real language of men' (Wu, p. 495). It is perhaps not surprising, therefore, that Wordsworth excised Coleridge's visionary supernatural poem, 'The Rime of the Ancient Mariner', from the second edition of 1800. We might ask, though, how 'real' the language of Wordsworth's poetry is. A well-educated middle-class man, Wordsworth generally avoided local dialects and some of his poetry is lexically and syntactically complex. For 'real' language, one might turn to the remarkable labouring-class poet John Clare, who still has yet to take his deserved place in the Romantic canon*. Despite the efforts of editors and patrons, Clare generally insisted in writing in an ungrammatical vernacular that is highly evocative of rural life: 'I miss the heath its yellow furze / Molehills and rabbit tracks that lead / Through beesom ling and teazel burrs' (Wu, p. 1230).

Whatever their differences, though, both Clare and Wordsworth are fundamentally poets of *place*. In his poetic autobiography *The Prelude* (1850), Wordsworth describes how his encounters with the frightening power of the Lake District landscape as a child were ultimately exhilarating and inspiring. This emphasis on the sublime* can also be found in Coleridge's poetry: for example, in 'This Lime-Tree Bower My Prison' (1800):

> I have stood
> Silent with swimming sense; yea, gazing round
> On the wide landscape, gaze till all doth seem
> Less gross than bodily, and of such hues
> As veil the Almighty Spirit, when yet he makes
> Spirits perceive His presence. (Wu, p. 615, ll. 38–43)

The experience of the sublime* initially stuns and overwhelms the perceiving self. (In his influential 1759 essay on the sublime*, Edmund Burke refers to this effect as 'astonishment' (p. 53)). However, it then leads to an expansion of the self and an engagement with the natural world that is spiritual rather than physical. One of the questions raised by this passage is whether by 'the Almighty Spirit' Coleridge simply means the conventional Christian God or whether he is taking up a heterodox pantheistic position, suggesting that God and the world are identical.

Wordsworth's poetry had a powerful impact on Byron, Keats, and Shelley, although all the three were also critical of him. Keats, for example, suggested 'we hate poetry that has a palpable design on us' (Wu, p. 1352) and distinguished his own 'poetical character' ('it is not itself – it has no self – it is everything and nothing') from the 'wordsworthian or egotistical sublime' (Wu, p. 1375). Keats wrote a remarkable set of odes* towards the end of his short life – perhaps most famously 'Ode to a Nightingale' (1820) and 'Ode on a Grecian Urn' (1820) – in which he invested this classical form with a new flexibility and inwardness. Their concern with permanence, transience, and creativity is also apparent in narrative poems* such as *Endymion* (1817) and 'Lamia' (1820). Although not obviously a political writer, Keats was attacked by conservative journals as a member of 'the Cockney School', which also included liberal-radical writers such as Leigh Hunt and William Hazlitt. Several critics, most notably Jeffrey Cox, have shown how positioning Keats as a coterie poet helps to bring out the political resonances of his work, although in some cases this has led to tenuous readings of certain poems.

Byron and Shelley were infamously dubbed by the conservative writer Robert Southey as members of the 'Satanic School' of poetry. Both men were friends who lived unconventional lives and wrote verse that was aesthetically and politically transgressive. The atheism and radicalism of Shelley's early work, such as *Queen Mab* (1813), continued throughout his career, as his poetry became much more complex and nuanced. Narrative poems* such as *The Revolt of Islam* (1817) and the verse drama *Prometheus Unbound* (1820), while set in exotic locations, presented revolutionary ideas in symbolic* form. And in lyric* poems such as 'Mont Blanc' (1817) and 'Ode to the West Wind' (1819), Shelley found a way of combining exploration of the relationship between the self and the natural world, with his political aims: 'to repeal large codes of fraud and woe' ('Mont Blanc', in Wu, p. 1077, ll. 80–81).

Unlike Shelley, Byron was an enormously popular poet and is often put forward as the first modern 'celebrity'. In *Childe Harold's Pilgrimage* (1812–18), the protagonist's* travels through Europe closely mirrored Byron's own; readers were fascinated by this apparent identification between the gloomy, tormented hero and the author. Similarly popular were the so-called 'Turkish Tales', such as *The Giaour* (1813) and *The Corsair* (1814), which also contain brooding hero figures, but have been shown by critics to be surprisingly complex in terms of how they represent race and gender. Byron's masterpiece is the satirical* epic* *Don Juan* (1819–24), a bawdy romp through contemporary Europe and England that uses the flexible *ottava rima** form to mercilessly mock his contemporaries. Byron's particular target was what he called 'cant': the insincere or hypocritical rhetoric that he thought was endemic in modern society.

With the exception of Byron, the poets who until recently made up the Romantic canon* were not particularly widely read during the Romantic period. Many more people knew the work of Felicia Hemans and Letitia Landon, for example, than that of Blake and Shelley. These and other Romantic women poets have only come to the fore of research and teaching in the last twenty years. Critics have debated whether it makes sense to talk about a 'feminine romanticism' that contrasts with that of the male poets in terms of 'thematic concerns, formal practices, and ideological positionings' (Mellor 1993, p. 3). This is something for you to think about when you study the period. For example, one might consider Charlotte Smith's *Elegiac Sonnets* (1784) and *Beachy Head* (1807). In their introspection and interest in the particularities of the landscape, one might see strong similarities with the poetry of Wordsworth and Coleridge. On the other hand, one might argue that Smith is very self-consciously writing from a female perspective, and to that end uses the language of sensibility* rather than that of the sublime*.

Conservative male critics of the Romantic period sometimes claimed that women writers should confine themselves to domestic, sentimental subjects and avoid commenting on public affairs. And yet some of the most important poetry in support of the abolition of the slave trade was written by women, perhaps most notably Hannah More's *Slavery: A Poem* (1788) and *A Poem on the Inhumanity of the Slave-Trade* (1788) by the labouring-class poet Ann Yearsley. The enormously popular poetry of Felicia Hemans, such as *England and Spain* (1808), *Modern Greece* (1817), and *Records of Women* (1828), addressed issues surrounding national identity, heroism, and history. Another significant 'public' poem is Anna Letitia Barbauld's *Eighteen Hundred and Eleven* (1812), which reflects anxiously on the state of Britain after nearly twenty years of war with France, and suggests that the nation's power and wealth may be illusory: 'But fairest flowers expand but to decay; / The worm is in thy core, thy glories pass away' (Wu, p. 52, ll. 313–14).

Like much poetry of the period, Romantic drama has been relatively neglected by lecturers and critics. This is not simply due to critical suspicion of popular culture, for Byron, Coleridge, Keats, Shelley, and Wordsworth all wrote plays (although most of them were not actually performed during the period). More successful playwrights included Elizabeth Inchbald, whose adaptation of Kotzebue's *Lovers' Vows* (1798) is controversially staged by characters in Austen's *Mansfield Park* (1814), and Joanna Baillie. In a series of plays, the most successful of which was *De Montfort* (1798; first performed 1800), Baillie sought to explore the nature of passion and sympathy in ways that resonate interestingly with many other texts of the period. (For a useful anthology of drama from the period, see Cox and Gamer.)

The most popular novelist was Sir Walter Scott, who was also a well-known poet. In *Waverley* (1814) and *Ivanhoe* (1820), he pioneered a form of historical fiction that was concerned with the construction of national identity and the relationship between modernity and the past. The Anglo-Irish novels of Maria Edgeworth, such as *Castle Rackrent* (1800) and *The Absentee* (1812), address similar issues. In their sense of the inescapability of history, both writers can be linked to the popular genre of Gothic* fiction. Often set in the medieval period, these texts sought to frighten their readers by facing their protagonists* (often innocent young women) with various dangers. As Fred Botting argues, these texts are concerned with 'threats associated with supernatural and natural forces, imaginative excesses and delusions, religious and human evil, social transgression, mental disintegration and spiritual corruption' (p. 2). In Anne Radcliffe's novels, such as *The Mysteries of Udolpho* (1794), apparently supernatural forces turn out to be illusory, and the true danger is shown to come from patriarchal* desire. In contrast, texts such as Matthew Lewis' *The Monk* (1795) present the supernatural as 'real' and revel in scenes of Satanic debauchery. A significant Gothic* trope is 'the double', a figure that is uncanny precisely because it is both strange and familiar. In Mary Shelley's *Frankenstein* (1818), the apparent opposition between the scientist Frankenstein and the Creature to whom he gives life frequently breaks down, showing the two characters to be doubles of each other and problematizing representations of the Creature as a monstrous 'Other' (Higgins 2008).

Another popular form of writing in the period was sentimental fiction, a genre that became powerful in the second half of the eighteenth century. A key example is Frances Burney's *Evelina* (1778) (see the previous chapter), which had significant influence on Jane Austen. Austen's novels depict the travails of young women trying to find their place in middle-class society. Their sensitivity to the failures of patriarchy* should not necessarily be seen as politically radical or feminist*. Rather, one could argue that she presents figures like Sir Thomas Bertram in *Mansfield Park* and Sir Walter Elliot in *Persuasion* (1818) to encourage male landowners to take their responsibilities more seriously; in that sense, she might be seen as a Burkean conservative.

You will probably already have a sense of the extent to which Romantic writers were interested in exploring the 'self'. It is no coincidence that the term autobiography was coined in 1797 (Treadwell, p. 3). The *Confessions* (1782–89) of the Genevan writer and philosopher Jean-Jacques Rousseau, with their emphasis on solitude, sensibility*, sincerity, and their attacks on the artifice of conventional society, were highly influential on British writers such as Wollstonecraft (see Dart). Her *A Short Residence in Sweden, Norway and Denmark* (1796) is a fascinatingly hybrid text, where accounts of Scandinavian society and meditations on politics mingle with descriptions of the sublime* transport and desperate melancholy. A very different example of autobiography, which nonetheless similarly combines the personal and the political, is Olaudah Equiano's *An Interesting Narrative* (1789). It tells the story of how as a child Equiano was captured by slave traders working off the African coast and ended up working as a slave on British ships. Eventually able to purchase his freedom, Equiano has a religious conversion to Evangelical Christianity. His book, prefaced with a letter to Parliament and the House of Lords, played an important role in the campaign for the abolition of the slave trade. Equiano's double view of himself, as both Englishman and African, reflects the complex interplay of racial and national identity in the period.

Three significant autobiographical writers came to prominence in the literary magazines of the 1820s. William Hazlitt, also a philosopher and critic, wrote familiar essays on a wide range of topics, from the nature of genius to bare-knuckle boxing. A committed republican, Hazlitt's autobiographical writing was (like Rousseau's) highly political: in 'My First Acquaintance with Poets' (1823), for example, his recollection of his youthful friendship with Wordsworth and Coleridge is tinged with regret at their political shifts and the apparent failure of the French Revolution to have a lasting impact on European politics (see Higgins 2005, pp. 102–26). Thomas De Quincey suggested that his *Confessions of an English Opium-Eater* would avoid the 'gratuitous self-humiliation' of writers like Rousseau, and yet his account of the nightmares induced by opium addiction shows the self threatened by alienation, loss, torture, and eventually absorption into the exotic 'Other': 'I was kissed, with cancerous kisses, by crocodiles; and laid, confounded with all unutterable slimy things, amongst reeds and Nilotic mud' (p. 73). De Quincey's sublime* hyperbole* contrasts interestingly with the emphasis on the local and the familiar in the essays of Charles Lamb. And yet these texts, too, reveal not only personal anxieties, but an attempt to make sense of the various national and racial 'Others' of which British writers were increasingly aware; and Lamb's day job as a clerk for the powerful East India Company meant that he was imbricated in the business of empire to as great an extent as any of his ostensibly more adventurous peers.

The myth of the Romantic genius is that *he* transcends normal society and creates his works in solitude. (Genius in the period was generally seen as a masculine characteristic.) And yet even this brief survey should at least hint at the extent to which all writers form part of a complex literary culture, which itself is made of various informal networks associated with particular publishers, periodicals, and places (see, for example, Cox; Russell and Tuite). Some Romantic texts, such as *Lyrical Ballads*, are obviously meant to be collaborative, but there is a sense in which all literature is collaborative and intertextual*. Every writer of the Romantic period had a set of peers, competitors, and forebears and these impacted on the work that she or he produced. It is therefore important when you come to study the period not to think about each text in a vacuum, but to consider the relationships between them.

Criticism and Literary Theory

This section will focus mainly on recent critical and theoretical approaches to Romantic literature, but it is important to note that some highly important and influential texts of this nature were written by the Romantics themselves. While concepts such as 'genius', 'imagination', and 'originality' have a long and complex history, it is certainly the case that, in the Romantic period, they were discussed (and celebrated) more intensely than had previously been the case. Whatever their many differences, key texts in Romantic theory, such as Coleridge's *Biographia Literaria*, Wordsworth's 'Preface' to *Lyrical Ballads*, Percy Bysshe Shelley's 'A Defence of Poetry', Keats' letters, Baillie's 'Introductory Discourse' to *Plays on the Passions*, and William Hazlitt's critical essays, share a suspicion of artifice and imitation (which they often associated with eighteenth-century poetry), and a belief in the creative, vital power of the individual imagination.

In philosophical terms, the Romantic approach to art and literature might be described as 'idealist', relating to the belief that the universe is not separate from consciousness but somehow dependent on the human mind for its existence. In contrast, much literary criticism of the last twenty years has been implicitly or explicitly 'materialist' in emphasis, suggesting or assuming that texts are not created by an autonomous authorial imagination but are part of a complex intersection of historically-specific events, practices, and discourses. The dominant mode in Romantic literary studies is probably best described as New Historicism, which has its roots in post-war Marxist criticism (Raymond Williams is a crucial figure here), but was articulated in its most influential form by Jerome McGann in *The Romantic Ideology* (1983). McGann's arguments are more complex than they are sometimes represented, but what he calls his 'ground thesis' is 'that the scholarship and criticism of Romanticism and its works are dominated by a Romantic Ideology, by an uncritical absorption in Romanticism's own self-representations' (p. 1). Such representations would include the notion that poets and poetry transcend politics and economics. One of McGann's targets is the influential critic M. H. Abrams, author of several important books and essays, including *Natural Supernaturalism* (1971). For McGann, 'Abrams has uncritically accepted a Wordsworthian-Coleridgean ideology of Romanticism' (p. 38). To put it crudely, McGann thinks that Abrams effectively *endorses* the way that Wordsworth's and Coleridge's poetry moves away from revolutionary ideas of a better future for all humanity and instead focuses on the transformation of the imagination of the individual poet. He also argues that Abrams' model of Romanticism does not properly take into account other important writers of the period, perhaps most crucially Byron.

Why *New* Historicism? The short answer is that New Historicism does not think of history as a sort of 'background' to literature, but tends to challenge any clear distinction between the two categories. Its key intellectual influences are notions of ideology from Marx and Althusser, Foucault's work on discourse and power, and deconstructionism* of Derrida and others (see Brannigan). Often, therefore, New Historicists are interested in the absences or *lacunae* in literary texts. For example, in a famous essay on Wordsworth's 'Lines Written a Few Miles Above Tintern Abbey', Marjorie Levinson argues that the poem represses the unpicturesque lives of those who actually lived around the abbey. Similarly, in *Culture and Imperialism* (1993), Edward Said explores the significance of slavery to *Mansfield Park*, as a practice about which the novel is mostly silent, and yet which enables its narrative to unfold.

More recently, critics have tended to emphasize the ways in which Romantic literature engaged with history, rather than sought to displace it. Either way, what seems to lie behind New Historicist approaches is an idea that literary criticism has the moral purpose in excavating and examining the history of inequality, whether related to class, gender, race, or other identity categories. It is hardly surprising, then, that important contemporary issues, such as feminism*, multiculturalism, and environmentalism, are reflected in recent critical trends. For example, the 'green' movement may seem like a relatively modern phenomenon, but the origins of modern ecology can clearly be seen in the Romantic period, as shown by Jonathan Bate (1991). So-called 'ecocriticism' has found the Romantic fascination with the relationship between human beings and the natural world particularly fertile ground for analysis (Bate 2000; McCusick).

Feminist* approaches to Romanticism initially focused on the novel and, particularly, on the work of Jane Austen and Mary Shelley (see Johnson; Kirkham; and Mellor 1988). Quickly, though, the approach broadened to consider other genres, and to question the past construction of a canon* of 'Big Six' male poets. The work of Anne K. Mellor and Stuart Curran is important here, as is Marlon B. Ross' book *The Contours of Masculine Desire* (1989), which considers the relationship between 'masculine' and 'feminine' Romanticism, an area that is still subject to vigorous critical debate. As a result of this sort of work, women poets of the period are now quite widely studied, although they are still sometimes in a marginal or tokenistic presence (see, for example, the recently published Blackwell book, *Romantic Poetry: An Annotated Anthology*). This raises difficult questions about how academics decide what texts and authors to teach. To what extent should we try to take account of the popularity of writers during their lifetimes? To what extent have women poets tended to be under-represented because (male) critics have disliked their choices of subjects or literary forms, or their styles of writing? How much of a role has straightforward sexism played? How do we judge the value of literary works and can this ever be separated from ideological considerations? For example, is Hemans a 'worse' poet than Wordsworth, and what does 'worse' actually mean? The above section on 'Key Authors and Texts' contains more on the 'Big Six' male poets than it does on women poets. This is partly because I am trying to take account of the writers that you are most likely to come across when you study at university, but it also inevitably says something about which texts I most value. It is good to be aware that no anthology, reading list, or survey, however carefully constructed, can give a neutral overview of the literature of a period.

Postcolonial* criticism and theory has had a powerful impact on Romantic literary scholarship. This began in the early 1990s with two groundbreaking studies: John Barrell's *The Infection of Thomas De Quincey* (1991) and Nigel Leask's *British Romantic Writers and the East* (1992). Edward Said's influential book *Orientalism* (1978) had presented the European construction of the Orient as rather a monolithic process, but Leask and Barrell combined psychoanalysis* and historicism to examine the private and public anxieties behind Romantic representations of the Orient and to show how complex and contested such representations were. A number of important studies and essay collections have followed, focusing on areas such as colonial disease, exploration, India, Native Americans, and slavery. This critical interest in the relationship between literature and colonialism/imperialism* is inextricably linked to an examination of the role of literary texts in constructing national identity. Important contributions to this field include Katie Trumpener's *Bardic Nationalism: The Romantic Novel and the British Empire* (1997), and Murray Pittock's *Scottish and Irish Romanticism* (2008). Taken as a whole, this body of scholarship has shown the extent to which Romantic literature and culture was *intrinsic* to imperialism*, colonialism, and nation-building and, furthermore, that the concerns of Romantic writers resonate strongly with modern discussions of Englishness, Britishness, devolution, and multiculturalism.

Thus although the current dominant approach to Romantic studies can be described as New Historicist, this term actually covers a variety of different approaches and interests. Furthermore, this paradigm* is continually being challenged and contested by critical work (most obviously Formalism*) that is suspicious of its claims and assumptions. The diversity and extent of critical and theoretical writing on Romantic-period literature can seem overwhelming and baffling, even to specialists. The trick, as always, is to keep in mind one's own interest in particular texts, contexts, and themes. Engaging with criticism and theory is a vital part of literary study, but it is never a substitute for our own interpretations of primary texts. These interpretations are always dependent on certain assumptions (implicit or explicit) – there is no neutral critical perspective – and engaging with secondary material allows us to reflect on our own assumptions, and thus to refine and develop our readings.

William Wordsworth's Poetry

This section will read closely William Wordsworth's poem 'Simon Lee', which was first published in *Lyrical Ballads*, a book that presented itself as revolutionary and experimental, an attempt to trace in common language the 'primary laws of our nature' through portrayals of 'low and rustic life' (Wu, p. 497). The extent to which this volume *was* revolutionary is debateable, but its poems clearly eschew the complexity, classical imagery, and tendency to periphrasis* of much eighteenth-century poetry (see the previous chapter). In its deliberate, provocative banality, 'Simon Lee' is typical of *Lyrical Ballads* and the sort of poem that Wordsworth's critics often attacked as sadly misguided. This section, I hope, has some interesting things to say about 'Simon Lee'; however, its principal purpose is to help you to develop your own analytical skills, whether they be applied to another poem from *Lyrical Ballads*, a poem by another author of the Romantic period, or, indeed, any literary text.

The poem's full title is 'Simon Lee, the Old Huntsman, with an incident in which he was concerned' (Wu, p. 368; further references are to this version of the poem). The 'hunting feats' (l. 25) of his youth have left Simon Lee a crippled, sick old man who, with his wife, can barely scratch out an existence from the 'scrap of land' (l. 59) they own. The narrator comes across him trying unsuccessfully to chop through 'a stump of rotten wood' (l. 84) and helps him by cutting through the stump with 'a single blow' (l. 93). This simplicity of plot is matched by the poem's simple language, but the poem's form is not straightforward, offering an elaboration of ballad* metre* and rhyme scheme. This would normally be abab (or ababcdcd), with lines of four feet* and three feet* alternating. The rhyme scheme of Wordsworth's poem, though, is less regular (ababcded), as is the metre*, with three feet* in the fourth, sixth, and eighth lines.

This sort of formal analysis is only useful if we are able to articulate its effects. It is perhaps worth noting that Wordsworth produced plenty of conceptually and syntactically complex poetry in blank verse* – see, for example, 'Lines Written a Few Miles Above Tintern Abbey', also in *Lyrical Ballads* – and so the fact that he chose to write 'Simon Lee' in the form he did may be significant. For me, there are two important effects. The awkwardness of the rhyme scheme and metre* reflect both the narrator's discomfort with the situation in which he finds himself and the poem's desire to unnerve and challenge its readers. Also, the simple, crude language, and the unstressed syllable at the ends of lines six and eight produces a tendency towards bathos*, for example:

```
X    /    X    /   X    /    X    /
```
And now he's forced to work, though weak –
```
X    /    X  /  X  /  X
```
The weakest in the village. (ll. 39–40)

The poem is self-conscious about its bathetic* tendencies and the apparent banality of its subject. The repeated references to Simon Lee's physical condition – 'His ankles they are swoln and thick / His legs are thin and dry' (ll. 35–36) – are deliberately commonplace and seem meant to discomfort the polite reader:

> For still, the more he works, the more
> His poor old ankles swell.
> My gentle reader, I perceive
> How patiently you've waited
> And I'm afraid that you expect
> Some tale will be related. (ll. 67–72)

There is a half-mocking irony here, as the speaker questions the reader's probable desire to take an edifying moral from this story of suffering. 'Gentle reader' may seem like a conventional phrase, but it points to the likely social status of those people who would have purchased *Lyrical Ballads*, and read the sentimental magazine verse about the unfortunate that was popular at the end of the eighteenth century. 'Gentle', here, does not simply mean 'kind', but also 'genteel' or 'well born'. Such people, in the main, would have had income from property and other sources and would not have had to work for a living. In contrast, the rural poor like Simon Lee could not have afforded to buy books, except in a few cases, and might well have been illiterate anyway.

In the next stanza, the speaker's teasing of the reader turns into admonishment:

> O reader! had you in your mind
> Such stores as silent thought can bring,
> O gentle reader! you would find
> A tale in every thing. (ll. 73–76)

Wordsworth here uses a form of apostrophe* to focus the poem on to the figure of the reader, who is imagined as someone who may not have the ability properly to interpret it. The repetition of 'gentle' once again emphasizes social status. 'Simon Lee' presents itself as trying to provoke and embarrass its readers into thinking seriously about what is being represented and to draw their own conclusions. In practice, though, we might see it as trying to *force* its readers to draw particular conclusions, while pretending to give them inter-pretative freedom.

The speaker's focus on the reader's social rank fits in with the rest of the poem. A number of critics have read 'Simon Lee' as a political text that medi-tates on the exploitation of the poor by the wealthy. In this view, it shows the failure of paternalism: the idea that a hierarchical society is knitted together by familial bonds in which the poor are like children who treat their betters with deference and obedience, and the wealthy are like parents who have an obligation to look after the poor. This idea lies behind much conservative writing of the Romantic period, such as Burke's *Reflections on the Revolution in France*. Simon Lee, it is clear, has not been looked after by his 'betters'. He still wears the 'livery-coat' (l. 9) that symbolizes his servitude in the 'Hall of Ivor' (l. 22), but this place, and perhaps the family who owned it, no longer exists. In this reading, therefore, having been used by the wealthy, Lee has been left crippled and virtually starving: there was of course no properly organized system of healthcare or social welfare in the period for someone in his position.

The poem's final stanza does not spell things out, but implies conclusions that may well have political resonances:

> The tears into his eyes were brought,
> And thanks and praise seemed to run
> So fast out of his heart, I thought
> They never would have done.
> – I've heard of hearts unkind, kind deeds
> With coldness still returning.
> Alas! the gratitude of men
> Has oftner left me mourning. (ll. 97–104)

The speed with which Lee's words of gratitude run 'out of his heart' shows by ironic contrast how far he has decayed from the days when he literally 'all the country could outrun'. Lee's gratitude leaves the speaker 'mourning' for the man that Lee once was. Gratitude may seem a positive emotion but, like the charity it provokes, it implies inequality: most obviously here between the strength of youth and the weakness of age, but perhaps also between the comfortable lives of Wordsworth and his readers, and the continual suffering of individuals like Simon Lee. We might recall Blake's disturbing lines, 'Pity would be no more / If we did not make somebody Poor' (Wu, p. 201), which suggest that the sentiment with which 'we' might view the poor, the sick, and the homeless is nothing to be celebrated but is consequent on fundamental social inequalities that pity does nothing to address and may actually make worse. As various critics have noted, the radical writer William Godwin, a significant intellectual influence on Wordsworth, attacked gratitude in similar terms (Jones, pp. 133–34). This is not necessarily to suggest that 'Simon Lee' is a politically radical poem – and there is plenty of evidence that Wordsworth had moved a long way from Godwin by 1798 – but it is clearly a poem that addresses substantial political issues through a very specific example.

This reading of 'Simon Lee' is not meant to be definitive. There are other aspects of the poem that I could have discussed in detail: for example, land ownership and landscape; rural labour; its relation to other representations of poverty in the period; the significance of 'hunting'; gender difference (the role of Ruth); and the tension between the poem's implied readers and its actual readers. I hope, though, to have offered some helpful ideas and suggestions about this text that should resonate with many other poems from *Lyrical Ballads*. Furthermore, I hope that my focus on the relationship between form, content, and context will help you in analysing other literary texts, however different they may be from 'Simon Lee'.

 ## Jane Austen's *Pride and Prejudice*

Pride and Prejudice (1813) is continually being reinterpreted and rewritten by film-makers and novelists. And yet modern renderings, however successful, cannot match the delicacy and precision of Austen's style. This section will analyse two passages with the aim of shedding light on the novel and helping you think about how to engage with other narrative texts. The first question we need to ask when analysing fiction is, 'whose perspective are we getting?' Consider, for example, our initial encounter with Bingley and Darcy:

> Mr Bingley was good looking and gentlemanlike; he had a pleasant countenance, and easy, unaffected manners [. . .]. His friend Mr Darcy soon drew the attention of the room by his fine, tall person, handsome features, noble mien; and the report which was in general circulation within five minutes after his entrance, of his having ten thousand a year. The gentlemen pronounced him to be a fine figure of a man, the ladies declared he was much handsomer than Mr Bingley, and he was looked at with great admiration for about half the evening, till his manners gave a disgust which turned the tide of his popularity; for he was discovered to be proud, to be above his company, and above being pleased; and not all his large estate in Derbyshire could then save him from having a most forbidding, disagreeable countenance, and being unworthy to be compared with his friend. (p. 6)

Pride and Prejudice is told in the third person ('he did this'; 'she said that') by an impersonal narrator (we should *never* assume that author and narrator are the same). The passage begins by giving what seems to be the narrator's perspective on the characters of Bingley and Darcy, but then, as is typical of Austen's writing, moves fluidly into giving the perspectives of people around them. Note how Austen uses free indirect style* at the end of the quotation: she is writing in the third person, but giving the point of view of the other characters at the ball. Darcy does not necessarily have 'a most forbidding, disagreeable countenance' – after all, he is earlier described as 'handsome' and 'noble' – but his behaviour has coloured people's perceptions of him. How Bingley and Darcy are described, therefore, can tell us something about the values of the genteel rural society that Austen depicts. Looks and money are important – Darcy's large income from land ownership of 'ten thousand a year' (the equivalent of several millions in today's money) is of great interest to everyone – but so is what we might call 'agreeableness'. The world that Austen's characters inhabit is small, relatively closed, and based on social interactions that have to appear relaxed and fluent, while being carefully controlled within certain boundaries. In that sense, the ball that Darcy and Bingley are attending typifies the society described in the novel.

The boundaries placed on women can be particularly strict: consider, for example, the way in which Elizabeth's muddy walk to Netherfield to visit her sick sister is interpreted by some characters as showing excessive independence (pp. 25–26). Young women are under pressure to be 'agreeable', which can often mean simply compliant to social pressures, in order to make themselves attractive so that they can succeed on the 'marriage market'. At the same time, they are faced by three major perils: life as an impoverished spinster dependent on the charity of relatives; a marriage that ensures their material comfort but provides no emotional sustenance (such as Charlotte's marriage to Collins); or seduction by an apparently agreeable villain that, even if it results in marriage, also results in exile and poverty, as in the case of Lydia and Wickham. One must never forget when reading Austen's novels that the society depicted provides virtually no opportunity for women to make their way in the world independently, and therefore that her heroines are under intense pressure to secure the right man.

To return to the quotation, Bingley's manners are 'easy': he is relaxed, relaxing, and pleasant to interact with. He is also 'unaffected'; that is, he does not seem to be performing, even though there is a sense in which he is: 'he was lively and unreserved [and] danced every dance' (pp. 6–7). Darcy, in contrast, refuses to perform: '[he] danced only once with Mrs Hurst and once with Miss Bingley, declined being introduced to any other lady, and spent the rest of the evening in walking about the room, speaking occasionally to one of his own party'. Ironically, this is interpreted as a sign of his affectation. Austen writes that, 'he was the proudest, most disagreeable man in the world, and every body hoped that he would never come there again' (p. 7). Note, once again, the use of free indirect style*. The narrator does not necessarily express or endorse this view of Darcy, but gives other characters' opinion of him a certain authority by conflating it with the narrative voice. *Pride and Prejudice* is fundamentally concerned with the problem of 'reading' character: Darcy initially appears agreeable, then disagreeable, and, towards the end of the novel, agreeable again. Elizabeth Bennett and others dangerously misread the character of the villain Wickham, who *appears* to be similar to Bingley (p. 54).

I want now to consider a very different example: Mr Collins' first letter to Mr Bennet, which nonetheless is similarly concerned with interpreting character. Here we get a first-person perspective, which discloses various aspects of Collins' personality and objectives.

> I have been so fortunate as to be distinguished by the *patronage* of the *Right Honourable* Lady Catherine de Bourgh, widow of Sir Lewis de Bourgh, whose bounty *and* beneficence has preferred me to the *valuable* rectory of this parish, where it shall be my endeavour to *demean myself* with grateful respect towards her Ladyship, and be ever ready to perform those rites *and* ceremonies which are instituted by the Church of England. As a clergyman, moreover, I feel it as a duty to promote and establish the blessing of peace in all families within the reach of my influence; and on these grounds I *flatter myself* that my present overtures of good-will are highly commendable, and that the circumstances of my being next in the *entail* of Longbourn estate, will be kindly overlooked on your side, and not lead you to reject the offered olive branch. I cannot be otherwise than concerned at being the means of injuring your amiable daughters, and *beg leave to apologise for it*, as well as to assure you of my readiness to make them every possible amends, – but of this hereafter. (p. 47; my italics)

Even bearing in the mind the formal requirements of letter writing in the period, this is pompous and periphrastic*; Collins makes his points in an excessively lengthy manner, which suggests the excessive importance he attaches to his own words. There is no need, for example, for 'bounty *and* beneficence', 'rites *and* ceremonies', or '*beg leave to apologise for it*': these phrases are all tautologous*. He also gives detail that is unnecessary for his meaning but which serves to emphasize (as he sees it) his own importance, for example '*Right Honourable* Lady Catherine De Bourgh' and '*valuable* rectory'. Austen's irony is important here: some of Collins' words have a double meaning of which he is unaware, but which disclose significant aspects of his personality to us and the other characters. 'Patronage' refers literally and precisely to 'the right of presenting a member of the clergy to a particular ecclesiastical benefice or living' (*OED*). But it also has connotations of 'patronising', which are borne out when we discover how much emphasis Lady Catherine places on her own rank. By 'demean myself', Collins simply means 'to behave', but 'demean' also has connotations of lowering or humbling, suggesting that Collins is excessively obsequious to those of higher rank. Similarly, *'flatter myself'* means to 'encourage' or 'cheer up', but 'flatter' has more obvious connotations of complimenting excessively, suggesting both Collins' undue sense of his own importance and his linked willingness to suck up to those he thinks are even more important.

The Bennets are careful close readers, and you should consider their analysis of Collins' letter (pp. 47–48). Mr Bennet is a likeable figure and we are likely to sympathize with his desire to mock Collins. But it is important to note that, as the narrator informs us a few pages on, the clergyman is the victim of bad parenting (p. 52). Bennet's easy assumption of superiority over Collins might tell us something about his own self-complacency, the refusal to discharge his paternal responsibilities that we see later in the novel contributes to the chaotic behaviour of Lydia. As with any text, close reading is vital: we need to think very carefully about how things are described, and who is doing the describing. Furthermore, although understanding character is important, it is by no means sufficient. We have already thought about the importance of the often ironic narratorial perspective, and we have also started to consider the sort of society that Austen describes. There is clearly a big gap between the implied reader of Collins' letter, and the actual readers that he gets. Perhaps, though, there is also a gap between us and the novel's implied reader. We may not be sensitive to the signs that would have been obvious to readers of the period, and we may not be familiar with generic conventions (relating to, for example, romance*, the sentimental novel, and the eighteenth-century formal letter) that have little to do with the sort of characterization that we associate with realist* fiction. We need to think hard about history. For me, the crucial word in the Collins quotation, and the whole novel, is 'entail', which means, here, 'the settlement of the succession of a landed estate' (*OED*). Austen's novels, ultimately, may not really be about romance* at all, but they are about the way in which (male) power is consolidated or redistributed through the ownership of property. Women are more than simply pawns in this process, and Austen is rightly celebrated for her creation of independent-minded heroines; but her novels nonetheless reflect on the severe restrictions placed on their actions and decisions in a highly patriarchal* society.

Further Reading

Butler, Marilyn (1982), *Romantics, Rebels and Reactionaries.* Oxford: Oxford University Press. Even after nearly thirty years, this is still probably the best introduction to the literature and culture of the British Romanticism; particularly helpful is its focus on historical context and on the connections between authors.

Chandler, James, and Maureen N. McLane (eds) (2008), *The Cambridge Companion to British Romantic Poetry.* Cambridge: Cambridge University Press. A useful, sophisticated overview; key chapters include: 'Romantic poetry and antiquity'; 'Romantic meter and form'; 'Romantic poetry, sexuality, gender'; 'Poetry, peripheries and empire'.

Jarvis, Robin (2004), *The Romantic Period: The Intellectual and Cultural Context of English Literature 1789–1830.* Harlow: Longman. A comprehensive, informative and accessible study of 'the intellectual and cultural background' to English literature of the Romantic period.

McCalman, Iain (ed.) (1999), *An Oxford Companion to the Romantic Age.* Oxford: Oxford University Press. A useful and rich resource, combining short encyclopedia entries with essays on various aspects of Romantic-period literature and culture.

Roe, Nicholas (ed.) (2005), *Romanticism: An Oxford Guide.* Oxford: Oxford University Press. An excellent introduction to Romanticism that comprises over forty essays on a wide range of topics. Divided into four sections: 'Romantic Orientations' (covering cultural contexts); 'Romantic Readings' (covering different critical approaches); 'Romantic Forms' (covering different genres); 'Romantic Afterlives' (covering the influence and effects of Romanticism). Each essay includes an annotated guide to further reading.

Ruston, Sharon (2007), *Romanticism.* London: Continuum. An accessible introductory study aimed particularly at students new to the period; includes a section on key critical approaches, a chronology, a glossary, and a guide to further reading.

'Romantic Chronology': http://english.ucsb.edu:591/rchrono/. A useful, detailed and sophisticated chronology of the Romantic period, which can be searched by date, topic, or entry.

'Romantic Circles': http://www.rc.umd.edu/. A scholarly website with a range of resources for students of Romantic literature. Particularly useful are the guide to scholarly resources, the critical essays, and the electronic editions.

Do not forget to keep a record of *all* the texts and websites you look at when researching for an assignment: you will need to list them in your bibliography.

8 The Victorian Period

Deborah Wynne

Chapter Overview

Historical Context

The 'Victorian Period' refers to Queen Victoria's reign (1837–1901). However, as a description of a period spanning sixty-four years, 'Victorian' is necessarily a shorthand term. It covers a period when Britain was transformed from a predominately rural society to an urban industrialized nation. Princess Victoria was supposedly reading Charles Dickens' *Oliver Twist* (1837) the night before her coronation; however, at this time most of her subjects lived in isolated rural communities and were illiterate. By the time she died in 1901, the motor car was replacing horse power, the telephone and cinema were transforming communication and entertainment, and most people in Britain were able to read and write. As the Victorian period advanced, there was a voracious appetite for literature, whether sensational cheap 'railway novels' bought to pass the time on journeys, or the books borrowed from 'circulating' (subscription) libraries and the newly created public libraries, or the part-issues of serialized novels which came out in monthly instalments. Never before had so many people been able to read and have access to affordable reading matter (see Sutherland for a useful discussion of Victorian publishing and reading practices).

Victorian writers were aware of the potential to reach vast numbers of readers and found a wealth of subject matter for their fiction, plays, and poetry in the dramatic social, political, cultural, and economic changes that were taking place. The 1840s, for example, was a decade of economic hardship, which saw the Irish Potato Famine, instability in the financial markets, and political unrest from the Chartists, who sought to improve working-class representation in Parliament. Numerous writers, such as the Brontë sisters, reflected the turmoil of the decade in their work. Charlotte Brontë's *Jane Eyre* (1847) exposes the harsh conditions in schools for the poor and the limited employment opportunities for impoverished women; Emily Brontë's anti-hero Heathcliff in *Wuthering Heights* (1847), found as a child on the streets of Liverpool, can be seen to represent the revolutionary power of the dispossessed and displaced; and Anne Brontë's *The Tenant of Wildfell Hall* (1848) exposes the problems faced by married women who lacked legal rights in terms of control of their own bodies and custody of their children. Literature, then, was not only a major form of entertainment, but also a forum for social debate in which writers and readers imaginatively engaged with important issues and developments.

The Victorian period also saw a number of major reforms. The 1867 and 1884 Reform Acts conferred democratic rights on the majority of men; the 1870 and 1882 Married Women's Property Acts allowed married women the right to retain control of their own property and earnings; and the 1870 Education Act increased educational opportunities for the poor (and thus led to even more readers demanding books, newspapers, and magazines). Many Victorian writers promoted these reforms by exposing social injustice. Elizabeth Gaskell, working among the unemployed and poverty-stricken workers of Manchester, depicted their appalling working conditions in her social-problem novels*, *Mary Barton* (1848) and *North and South* (1855). Similarly, Dickens in *Hard Times* (1854) represented the plight of workers in the industrial north. Both *North and South* and *Hard Times* were serialized in Dickens' own weekly magazine *Household Words*, thus reaching a much wider readership than if they had originally been published in more expensive book form.

Poets also engaged with the important events and developments of their age. For example, Thomas Hood's 'The Song of the Shirt' (1843) drew attention to the plight of seamstresses who worked long hours for little money; similarly, the poetry of Ebenezer Elliot sought to improve the condition of the poor by attacking the restrictive Corn Laws and promoting free trade. Poets also responded to the intellectual debates of the period. When Charles Darwin's *On the Origin of Species* was published in 1859, many readers were made aware of recent geological discoveries offering evidence of the evolutionary development of species over millions of years. These scientific theories were deeply disturbing to many Victorians, whose beliefs in religious explanations of the origins of human beings were called into question, even undermined. George Eliot, for example, found that her religious faith could not be sustained in the new climate of scientific discovery. The poet Alfred Tennyson also responded to the disturbing notion of a Godless universe where Nature, amoral and uncaring, is *the* controlling force. In his moving elegy* for his dead friend Arthur Hallam, *In Memoriam* (1850), Tennyson dramatically outlines his crisis of faith and his return to belief, eloquently speaking for many who felt disorientated by the new developments in science.

The mid-Victorian period was, however, also a period of prosperity and optimism, where Britain, as the first industrialized nation, began to attain unprecedented levels of wealth, international prestige, and overseas territories, known as the 'British Empire'. The Empire expanded as the century progressed; it included India (administered by the East India Company and the British Government), the Caribbean, Canada, New Zealand, Australia, and parts of Africa. This expansion was facilitated by improvements in transport and developments in manufacturing and trade. British pride in its manufacturing achievements culminated in the Great Exhibition of 1851, held in the Crystal Palace in Hyde Park. All nations were invited here to exhibit their manufactures, arts and crafts and raw materials. This exhibition was a display of the material exuberance of the age, and the prosperity of the mid-Victorian period resulted in an increase in consumerism and the development of shopping centres. This is reflected in the realist* literature and art of the period, with its attention to the details of everyday life, from chairs and tables to clothes and ornaments. The development and popularity of photography (first invented in the 1830s) was part of this cultural obsession with recording reality. Similarly, artists such as the Pre-Raphaelite Brotherhood (which included the poet and painter Dante Gabriel Rossetti) also believed that the painstaking representation of the real world was both morally and aesthetically important.

As the century progressed, the reforms of the early and mid-Victorian period led to higher expectations and aspirations among women and the working classes. So-called 'New Women' wanted greater educational opportunities, the vote, equal rights with men, and access to the workplace in order to earn enough to support themselves independently. Writers responded to the growth of feminism* with the representation of new types of heroine, such as the freethinking Lyndall in Olive Schreiner's *The Story of an African Farm* (1883), the feminist* activists, Olive and Verena, in Henry James' *The Bostonians* (1886), and Sue Bridehead, who holds anti-marriage views, in Thomas Hardy's *Jude the Obscure* (1895). The development of feminism* progressed alongside the development of socialism, a movement demanding greater rights for workers, social equality, better working conditions, and greater working-class representation in Parliament. Industrial production, with its relentless churning out of machine-made mass-produced goods, led some Victorians to promote more traditional working practices. William Morris, for example, set up his own company in 1861, Morris and Co., offering products ranging from wallpaper to glassware, made by craftsmen and women using traditional techniques. These were very fashionable, but ironically, considering Morris' socialist views, only the wealthiest members of society could afford to buy them.

The later decades of the nineteenth century were characterized by anxieties centred on notions of race, class, gender, and sexuality. The British Empire was expanding, but Britain had to face competition from the imperialist* ambitions of other European countries. This created numerous conflicts: a territorial dispute over the Holy Land led to the Crimean War (1853–56) between Britain and its allies (principally the French and the Ottoman Turks) and Imperial Russia. In India, the 1857 rebellion (known at the time as the 'Indian Mutiny') exposed religious, cultural, and political tensions engendered by the British imperial presence. In this climate of instability, numerous oppositional voices could be heard. Irish nationalism, for example, engendered a revival of traditional Irish culture and the violent activities of the Fenians, who demanded Irish independence. The British also found themselves involved in conflicts in South Africa, resulting in the Boer Wars of 1880–81 and 1899–1902. Perceived threats from abroad were represented in late-Victorian Gothic* novels; for example, Bram Stoker's *Dracula* (1897) highlights the possibility of 'reverse colonisation', where a vampire from the East invades and 'colonizes' Britain. These fears of Otherness* were inextricably linked to new anxieties about sexual identity, particularly after Oscar Wilde's trials in 1895, when the figure of the homosexual emerged into public consciousness. The so-called 'decadence'* of the late nineteenth century was denigrated in the popular press; however, many artists and writers of the *fin de siècle** embraced 'decadence'* as a way of pushing the boundaries of art in new directions.

With Queen Victoria's death in 1901 the Victorian era officially came to an end. Yet there were numerous overlaps between the late-Victorian world and the new century; the use of the car, the portable camera and the telephone, as well as with the entertainment industry centred on film, popular fiction and magazines, all had their origins in the Victorian period. Its cultural legacy, after a brief reaction in the early decades of the twentieth century, has been profound and enduring, as Cora Kaplan shows in her recent book *Victoriana* (2007).

A good way to begin an investigation into the historical context of a Victorian text is to consider its date of publication. For example, a novel which appeared in 1859–60 (as did Collins' *The Woman in White*) may be responding to events around the same time. A preliminary investigation into the developments of the late 1850s would reveal the passing of the Matrimonial

Causes Act in 1857, which made divorces easier to obtain. You may then consider *The Woman in White*'s representation of a failed marriage and re-marriage in the light of this major social change. The late 1850s also saw the development of voluntary rifle corps throughout Britain, formed because of widespread (and, as it turned out, unfounded) fears of a foreign invasion. Knowledge of these fears about national security helps to put Collins' representation of the encroachment of the secret Italian 'Brotherhood' into a specific context. Reading a text in relation to its historical context not only enriches our understanding of that text, but also suggests new lines of enquiry and alternative ways of reading.

Key Authors and Texts

For many, Charles Dickens is the archetypal Victorian novelist; his work was not only enormously popular with its original readers, but is also widely studied today. All of his novels have been adapted for film and television, ensuring that most people have heard of the characters Oliver Twist and David Copperfield, even if they have not read the novels. Dickens' career stretches over nearly four decades and his writing offers some of the most important ideas and images of the Victorian period. Novels such as *Oliver Twist* (1837), *The Old Curiosity Shop* (1841), *David Copperfield* (1850), and *Great Expectations* (1861) focus on representations of children's experiences, particularly the orphaned child. This was an innovation which reflected the importance placed by many Victorians on childhood development, and it is not surprising that the period also saw the development of literature for children: Lewis Carroll's *Alice* books, for example, appeared in 1865 and 1872.

Dickens' earlier novels are characterized by a mixture of comedy and melodrama*; however, his later novels were increasingly satirical*, exposing social abuses and human absurdity. *Hard Times* satirizes* the excesses of Utilitarianism and the uncaring attitudes of industrialists and educators; *Bleak House* (1853) satirizes* the British legal system, while *Our Mutual Friend* (1865) focuses on dirt, both metaphorical and literal, as a way of commenting on the corruption in British society. *Great Expectations* shares the sharp satirical* tone of Dickens' later work, but here he returns to an exploration of childhood experience; like the earlier *David Copperfield*, *Great Expectations* is a classic *Bildungsroman**, exploring the protagonist's* growth from boyhood to maturity, using a sophisticated first-person narrative.

Dickens' novels have an epic* quality; they usually depict a wide array of characters from all walks of life and offer a panoramic view of society. By comparison, the novels of Charlotte and Emily Brontë seem to work on a much smaller scale. However, Charlotte Brontë's *Jane Eyre* (1847) and *Villette* (1853) and Emily Brontë's *Wuthering Heights* (1847) are dramatic explorations of important areas of human experience. *Wuthering Heights*, for example, may be restricted to the depiction of two families living in close proximity in an isolated moorland region, yet the range of human emotion Emily Brontë represents, as the conflict between the protagonists* intensifies, itself has epic* qualities. Similarly, *Jane Eyre* and *Villette*, both exploring the complex inner lives of their female first-person narrators, suggest that women's experiences of social restriction and the resulting mental pain are worthwhile subjects for the novel.

Other women writers emerged as important voices during the Victorian period. Elizabeth Gaskell, the wife of a Manchester-based Unitarian minister, wrote social-problem novels* about the industrial north. *Mary Barton* depicted the sufferings of the poor and describes how one disaffected worker, John Barton, murders the son of a factory owner. The heroine of *North and South*, Margaret Hale, receives a culture shock when she moves with her family from the rural south to the industrial north. The novel ends with her marriage with a mill-owner, suggesting that divisions between the wealthy south and the industrial north can eventually be reconciled. Gaskell is also renowned for her sophisticated psychological insights into the female condition. In *Ruth* (1853), for example, she depicts the sufferings of an unmarried mother, while *Cousin Phillis* (1864) offers a sensitive portrayal of a young woman's breakdown following a disappointment in love.

Another major female writer of the period was George Eliot, the pseudonym of Mary Anne Evans. She found a male pseudonym useful, not only to avoid having her work judged unfairly (women writers were sometimes treated patronizingly by Victorian reviewers), but also as a way of concealing her identity. She lived with George Henry Lewes, a married man unable to divorce his wife, and because of this she was considered unrespectable by many Victorians. A professional journalist and sub-editor before she began writing fiction, Eliot is one of the most important innovators of the novel, doing much to develop the genre into an art form. She used the realist* novel as a sophisticated vehicle for her commentaries on the cultural, social and political developments that shape the life of the individual, as well as exploring the interior lives of her characters. Her early novels, *Adam Bede* (1859) and *The Mill on the Floss* (1860), focus on the ways in which individuals find themselves in conflict with their communities. In the latter novel, her heroine Maggie is forced to make difficult moral decisions about whether she should act for self-fulfilment or to keep faith with the values of her family and community. It is perhaps telling that Maggie drowns, as though Eliot felt that there was no solution to the conflict between individual needs and social demands. Her masterpiece, *Middlemarch* (1871–72), has the sub-title *A Study of Provincial Life*, and here Eliot saw herself combining the roles of novelist and social critic. *Middlemarch* is an epic* novel, for although she focuses on a small provincial town and its surroundings, she shows the ways in which vast social changes (in this case the first Reform Bill of 1832 and developments in scientific knowledge) impinge on everyday life. In her final novel, *Daniel Deronda* (1876), Eliot looks beyond the provincial and the rural to explore issues such as Jewish identity within cosmopolitan and urban settings. Eliot paved the way for later writers such as Henry James (whose *The Portrait of a Lady* (1881) reworks *Daniel Deronda*'s feminist* themes centred on female autonomy and marriage) and Thomas Hardy, who found Eliot's intense focus on provincial life useful in the development of novels based on his fictional region, 'Wessex'.

Hardy considered a small geographic region capable of furnishing him with enough material to consider all aspects of human existence. His early *Under the Greenwood Tree* (1872) was a comic depiction of rural society in Dorset. However, Hardy found comedy an inappropriate medium for his vision, and later novels, such as *Far From the Madding Crowd* (1873), *Tess of the D'Urbervilles* (1891), and *Jude the Obscure* (1895), were profoundly tragic in tone and controversial in that Hardy felt that a realistic depiction of sexual relationships, and the problems of married life, were important to his artistic vision. For example, in *Tess of the D'Urbervilles*, the heroine Tess, a milkmaid, bears a child out of wedlock. The child dies and she tries to rebuild her life, agreeing to marry the middle-class Angel Clare. When she confesses on her wedding night that she is not a virgin, Angel abandons her, despite the fact that he admitted to a previous sexual liaison with another woman. Tess, virtually destitute, is forced to accept help from her seducer Alec. When the repentant Angel returns from abroad, Tess, distraught, kills Alec and is eventually hanged for the crime. What shocked many Victorian critics was that Hardy chose to subtitle this novel about a 'fallen' woman, 'A Pure Woman'. Hardy defended his position as a writer in an angry essay, 'Candour in English Fiction' (1890), in which he argued that 'Life being a physiological fact, its honest portrayal must be largely concerned with [. . .] the relations of the sexes [. . .]. To this [. . .] English society opposes a well-nigh insuperable bar'. Hardy abandoned novel writing largely because of the fact that many Victorian magazine editors and libraries imposed censorship on authors. He went on to develop a successful career as a poet.

For many popular Victorian writers, however, there were ways of avoiding censorship and some skilfully managed to treat so-called shocking themes, such as bigamy, adultery, and murder, without offending editors. For example, a new type of fiction emerged in the 1860s: the sensation novel*. Also known as 'the novel-with-a-secret', this popular genre was designed to shock readers with its depictions of mysteries, crimes, and secrets in the context of con-temporary genteel life. Wilkie Collins' *The Woman in White* (1859–60) was the first of the sensation novels*, describing how two aristocratic men plot to steal the fortune of a young lady before incarcerating her in a lunatic asylum; an amateur detective later tracks down the conspirators, discovering their dark secrets. Collins' *The Moonstone* (1868) is equally sensational, with the theft of a magnificent diamond at the centre of the plot. However, this novel depicts a professional detective, and is considered by many to be the first example of the detective novel.

Sensationalism continued to be a major feature of Victorian popular fiction. The late-Victorian period saw the development of a new type of sensational novel which drew upon earlier Gothic* novels; here the unknown terrors of urban life and of unconscious impulses became linked. Robert Louis Stevenson's *The Strange Case of Dr Jekyll and Mr Hyde* (1886) focused on this fear of the modern city. The respectable Dr Jekyll contains within himself an 'unknown' force in the form of the murderous Mr Hyde. Another example of *fin-de-siècle** Gothic* is Bram Stoker's *Dracula* (1897), where the Transylvanian vampire buys property in London to use as a base from which he can pursue his sinister designs on the British population. Oscar Wilde's novel *The Picture of Dorian Gray* (1891), also explores the hidden aspects of human psychology and the opportunities afforded by the modern city for hiding crimes. His play *The Importance of Being Earnest* (1895), offers another exploration of the need for a double life, although here he employs the different registers of farce* and comedy, rather than the Gothic* genre.

Although the Victorian period was known as the 'Age of the Novel', many major poets published challenging and innovative work throughout the nineteenth century. The popular poet Alfred Tennyson, who became Poet Laureate* in 1850, produced some of the finest lyrics* of the age. His powerful representations of emotion, particularly the feelings of love, loss, and grief, as well as his detailed references to the natural world, make his poetic style distinctive. *In Memoriam* (1850), his long elegy* for his dead friend Hallam, is an important example of Victorian literature's concern to chart the complexities of human emotion and processes of mourning. Yet Tennyson's work covers a wide range of topics, from women and education in *The Princess: A Medley* (1847), to inter-class love, madness, masculinity, and warfare in *Maud* (1855), a long and sensational dramatic monologue*. Tennyson's interest in female experience is evident in 'The Lady of Shalott' (1842), a lyrical narrative poem* describing the tragic fate of a Lady condemned to die if she directly engages with the world beyond her prison-tower. Tennyson also responded to contemporary events in poems such as 'The Charge of the Light Brigade' (1854), which celebrated British heroism during the Crimean War.

Robert Browning was another prominent poet who explored the complexities of the mind. He used the form of the dramatic monologue* to great effect. For example, 'My Last Duchess' (1842), set in Renaissance Italy, is spoken by a Duke who demands certain qualities of pride and restraint in his wife.

Having failed to behave in the way he expects, she is murdered. The Duke states: 'I gave commands. / Then all smiles stopped together' (Abrams, p. 1256, ll. 46–47). Her portrait, he suggests, is much more satisfactory to him than the real woman. Browning continued to represent the thought processes of criminals in later poetry such as his sensational long poem, *The Ring and the Book* (1868–69), which appeared in serialized form, depicting a murder trial from the seventeenth century. Browning's dramatic monologues* energetically convey the ways in which thought processes develop and capture the quirky traits of his speakers, which range from Spanish monks to Italian painters to questing knights.

A number of women poets also flourished during the Victorian period. Elizabeth Barrett Browning (who married Robert Browning) wrote a long feminist* poem depicting the struggles of a female artist, *Aurora Leigh* (1856). Christina Rossetti's poem for children, *Goblin Market* (1862), is a dramatic, sensuous, and ambiguous poem which depicts the story of two sisters, one of whom consumes forbidden goblin fruit and whose health and well-being declines. She is rescued by her sister, who is prepared to sacrifice herself by meeting the goblin men to find the antidote. The poem has attracted considerable critical attention, not least because of its strange combination of sexual and religious imagery.

Victorian drama tended to be characterized by the popular genres of melodrama* and farce* until the late-Victorian period, when innovations by emerging playwrights injected new energies into the theatre. Many of these were influenced by the Norwegian playwright Henrik Ibsen, whose work dealt with contemporary social issues. George Bernard Shaw's career as a dramatist began at this period with plays such as *Mrs Warren's Profession* (1893) about prostitution, and his exploration of ideal masculinity in *Arms and the Man* (1894). Oscar Wilde, with his social comedies of modern life, such as *An Ideal Husband* (1895) and *The Importance of Being Earnest* (see the 'Case Study', below), exposed the ways in which social conventions encouraged secrecy and duplicity.

Each Victorian text does not, of course, exist in isolation, and it is helpful when studying Victorian literature to consider how it might relate to other key texts of the period. For example, *Middlemarch* attempts to show the impact of national movements and changes by studying its effects on the community of a small town. Yet Eliot's novel can be usefully seen as building upon the epic* novels of Dickens, such as *Bleak House*, which shows how the law impacts upon everybody, rich and poor, or Thackeray's *Vanity Fair* (1848), which depicts middle-class British people's lives affected by the events of the Napoleonic Wars. By examining Eliot's project alongside these earlier texts of British national life, it becomes possible to see what new things she was trying to achieve, and what legacies she was inheriting.

Criticism and Literary Theory

It would be difficult to engage with the literature of the Victorian period without considering the concept of realism*. For Victorian critics, realism* was discussed as an imaginative portrayal of the real world, although for some later twentieth-century critics, such as Virginia Woolf, realism* was both naïve and inartistic. Yet in recent years, critics have made important revaluations of the literature of the Victorian period, and literary realism* has attracted its defenders. George Levine, for example, in *The Realistic Imagination* (1981), has argued that far from being naïve, Victorian realism* involves a self-conscious use of language:

> No major Victorian novelists were deluded into believing that they
> were in fact offering unmediated reality; but all of them struggled to
> make contact with the world out there, and, even with their knowledge
> of their own subjectivity, to break from the threatening limits of solipsism,
> of convention, and of language. (p. 8)

Realism* was not a simple attempt to hold up a mirror to the real world; as Dickens maintained, literature depended for its power on writers' 'fanciful' treatment of the truth, their ability to shape their vision of reality imaginatively. The critical focus on realism*, and the debates about its value and techniques, have enabled critics to reread texts which were once dismissed as merely entertaining and inartistic; these new interpretations have highlighted both the richness and sophistication of Victorian novels and other literary forms.

An important defence of Victorian literature came from twentieth-century Marxist critics. Raymond Williams, for example, in *The English Novel from Dickens to Lawrence* (1970), saw Victorian literature as crucial in the formation of the new identities and 'structures of feeling' which emerged throughout the Victorian period. Industrialization and urbanization brought about the alienation of individuals and their communities, and Victorian novels, Williams argues, played an important role in 'show[ing] people and their relationships in essentially knowable and communicable ways' (p. 14). Other critics concerned to explore literature as political, particularly those influenced by Michel Foucault's theories on the disciplinary structures of social power, read Victorian literature as part of the processes of oppressive state power. D. A. Miller's *The Novel and the Police* (1988), for example, examines novels by writers such as Dickens, Anthony Trollope, and Wilkie Collins, arguing that their novels 'police' readers in similar ways to social institutions such as schools and prisons.

New perspectives on Victorian literature have emerged from such Marxist and Foucauldian approaches. Catherine Gallagher in *The Industrial Reformation of English Fiction* (1985) examines the ways in which writers of social-problem novels*, such as Dickens and Elizabeth Gaskell, responded to the social and political ideologies of their time. She demonstrates the ways in which such novels contributed to and responded to a range of other texts and social discourses. Another influential historicist critic is Gillian Beer, whose book, *Darwin's Plots: Evolutionary Narrative in Darwin, George Eliot and Nineteenth-Century Fiction* (1983), examines the ways in which the scientific theories and discourses of the Victorian period permeated literature. She demonstrates how George Eliot's work in particular, with its references to biology and natural history, engaged with Darwin's theory of natural selection. For example, in *Middlemarch* Eliot represents two scientists, the doctor, Lydgate, and the clergyman naturalist, Farebrother, both of whom struggle to discover truths about biological processes against a background of philistine complacency and provincial incompetence. Eliot uses the organic image of the web as a way of describing the various interconnected strands of the human community. Historicist critics have highlighted the sustained engagement of Victorian writers with the great debates, discoveries, and events of the period.

Feminist* critics have also given considerable attention to Victorian texts. This was a time when the professional women writers emerged and, as the nineteenth century progressed, numerous women made a living by writing novels, poetry, plays, and by journalism. Sandra Gilbert and Susan Gubar, in *The Madwoman in the Attic: The Woman Writer and the Nineteenth-Century Literary Imagination* (1979), argue that for many nineteenth-century women writers the issue of self-expression was fraught with anxiety. Uneasy about publicly voicing their sense of protest against the restrictions imposed upon women, such as the lack of a full education and the inhibiting codes of 'proper' femininity, women writers tended to vent their anger in covert ways. For example, in Charlotte Brontë's *Jane Eyre*, Jane, the quiet governess employed by the wealthy landowner, Mr Rochester, feels a sense of imprisonment. Aware that because of her gender she is unable to seek adventure abroad or to shape her own future, Jane cannot openly express her anger. Gilbert and Gubar argue that this is vented on her behalf via her 'double', the West Indian Bertha Mason, Mr Rochester's 'mad' wife, who regularly escapes from her literal imprisonment in his attic to rampage destructively through his house. As the title of their book suggests, many nineteenth-century women writers, such as the poets Christina Rossetti and Elizabeth Barrett Browning, and novelists such as George Eliot, found similar covert strategies through which to express those ideas considered to be unladylike or extreme.

In recent years, growing numbers of postcolonial* critics have reinterpreted Victorian literature to take account of its representations of race, ethnicity and the 'foreign', and have drawn attention towards the blindness of many

Western scholars who have failed to address these issues. For example, Gayatri Chakravorty Spivak, in an important 1985 essay on *Jane Eyre*, criticizes previous feminist* approaches to the novel for ignoring its imperial contexts. Other significant works in this area include Patrick Brantlinger's *Rule of Darkness* (1988), which explores the ways in which Victorian authors responded to the Empire, and John Kucich's *Imperial Masochism* (2006), which examines how notions of guilt and suffering inform Victorian literary representations of colonization.

Feminist* and postcolonial* approaches to Victorian literature have influenced critics working within the fields of gender studies and queer theory*, both of which explore representations of gender, sexuality, otherness, and same-sex relationships. Eve Kosofsky Sedgwick, in her influential books *Between Men* (1985) and *Epistemology of the Closet* (1990), examines a number of Victorian novels by authors such as Charles Dickens, Henry James, Oscar Wilde, and Robert Louis Stevenson to demonstrate how the homoerotic and 'homosocial'* (here the bonds forged by men within the contexts of male-only institutions) generate anxiety and tension concerning the 'proper' boundaries of masculine identity. The male cultures outlined in the texts she discusses are all shown to be oppressive to women; however, these male homosocial* worlds do not always exclude the feminine, and this, she argues, leads to a sense of panic. This idea has also been explored by Elaine Showalter in *Sexual Anarchy* (1991), an examination of gender panic at the end of the century. One example she explores is the relationship between Dr Jekyll and his violent, uncontrollable alter-ego, Mr Hyde, in Stevenson's *Dr Jekyll and Mr Hyde*. Showalter sees Jekyll's description of his relationship with Hyde in terms of anxieties about homosexual desire.

In recent years, many scholars have attempted to retrieve some of the thousands of Victorian authors whose work has been overlooked, under-read, or simply fallen out of fashion. Some of these writers and texts are important to our understanding of the diversity and richness of the Victorian period. For example, the lesbian poets Katherine Bradley and her niece, Edith Cooper, who collaborated under the pseudonym 'Michael Field', have received considerable critical attention for their representations of female same-sex desire. Other neglected writers include Charlotte M. Yonge, whose bestselling novels were inflected with her High Anglican beliefs, and who also edited her own magazines for girls and young women. The novelist Charles Reade, once a great name in Victorian letters, has only recently been rediscovered. Victorian literature, as critics are continually reminding us, is a rich and vast territory. The boundaries of the term 'Victorian' have expanded considerably, creating an awareness of the diversity of Victorian culture.

Clearly, it would be impossible to incorporate all critical approaches when writing an essay on a Victorian text. However, many texts lend themselves to particular approaches, and it would be sensible to take this into account. For example, a novel such as *Jane Eyre*, with its heroine seeking work, independence, and equality in marriage, seems almost to ask to be interpreted from a feminist* point of view. However, a strong essay would include other approaches to supplement a feminist* reading, such as a postcolonial* interpretation of Bertha, or a Marxist analysis of the servant, Mrs Fairfax, or a 'queer'* reading of Jane's fascination with her rival Blanche Ingram. A student who is aware of diverse ways of reading is more likely to gain more from a text than a student who seeks only to present their own opinion. Indeed, by examining a range of interpretations and approaches, one is able to strengthen and clarify one's own opinion of a text.

 ## Charles Dickens' *Great Expectations*

Great Expectations was first published in *All The Year Round*, Dickens' own weekly magazine which, at two pence per issue, was affordable to a wide readership. The first of thirty-six instalments appeared on 1 December 1860, and the three-volume book was published in 1861. (For details of the publishing contexts and reception of *Great Expectations*, see Wynne, pp. 83–97.) The first volume covers the orphan Pip's childhood; he is brought up by his tyrannical sister, Mrs Joe, and her kindly husband, Joe the blacksmith. In this section he meets Magwitch, the convict, and encounters the wealthy eccentric Miss Havisham and her beautiful and haughty ward Estella. The second volume depicts Pip, the inheritor of a fortune from a mysterious benefactor, determined to become a gentleman in London, and it ends when the benefactor discloses himself as Magwitch. Having presumed that Miss Havisham had enriched him, Pip is distraught to find that his fortune originated with a convict. The third volume shows the unravelling of Pip's 'great expectations' and his growth to maturity, signalled by his rejection of his inheritance and acceptance of his two surrogate 'fathers', Magwitch and Joe. The novel's opening, when Pip declares, 'My father's family name being Pirrip, and my christian name Philip, my infant tongue could make of both names nothing longer or more explicit than Pip. So, I called myself Pip, and came to be called Pip' (p. 3), reveals his desire to distance himself from his family. Pip avoids using the more straightforward expression 'my family name' and even rejects the Christian name bestowed upon him by his parents. After meeting Miss Havisham, Pip longs to escape his working-class origins by becoming a gentleman; however, he expects to wait passively until his 'great expectations' transform him into a suitable bridegroom for Estella. Pip's fantasies lead nowhere; the title of the novel is ironic, for Pip's belief in the transforming power of his 'great expectations' turns out to be illusory.

Outlining Pip's evolution from ignorance to knowledge and idleness to labour, *Great Expectations* is a *Bildungsroman**, a novel of development. Pip narrates his own psychological journey in a narrative which involves a complex negotiation between the mature man who narrates his own story (in sophisticated language: 'my infant tongue could make of both names nothing longer or more explicit than Pip'), and the younger Pip who fails to recognize his entrapment within the plots developed by the 'benefactors', Miss Havisham and Magwitch.

Great Expectations is, like many Victorian novels, a substantial book to read, and it may seem difficult to know where to begin a study of the text. It is useful to select a key chapter to read carefully, in order to identify themes and to explore the writer's use of language. Noting apparently odd images, unusual words, and repetitions can help in identifying important features of a novel. Chapter 8 is significant, for it depicts a transitional moment in Pip's life when he visits Miss Havisham for the first time and becomes aware of his own position as a member of the working classes. A closer examination of the chapter not only reveals the novel's central themes, but also shows the distinctive features of Dickens' style and how these work to create meaning.

Chapter 8 shows the child Pip poised between the world of Joe's forge (he thinks he is destined to become a blacksmith) and the world of gentility, represented by Satis House (the home of Miss Havisham and Estella). Before he leaves for Satis House, Pip observes the idle tradesmen in the town, each of them standing in their shop doorways. However, one tradesman alone is absorbed in his work: 'The watch-maker, always poring over his little desk [. . .] seemed to be the only person in the High Street whose trade engaged his attention' (p. 54). Why does Dickens single out the watchmaker as the only man at work? This detail may seem insignificant; however, when Dickens describes Miss Havisham's room a little later in the chapter, we are informed that she has stopped all of her clocks at twenty minutes to nine (p. 57). The industrious watchmaker and the leisured woman who attempts to stop time are clearly linked, suggesting that time and labour are important themes in the novel.

The importance of time (whether it is wasted time, the inevitability of the passing of time, human measurements of time, or time viewed as a commodity) is emphasized repeatedly in this chapter, which begins with the image of the busy watchmaker (whose 'time is money'). Consider, for example, Pip's account of his first sighting of Miss Havisham:

> She was dressed in rich materials – satins, and lace, and silks – all of white.
> Her shoes were white. And she wore a long white veil dependent from her

hair, and she had bridal flowers in her hair, but her hair was white. [. . .] She had not quite finished dressing, for she had but one shoe on – the other was on the table near her hand – her veil was but half arranged, her watch and chain were not put on, and some lace for her bosom lay with those trinkets, and with her handkerchief, and gloves, and some flowers, and a prayer-book, all confusedly heaped about the looking-glass. (p. 57)

It is evident here that Miss Havisham is in a state of transition: not quite fully dressed, in bridal clothes about to get married, but not married (she is *Miss* Havisham), she has shoes and gloves for outdoor wear, but she is fixed indoors. Dickens makes another reference to watches, but Miss Havisham does not wear hers (and she never will, for she has deliberately broken it). The confusion of Miss Havisham's position is further emphasized by the fact that although she wears the clothes of a young bride, time has turned her hair white. As Pip continues to scrutinize her he notes that her wedding-dress had 'lost its lustre and was faded and yellow' (p. 58). We later discover that after being jilted on her wedding day, she refused to leave Satis House or change anything from that moment. Her attempt to fix one moment in time is impossible, for inevitably she ages and decays and her possessions deteriorate. Pip's sighting of Miss Havisham disturbs him, for it reminds him of death (the moment when time actually does stop for each individual life). She resembles a skeleton, wearing a rich dress, which he saw dug up from a church vault and of a 'ghastly waxwork at the fair' (p. 58). In other words, she seems both dead and alive at the same time, just as she is bride and virgin, poised to leave her room, yet trapped inside; she is fixed in a state of transition.

Pip's own transition from labouring boy to gentleman becomes evident in this chapter, as he realizes that his class position is inferior to that of Miss Havisham and Estella. He also becomes aware of gender difference, for the feminine world of Satis House (signified by the profusion of 'feminine' objects on Miss Havisham's dressing table) is very different from the more masculine world of the blacksmith's forge. When the two children play cards, significantly a game of 'beggar my neighbour', Estella repeatedly 'beggar[s] him' (p. 60) as though to emphasize his poverty and helplessness. Encouraged by Miss Havisham to abuse Pip, to 'break his heart', Estella mocks Pip's speech, his 'coarse hands' and 'thick boots' (p. 60), emphasizing his sense of inferiority: 'I had never thought of being ashamed of my hands before [. . .]. Her contempt was so strong that it became infectious, and I caught it' (p. 60). If we pause on the word 'infectious', a word we associate with disease, we can see that it is particularly apt, for from this moment Pip is unable to feel at ease with himself and accepts her estimation of him as inferior, 'contemptible'. He states: 'I was so humiliated, hurt, spurned, offended, angry, sorry – I cannot hit upon the right name for the smart' (p. 62). This lack of a language with which to describe his emotion is significant, indicating how the 'infection' he has caught has struck deeply at his sense of identity. Pip, as narrator, struggles to express the deep emotion he feels and his failure indicates the limitations of language itself.

Chapter 8 continues to emphasize the power of time, the importance of labour, and the inadequacies of language. When Pip is dismissed by Miss Havisham, he explores the grounds of Satis House; once a thriving brewery, it is now empty of life: 'no horses, no stable, no pigs in the sty, no malt in the storehouse, no smells of grains and beer in the copper or the vat' (p. 63). The long list of negatives here suggests that once labour ceases, death takes hold (a point that is relevant to Miss Havisham's static, dead-alive existence). Pip watches Estella climb the steps of the deserted brewery, 'as if she were going out into the sky' (p. 64), before he suffers a hallucination:

> I turned my eyes [. . .] towards a great wooden beam in a low nook of the building [. . .] and I saw a figure hanging there by the neck. A figure all in yellow white, with but one shoe to the feet; and it hung so, that I could see that the faded trimmings of the dress were like earthy paper, and that the face was Miss Havisham's, with a movement going over the whole countenance as if she were trying to call me. (p. 64)

If we link the image of the young girl climbing 'into the sky' with the vision of the older woman hanging, apparently dead, yet with a moving face, it suggests that Estella may become another Miss Havisham, that the older woman has perhaps already 'infected' her with her 'dis-ease'. This image of the dead-alive bride is a powerful and disturbing one. Is it a warning to Pip from his unconscious mind? Is it a sign of Pip's newly 'infected' state? Is it an indication to the reader that death is the end of all our 'great expectations'? A good student of literature will think carefully about such questions, and return to the text again and again, until some answers (however provisional they may be) emerge.

 ## Oscar Wilde's *The Importance of Being Earnest*

The Importance of Being Earnest (1895) at first sight seems far removed from *Great Expectations*, yet they share much in common. Both explore the nature of identity and origins, represent passive men as dandies avoiding work, depict older female eccentrics who have the power to control the destinies of the younger generation, and portray an array of fragmented and distorted characters. However, while Dickens' *Bildungsroman** presents the hero moving from idleness towards industriousness and moral integrity, Wilde's heroes, Jack and Algy, remain passive and idle throughout: Jack finds his identity only when he is told who he is by Lady Bracknell, and marries Gwendolen not when he has developed the quality of 'earnestness' (as the title of the play suggests), but when he fortuitously discovers that his real name is 'Ernest'. Yet despite Wilde's focus on the 'exquisitely trivial' – which, he suggests, we should treat 'very seriously' (Raby, p. 39) – *The Importance of Being Earnest* is as much a critique of Victorian society and its class system as *Great Expectations*.

Wilde's comedy draws upon a number of theatrical traditions, including farce* and the comedy of manners*, such as Sheridan's *The School for Scandal* (1777). Wilde's depiction of sexual mores, like Sheridan's, has the potential for scandal; for example, in Act 1, when Jack refers to Cecily, his 'pretty ward who is only just eighteen' (p. 313), Victorian audiences would probably have been aware that 'ward' was often the euphemism for 'mistress'; similarly, Algy's references to 'Bunburying' may suggest concealed sexual adventures; yet in neither instance is there any exposure of misdemeanour. The point Wilde emphasizes is that polite society is based on boring rituals, and his male protagonists*, Jack and Algy, feel the need to lead complicated double lives in order to escape the tedium. His heroines, Gwendolen and Cecily, also avoid boredom by creating fictional lives for themselves through their 'sensational' diaries.

Wilde's depiction of the emptiness and artificiality of society suggests that there is no stable basis for identity, including gender identity, and he uses the concept of inversion as a way of disrupting notions of the 'natural' order. For example, the play overturns the presumption that men possess more authority than women; both Gwendolen and Cecily, contrary to notions of proper Victorian femininity, actually arrange their courtships and marriage proposals to Jack and Algy, the men having no choice but to passively take part in their schemes. Far from benefiting from the gender power associated with the Victorian man of leisure, Jack and Algy find themselves bound by controlling feminine forces. Lady Bracknell is a prime example of controlling femininity, telling her daughter, 'When you do become engaged to someone, I, or your father, should his health permit him, will inform you of the fact' (p. 308). That Lady Bracknell is more of a patriarch* than Jack or her own husband suggests that gender roles are social constructions capable of being subverted and inverted.

Issues of class and gender are crucial in *The Importance of Being Earnest* and a student wishing to explore these topics would do well to examine the historical context of Wilde's play, which was first performed in 1895. A number of significant facts emerge: first, that the socialist movement was gaining increasing working-class support at the end of the century; secondly, that feminists* (labelled 'New Women') were demanding greater access to higher education and the workplace; and thirdly, that Wilde was arrested in 1895 and imprisoned for committing homosexual acts. These changes in working-class culture, the development of new roles for women, and an awareness of the figure of the 'homosexual' caused considerable anxiety to those who promoted the status quo.

In order to see how Wilde deals with the issues of gender and class, it is worth examining Lady Bracknell, a major character in the play who both acts as a patriarchal* mother and staunchly defends the rights of the aristocracy. In Act 1 she reacts negatively to Jack's announcement that he is ignorant of his parents (as a baby he was found in a handbag deposited in the cloakroom at Victoria Station), exclaiming:

> Mr Worthing, I confess I feel somewhat bewildered by what you have just told me. To be born, or at any rate bred, in a hand-bag [. . .] seems to me to display a contempt for the ordinary decencies of family life that reminds one of the worst excesses of the French Revolution. And I presume you know what that unfortunate movement led to? As for the particular locality in which the hand-bag was found, a cloak-room at a railway station might serve to conceal a social indiscretion – has probably, indeed, been used for that purpose before now – but it could hardly be regarded as an assured basis for a recognized position in good society. (p. 311)

Lady Bracknell's objections to Jack as her daughter's suitor are absurd, and much of the comedy lies in her seriously thinking that the infant Jack was somehow responsible for his origins, and thus making a political gesture by beginning life in an unconventional way. Yet, why does Lady Bracknell associate Jack's unusual situation with 'the worst excesses of the French Revolution'? A historical investigation would reveal that the French Revolution of 1789 led to the execution of the French monarch and the emergence of a modern state based on republicanism, democracy, and secularism. For Lady Bracknell, the idea of revolution (and there were further revolutions throughout Europe in 1848) is an ever-present threat to her social world based on inherited privilege, leisure, and the exploitation of the poor. Her speech reveals her fear, indicating her role in policing the boundaries of 'polite' society and excluding those associated with social change. Because Jack does not know his parents, he could be from a 'lower class', and thus pose a threat to her.

Lady Bracknell also embodies aspects of gender inversion. In Act 3 she enters Jack's country home uninvited in order to prevent her daughter making an 'unsuitable' marriage. She states:

> Apprised, sir, of my daughter's sudden flight by her trusty maid, whose
> confidence I purchased by means of a small coin, I followed her at once
> by a luggage train. Her unhappy father is, I am glad to say, under the
> impression that she is attending a more than usually lengthy lecture
> by the University Extension Scheme on the Influence of a Permanent
> Income on Thought. I do not propose to undeceive him. Indeed
> I have never undeceived him on any question. I would consider it
> wrong. (p. 346)

Lady Bracknell here indicates an inversion of traditional ideas about gender
identity that women are best suited to the public sphere, while men should be
left at home, sheltered from the truth about their wives and daughters.
Gwendolen appears to have attended a university course of lectures, thus
affirming her status as an educated 'New Woman', while the 'trusty' maid
shows little feudal attachment to her employers, concerned only with money.
Lady Bracknell, in an inversion of the moral order, sees telling the truth as
'wrong'. Gwendolen shares her mother's view of gender roles when she
states: 'Outside the family circle, papa, I am glad to say, is entirely unknown.
I think that is quite as it should be. The home seems to me to be the proper
sphere for the man' (p. 334). Although Wilde presents these inversions of
traditional gender stereotypes as comic, his play appears to relish the idea of
the world being turned upside down. The male protagonists*, Jack and Algy,
are not so much part of the stable basis of patriarchal* society as radically
unsure of their roles. Having adopted different personae for different locations and situations, their strategies to evade responsibility expose all aspects
of identity as unstable.

An examination of the historical context of the play reveals ruling-class
characters such as Lady Bracknell as representatives of a class system which
was beginning to seem obsolete. However, her ability to wield power indicates that traditional notions of gender roles were becoming outdated. *The
Importance of Being Earnest* points towards the possibility of dynamic social
and cultural changes. Indeed, it continues to exist as a powerful commentary
on the British class system and gender stereotypes.

Further Reading

Bristow, Joseph (2000), *The Cambridge Companion to Victorian Poetry*. Cambridge:
    Cambridge University Press. A comprehensive overview: key chapters include
    'Reforming Victorian Poetry: Poetics After 1832'; 'The Dramatic Monologue';
    'Victorian Poetry and Science'; 'The Victorian Poetess'. Also includes a guide to
    further reading.
David, Deirdre (2000), *The Cambridge Companion to the Victorian Novel*. Cambridge:
    Cambridge University Press. A comprehensive overview: key chapters include

'Industrial Culture and the Victorian Novel'; 'Gender and the Victorian Novel'; and 'Race and the Victorian Novel'. Also includes a guide to further reading.

Davis, Philip (2002), *The Victorians (The Oxford Literary History Volume 8)*. Oxford: Oxford University Press. An impressively rich, detailed, and wide-ranging study of Victorian literature and culture.

Moran, Maureen (2006), *Victorian Literature and Culture*. London: Continuum. An accessible introductory study aimed particularly at students new to the period; includes a section on key critical approaches, a chronology, a glossary, and a guide to further reading.

Purchase, Sean (2006), *Key Concepts in Victorian Literature*. Basingstoke: Palgrave. An accessible introduction with short entries on a range of topics divided into sections on 'Contexts', 'Texts', and 'Criticism'.

Tucker, Herbert F. (1999), *A Companion to Victorian Literature and Culture*. Oxford: Blackwell. A useful reference work comprising twenty-nine essays on topics ranging from 'Victorian Sexualities' to 'Publishing'. Includes essays focusing on the major literary genres.

'19: Interdisciplinary Studies in the Long Nineteenth Century': http://www.19.bbk.ac.uk. A scholarly journal 'dedicated to advancing interdisciplinary study in the long nineteenth century'. Each issue covers a particular theme; for example, 'Victorian Fiction and the Material Imagination'.

'The Victorian Web': http://www.victorianweb.org/. A valuable, rich resource covering the literature, culture, and history of the period.

Do not forget to keep a record of *all* the texts and websites you look at when researching for an assignment: you will need to list them in your bibliography.

Part IV
Studying Twentieth-Century and Contemporary Literature

9 Literature 1901–1945

Ashley Chantler

Chapter Overview

Historical Context

You will approach this period already aware of the significance of the First World War. But you might be surprised to find that many of the set texts at university do not seem to be 'about' the War and that they are complex and confusing. The work of Joseph Conrad, T. S. Eliot, Ford Madox Ford, James Joyce, Jean Rhys, Virginia Woolf, and W. B. Yeats can certainly seem deliberately and frustratingly demanding. One of the reasons for this is encapsulated in a statement by Eliot, in his 1921 essay 'The Metaphysical Poets'. What he says can be applied to many of the key writers of the time.

> We can only say that it appears likely that poets in our civilization,
> as it exists at present, must be *difficult*. Our civilization comprehends
> great variety and complexity, and this variety and complexity, playing
> upon a refined sensibility, must produce various and complex results.
> (1953, p. 118)

Even before the War authors such as Eliot considered the world to be a complicated, confusing, and probably unknowable place, and were reflecting this by producing 'various and complex results'. To get to grips with the writers' sense of 'complexity', it is necessary for us to go back to before 1914–18, and in so doing we can engage with what your tutors will refer to as 'modernism'.

As with 'Romanticism' and 'Romantic', 'postmodernism'* and 'post-modernist'* (see 'The Romantic Period' and 'Literature 1945–1990', respectively), critics are still debating the nuances, scope, and indeed usefulness of 'modernism' and 'modernist'. You do not need to worry about this. In the first year of university, it is enough for you to understand the generally agreed uses of those terms.

The Oxford Companion to Literature notes that modernism:

> may be seen as a literary movement, spanning the period from the
> last quarter of the 19th cent[ury] in France and from 1890 in Great Britain
> and Germany to the start of the Second World War. It may also be
> viewed as a collective term for the remarkable variety of contending
> groups, movements, and schools in literature, art and music throughout
> Europe over the same period: Symbolism, Post-Impressionism, Decadence,
> Fauvism, Cubism, Expressionism, Imagism*, Vorticism*, Futurism, Dada,
> Surrealism, and so on. (Drabble, p. 682)

We need to be careful, though, not to take 'literary movement' as meaning a group of writers with agreed or shared aims. Modernism is messy. Writers such as Eliot, Ford, Joyce, and Woolf are often grouped under the umbrella term 'modernist' because they tend to be seen as rejecters of what preceded them, breaking free from all things Victorian (see the previous chapter). Indeed, statements by many of the modernists themselves (this was the age of the literary manifesto; see Kolocotroni *et al*) support this view: 'BLAST years 1837 to 1900' by Wyndham Lewis and the Vorticists*, for example, and 'Make it new!' by Ezra Pound and the Imagists*. But how each modernist chose to challenge and write against 'years 1837 to 1900', how each made their writing 'new', was often rather different.

David Lodge reinforces the view that the modernists were rejecting their Victorian antecedents:

> Modernist fiction [. . .] is experimental or innovatory in form, displaying
> marked deviations from preexisting modes of discourse, literary and
> non-literary. Modernist fiction is concerned with consciousness, and
> also with the subconscious and unconscious workings of the human
> mind. Hence the structure of external 'objective' events essential to
> traditional narrative art is diminished in scope and scale, or presented
> very selectively and obliquely, or is almost completely dissolved, in order
> to make room for introspection, analysis, reflection and reverie. [. . .]
> To compensate for the diminution of narrative structure and unity,

alternative methods of aesthetic ordering become more prominent, such as allusion* to or imitation of literary models or mythical archetypes*, and the repetition-with-variation of motifs, images, symbols* [. . .]. Modernist fiction eschews the straight chronological ordering of its material, and the use of a reliable, omniscient and intrusive narrator. It employs, instead, either a single, limited point of view, or a method of multiple points of view, all more or less limited or fallible [. . .]. (1993, pp. 45–46)

There is much here that will help you get a grasp on modernist fiction, and aspects of modernist poetry, but it is important to remember that modernism was also to do with ways of thinking. Modernist experimentation was born not solely from an aesthetic 'dislike for [Victorian] poetry' (Ford 1913, p. 22), nor from a youthful desire to rebel against the old novelists, but because the 'preexisting modes of discourse' were not the best vehicles with which to engage with the 'great variety and complexity' of the modern world or to incorporate new ideas about the self. Katherine Mansfield wrote in 1919 a letter: 'we have to [. . .] find new expressions, new moulds for our thoughts and feelings' (Kolocotroni *et al*, p. 363). It is helpful, then, to not see modernism as a complete severing of the present from the past, rather as the culmination of various 'events'.

Towards the end of Matthew Arnold's 1867 poem 'Dover Beach', the speaker says:

Ah, love, let us be true
To one another! for the world, which seems
To lie before us like a land of dreams,
So various, so beautiful, so new,
Hath really neither joy, nor love, nor light,
Nor certitude, nor peace, nor help for pain (p. 77, ll. 29–34)

After Darwin and significant geological discoveries (see the previous chapter and Maria Frawley's 'The Victorian Age, 1832–1901'), so in the light of scepticism about the Bible's authority, God and religion, Arnold suggests that there is no 'certitude'. By the turn of the century, most of the major writers capture this sense of uncertainty. In the words of H. G. Wells, in 1916:

The nineteenth century was a period of unprecedented modification of social relationships; but great as these changes were, they were trivial in comparison with the changes in religious thought and the criticism of moral ideals. [. . .] The opening decade of the twentieth century was a period of [. . .] great social disorganisation and confused impulses. (p. 161)

As one of the speakers in Ford's 'Grey Matter' (1904) says:

> Where shall I,
> The woman, where shall you take part,
> My poet? Where has either of us scope
> In this dead-dawning century that lacks all faith,
> All hope, all aim, and all the mystery
> That comforteth[?] (1997, p. 23, ll. 21–26)

A significant difference between Arnold's mid-Victorian speaker and Ford's early twentieth-century speaker is that the former makes statements, the latter asks questions. Indeed, the turn of the 'dead-dawning century' and modernism might be characterized by a crisis of knowledge, by epistemological uncertainty. (An important contribution to this crumbling of certainty was the thoroughgoing scepticism of the nineteenth-century German philosopher Friedrich Nietzsche; see Stern.) The phrase 'I don't know' (p. 12), from Ford's *The Good Soldier* (1915), echoes in some form throughout modernist literature.

> For the life of to-day is more and more becoming a life of little things.
> We are losing more and more the sense of a whole, the feeling of a grand
> design, of the co-ordination of all Nature in one great architectonic scheme.
> We have no longer any time to look out for the ultimate design. We have
> to face such an infinite number of little things that we cannot stay to
> arrange them in our minds, or to consider them as anything but as
> accidents, happenings, the mere events of the day. And if in outside
> things we can perceive no design but only the fortuitous materialism of a
> bewildering world, we are thrown more and more in upon ourselves for
> comprehension of that which is not understandable and for analysis of
> things of the spirit. (Ford 1911, p. 62)

The rapid expansion of cities and transport links (see Whitworth); the development of new technologies and media; questions about religion, morality, class, and consciousness (Lunn); concerns about Empire, colonialism and imperialism* (Booth and Rigby; Childs; Matthews); the advances of science and rise of psychology (Watts), culminating in the publication of Sigmund Freud's *The Interpretation of Dreams* (1900): these led writers to draw in to the individual and the individual point of view. As Ford says: 'we are thrown more and more in upon ourselves for comprehension'. Communal truths, 'grand narratives' (see Lyotard in the following chapter), were increasingly replaced by (fragile) personal truths as each person looked at the world in his or her own (uncertain, fallible) way. Henry James' analogy for this is each person standing at the window of his/her own separate room in a vast house:

He and his neighbours are watching the same show, but one seeing more where the other sees less, one seeing black where the other sees white, one seeing big where the other sees small, one seeing coarse where the other sees fine. And so on, and so on. (p. 7)

For the modernists, there was no longer a common phenomenological world, as implied by much Victorian realism*, just personal points of view. Compare, for example, the opening of George Eliot's *The Mill on the Floss* (1860), with its clear and detailed rendering of the landscape, with the impressionistic opening of Conrad's *Heart of Darkness* (1902). As Virginia Woolf writes, in 'Modern Fiction' (1919), of the relationship between the internal and external world:

Examine for a moment an ordinary mind on an ordinary day. The mind receives a myriad impressions – trivial, fantastic, evanescent, or engraved with the sharpness of steel. From all sides they come, an incessant shower of innumerable atoms; and as they fall, as they shape themselves into the life of Monday or Tuesday, the accent falls differently from of old [. . .]. Life is not a series of gig-lamps symmetrically arranged; life is a luminous halo, a semi-transparent envelope surrounding us from the beginning of consciousness to the end. (2008, p. 9)

The world for the modernists was mutable and ultimately unknowable; the self isolated, unstable, unsure.

The First World War compounded this view, and for many writers, modernist or not (see, for example, Hardy, Sassoon, and Owen), it prompted further questions, many begun with Darwin, about the dichotomies of human/animal, civilized/bestial, and sane/mad. Jean Rhys distils the post-War position of despair about humanity in her 1939 novel *Good Morning, Midnight*:

I'm very much afraid of the whole bloody human race. [. . .] Who wouldn't be afraid of a pack of damned hyenas? [. . .] What I really mean is that I hate them. [. . .] I hate the whole bloody business. It's cruel, it's idiotic, it's unspeakably horrible. I never had the guts to kill myself or I'd have got out of it long ago. (pp. 144–45)

Evolution does not necessarily mean positive progress, and in the light of the War, looking coldly at who we are, perhaps suicide is an act of sanity rather than madness.

The War also raised questions about the purpose of art and the role of the writer. Here is Ford in an article published on 8 August 1914:

We go out. We writers go out. And, when the world again has leisure to think about letters, the whole world will have changed. It will have changed in morality, in manners, in all human relationships, in all views of life, possibly even in language, certainly in it estimates of literature. What then is the good of it all? I don't know. (1914, p. 174)

But Ford and many of his contemporaries did not abandon literature as a vehicle for comprehending the post-War world, they just chose different styles and forms for doing so. (See Faulkner, pp. 19–21, on one characteristic of modernism being 'an acute awareness of the problems of art, an unremitting self-consciousness'.) Indeed, if there is one thing that might be said to connect the writers of the period it is the view that literature can, however tenuously, however personally, help make some sense of the cruelty and suffering witnessed and endured, and of the 'variety and complexity' (Eliot) of the world. A line from the end of Eliot's *The Waste Land* (1922), much quoted by critics, perhaps encapsulates the difference between many of the post-War writers and those affected by the Second World War: 'These fragments I have shored against my ruins' (p. 69, l. 431). The post-War writer, like the mid-Victorian Matthew Arnold ('Ah, love, let us be true / To one another!'), still searches for positives in an agnostic, barbarous, and uncertain world, still attempts to stop the self falling into an existential slough, to find, as Marlow says in Conrad's *Heart of Darkness*, 'Rivets [. . .] to stop the hole' (p. 51). The post-1945, postmodernist* position is encapsulated in *Waiting for Godot*'s (1953) 'Nothing to be done' (Beckett, p. 1): there is no point searching for positives because there is none (see the following chapter).

Another old way of thinking that was being challenged before the War was to do with the role of women. If the Romantic period saw the birth of feminism* and the Victorian period the growth of feminism* and rise of the 'New Woman' (see 'Historical Context' in 'The Romantic Period' and 'The Victorian Period'), the early twentieth century saw the rise of the suffragette (a woman seeking, through organized protest, the right to vote) and the first of several major steps in the feminist* 'movement'. (For a discussion of 'Suffragette Fiction and the Fictions of Suffrage', see Joannou.) In 1903, Emmeline Pankhurst founded the Women's Social and Political Union (WSPU) and in a 1908 lecture argued:

Government without the vote is more or less a form of tyranny. [. . .] In this country they tell us that we have representative government. So far as women are concerned, while you have representative government for men, you have despotic government for women. (Matthews, pp. 144–45)

The suffragettes were divisive figures, even among women (Woolf wrote negatively of them), but their direct action and the publicity they garnered –

1911 saw suffragette riots in London – was effective in raising public awareness, and in 1918, women over 30 were given the right to vote.

The War also contributed to the changing public perception of women. As H. G. Wells writes, in *What is Coming? A Forecast of Things After the War* (1916), regarding 'every sort of occupation' undertaken by women during the War, from 'clerking', 'automobile driving', and 'police work' to hard labour in the munitions factories:

> There is scarcely a point where women, having been given a chance, have not more than made good. [. . .] Not the most frantic outbursts of militancy after this war can prevent them getting [the vote]. The girls who have faced death and wounds so gallantly in our cordite factories [. . .] have killed for ever the poor argument that women should not vote because they had no military value. Indeed, they have killed every argument against their subjection. (pp. 175–76)

In 1928 (ten years after the War), the minimum voting age for women was reduced to twenty-one.

Some people would prefer a tidy version of history. Thankfully, it is messy and complex. The modernists were not a coherent group of writers with shared aims, but there are connections between their work and it differs in many respects from its literary predecessors; not every 1901–1945 writer was a modernist; the First World War was the defining event of the period, but not the only one, and it was responded to by writers in various ways; to understand what is now seen as the dominant thinking of the period, one must go back into the nineteenth century. As students of literature, it is best, then, to embrace the mess (which of course gives you a certain freedom), if only to get some grasp on why many writers of the period, to return to Eliot, are *'difficult'*.

Key Authors and Texts

One of the things you will soon become aware of when reading about any period of literature is that its major authors were rarely sequestered in dusty garrets, cut off from and uninterested in their contemporaries, penning masterpieces in isolation. Pick any author and you will be able to make connections with other writers. If we take Ford Madox Ford as an example: Ford collaborated with, published and later wrote a book about Conrad; he advised, published and was published by Ezra Pound; he praised Eliot's early poetry and his poem *Antwerp* (1914) was praised by Eliot; in his literary periodical the *English Review* (founded 1908) he published, among others, Rupert Brooke, H. D. (Hilda Doolittle), Thomas Hardy, Henry James, Lawrence, Wyndham Lewis, Wells, and Yeats, and when editing the *transatlantic review* (founded 1924) published E. E. Cummings, Ernest Hemingway, Joyce, Rhys (with whom he also had an affair), Gertrude Stein, and William Carlos Williams; and his poetry appeared in various periodicals and anthologies alongside Owen's and Sassoon's. A trivial biographical link can be made between Ford and Woolf: in 1917, he consulted the appropriately named Dr Head, a neurologist and shell-shock specialist, who had treated Woolf before the War and 'is thought to be a character source for Sir William Bradshaw in *Mrs Dalloway*' (Saunders, vol. 1, p. 38).

A more complex, interesting, and valuable diagram could be drawn, also with Ford at the centre, which makes connections between his poetry and fiction and that of the writers above. The link with Woolf would then be far from trivial: both were interested in consciousness, subjectivity, epistemological uncertainty, gender, marriage, class, time, aesthetic expression, and the effects of the War. As Derek Alsop writes at the end of the chapter 'Literature 1714–1789', the excitement of studying literature at university is not just about reading new texts but making connections between them. And your tutors will be excited by your seminar contributions and assignments if you go beyond the individual text, to show that it does not exist in isolation and that you are aware of its relationship with the texts around it.

Conrad's *Heart of Darkness* (1902; first published 1899 as 'The Heart of Darkness' in *Blackwood's Magazine*) was the first novel that deeply affected me when I was an undergraduate. Its images haunted, and haunt me still: the strange women 'knitting black wool as for a warm pall' (p. 26); the dying slaves 'half effaced within the dim light, in all the attitudes of pain, abandonment, and despair' (p. 35); the man's blood in Marlow's shoes making his feet 'so very warm and wet' (p. 77); and of course Kurtz, lying dying on the boat, his 'ivory face' showing 'craven terror', whispering his last words, 'The horror! The horror!' (p. 112). But I was also affected intellectually: it was the first novel I had read that I sensed I would never nail down – and after school, where banging six-inch nails was expected, that was exciting. Is Marlow a reliable or unreliable narrator? Is the first narrator's version of Marlow's story as verbatim as possible or did he intentionally change parts? Is/was Marlow a racist and/or a sexist? Perhaps the first narrator is a racist and/or a sexist? Are the cannibals the most civilized people in the novel? What were the 'unspeakable rites' (p. 83) that Kurtz presided over? Did Marlow have sexual feelings for the 'savage and superb' black woman (p. 99)? What did Kurtz mean by 'The horror'? Should Marlow have lied to Kurtz's 'Intended' (pp. 117–23)? None of these questions can be answered definitively; the reader will never know. But that, I realized, was the point.

Victorian realist* fiction tends to put the reader in a position of knowing, so by extension suggests that we can know: ourselves, others, society, the world. Conrad, at the turn of the twentieth century, must show otherwise if he is to reflect the shift in thinking: he puts his readers into a position of epistemo-logical uncertainty (see Watt), so suggests that nothing is certain, except death. This is, perhaps, a bleak view, but the novel shows that we find 'rivets' (p. 51) to stop us going mad or committing suicide: religion, family, work, hobbies, stories. Ultimately, they are absurd, but they do the job – if we do not question them.

Conrad's other masterpieces include *Lord Jim* (1900), *Nostromo* (1904) and *The Secret Agent* (1907), all of which are linked textually (and the last two biographically) to his friend and occasional collaborator Ford Madox Ford. Ford's *The Good Soldier* (1915) raises complex and perhaps troubling epistemo-logical and ontological questions, but unlike *Heart of Darkness* does not use a frame narrative. We are trapped with a single narrator, John Dowell, who is writing about his past before he fully understands it (Victorian first-person narrators often seem to know what story they are going to tell before they begin), so every so often he has to revise what he has said, and so revise the past:

> looking over what I have written, I see that I have unintentionally misled you when I said that Florence [his wife] was never out of my sight. Yet that was the impression that I really had until just now. When I come to think of it she was out of my sight most of the time. (pp. 63–64)

Not only does this make the reader feel uncomfortable about Dowell's ability to understand the past (how many moments of realization will there *not* be, and how much has he forgotten or sublimated?), it also prompts one to mis-trust not only his new impressions but everything he has seen in the past. In a key scene, for example, Florence puts 'one finger' on the wrist of Edward Ashburnham (p. 37), Dowell's best friend and the person with whom Florence will soon start a nine-year affair. Dowell does not know how to read the ges-ture: 'don't you see what's going on?' he is asked by Leonora, Ashburnham's wife, to which Dowell replies, 'No! What's the matter?' (pp. 37–38). What other scenes are there that he did not understand, and will perhaps never interpret correctly? And 'correctly' according to whom? There is not a 'cor-rect' reading of the finger on the wrist; there is not a single interpretation. It meant one thing to Florence, another for Ashburnham, another for Leonora, another Dowell. There was not one finger; there is not one stable truth. There are points of view, impressions, personal interpretations.

Dowell does not know the past (there is no such thing as *the* past), nor does he fully understand other people. Perhaps more troubling, though, he does not even understand himself. After Florence has died, Dowell blurts out unconsciously: 'Now I can marry the girl' (p. 73), referring to Nancy, Ashburnham's ward. As Dowell says:

> Now that is to me a very amazing thing – amazing for the light of
> possibilities that it casts into the human heart. For I had never had the
> slightest conscious idea of marrying the girl; I never had the slightest
> idea even of caring for her. [. . .] It is as if one had a dual personality,
> the one I being entirely unconscious of the other. (pp. 72–73).

Dowell's 'Now I can marry the girl', like a Freudian slip, emerges to reveal
something about himself of which he was previously unaware. But what if
he had not made the slip, aloud or in his head? How much of himself is
Dowell not conscious of, and will remain so? In terms of self-knowledge, he
is incomplete, a fragment of a whole that will never be, can never be, known.
And if we cannot know ourselves, we certainly cannot know other people.
As Ford puts it in his 1910 poem 'Views':

> I have [my] Rome; and you, you have a Me,
> You have a Rome and I, I have my You;
> Oh passing lonely souls we sons of men!
> My Rome is not your Rome: my you, not you
> Oh passing lonely. . . . For, if man knew woman
> I should have plumbed your heart; if woman, man
> Your me should be true I. . . . (1997, p. 45, ll. 25–31)

There is not one 'I'; not one 'you'. Neither is there one 'Rome'. There are
impressions: unstable views of the self, others, the world, and the past. What
do we know for certain about existence? Very little, *The Good Soldier*, like *Heart
of Darkness*, suggests, except that it will end, and possibly grotesquely, or
comically, with little dignity or honour.

At school, I probably thought that all First World War poetry was about
death, from the positive uncertainty of the opening of Rupert Brooke's 'The
Soldier' (1915) – 'If I should die, think only this of me' (Silkin, p. 81, l. 1) – to
Owen's concluding bitter certainty that 'Dulce et decorum est / Pro patria
mori' is a 'Lie' (Silkin, p. 193, ll. 21–22). 'Dulce Et Decorum Est' (1920) and
Owen's equally famous 'Anthem for Doomed Youth' (1920) trouble me, partly
because of the similes and rhyme (these are part of a larger concern regarding
turning war into an aesthetic experience), but mainly because the poems,
along with several by Isaac Rosenberg and Sassoon, loom so large in anthologies and the teaching of First World War poetry that students tend to have a
narrow view of a vast literary field. Not only did writers as diverse as E. E.
Cummings, Ford, Hardy, A. E. Housman, Rudyard Kipling, Lawrence, and
Pound write War poetry worthy of study, there is also a large body of poetry by
women: partners, mothers, friends, Voluntary Aid Detachment nurses, muni-
tion workers, conscientious objectors, suffragettes, those in the Intelligence

Service, War Relief offices, the Red Cross, and British women's hospitals in France. (There are also, of course, poems by authors from Europe.) For a more informed view of poetry about the War, it is best, then, to read beyond the set texts. Jon Silkin's *The Penguin Book of First World War Poetry* (1996) is a good place to start as it contains poems by the men mentioned above and several quite well-known, but still marginalized, poems by women: Alice Meynell's 'Summer in England, 1914' (1914), May Wedderburn Cannan's 'Lamplight' (1917), Charlotte Mew's 'The Cenotaph' (1919), and Margaret Postgate Cole's 'The Veteran' (1930). Also look at Catherine W. Reilly's excellent *Scars upon My Heart: Women's Poetry and Verse of the First World War* (2007). Reilly has included a mix of established and amateur women poets, the work of the latter being rather weak in terms of poetic technique and subtlety but important to help us more fully understand what people were thinking during and after the War.

The most important story in Joyce's *Dubliners* (1914) is the concluding 'The Dead'. It is here that Joyce really begins to move towards the radical, exhilarating experimentation of his three masterpieces: *A Portrait of the Artist as a Young Man* (1916), *Ulysses* (1922), and *Finnegans Wake* (1939). Ford correctly said that Joyce 'cannot properly be approached without several readings and without a great deal of thought' (2002, p. 218), and two words in the opening sentence of 'The Dead' – '*Lily*, the caretaker's daughter, was *literally* run off her feet' (p. 175; my italics) – will show you why. They will also help you understand what Joyce builds on in his later fiction. Lilies are associated with, among other things, virginity (innocence, purity, youth) and death. 'Lily', then, does not mean one thing or another. And Lily the person is not one thing or another: is she a virgin or not? Is she naïve or knowledgeable, innocent or manipulative? Is she a flirt or a good girl, naughty or sweetly Catholic? Is she a child or an adult? Joyce then gives us a shocking cliché: 'literally run off her feet'. The awful prose jars, but in the light of the story (Joyce requires 'several readings'), which is in part a meditation on what people say and what people mean, and what objects mean depending on point of view (the world is a lily), 'literally' does not mean 'literally': Lily was not 'run off her feet'. The word points up the non-meaning of the phrase. Joyce is thus not only getting us to think about the complexity of character, but also about the words we use to describe the world, so see the world, as we see it through language (to paraphrase Ludwig Wittgenstein). We return, then, to Ford and the issue of whether we can ever fully understand ourselves, others, the world, the past, if we cannot see through untainted eyes. We also move on to *A Portrait of the Artist as a Young Man* and Stephen Dedalus stating: 'When the soul of a man is born in this country there are nets flung at it to hold it back from flight. You talk to me of nationality, language, religion. I shall try to fly by those nets' (p. 171). We are captured by that trinity, whether we like it or not, whether we realize it or not. Whether it is possible to 'fly by them', so be free (there are parallels here with Nietzsche on 'self-determination' (p. 19)), is answered in *Ulysses* and *Finnegans Wake*. It is perhaps possible to have moments of freedom, but you cannot avoid the structures and strictures of the trinity for long unless you are truly, madly ungrammatical (so mad). Even the apparently free unconscious becomes bound when transformed into language. *Finnegans Wake*, a dream-sequence of H. C. Earwicker, ends and begins: 'A way a lone a last a loved a long the // riverrun, past Eve and Adam's, from swerve of shore to bend of bay, brings us by a commodius vicus of recirculation back to Howth Castle and Environs' (pp. 638, 3). It is a beautiful sentence. And that judgement transforms it: we cannot help but return to old words, correct grammar, taught standards, shocking cliché. When we speak, we are constrained and we constrain. Unbounded, ongoing freedom is, therefore, unthinkable, because we think and express with taught language.

Joyce's Irish compatriot W. B. Yeats is another writer who requires 'several readings', but also some secondary reading, especially on his relationship with Ireland and Irish writers (see Foster; Matthews; Stead). We can break into his poetry through the issue of freedom. In 'The Lake Isle of Innisfree' (1890), for example, the speaker, standing 'on the roadway, or on the pavements grey' (p. 60, l. 11), yearns to escape to the solitude of a pre-industrial idyll: to 'a small cabin' in a 'bee-loud glade' (ll. 2, 4). But the repetition of 'I will arise and go' leaves one unconvinced that the speaker will do so; the speaker seems likely to remain trapped in the city and with his/her anxious 'I'. In another early poem, 'When You Are Old' (1892), freedom – here from the ageing body and the burden of being alone – seems at first to come from escaping into the past. Close reading, however, reveals that the past is/was not wholly positive: the youthful eyes had 'shadows deep' (l. 4), for example, and there were 'sorrows' in the person's 'changing face' (l. 8). Freedom, the poem seems to suggest, can really only come from death. The two poems are good examples of how Yeats' early work can, in its lyricism and imagery, seem simplistic and optimistic, perhaps sentimental, romantic or nostalgic, but is often fraught with internal tensions and contradictions.

In a review of Yeats' 1914 collection *Responsibilities*, which like Joyce's 'The Dead' marks a change in his writing, Ford noted that Yeats seemed to be striving after 'harsh effects, harsh words', 'evolving a new method and adumbrating a new point of view' (2002, p. 166). Similarly, Eliot observed that Yeats' mature style was 'violent and terrible', and that he had achieved a 'freedom of speech' (Stead, p. 32). With poems such as 'The Grey Rock', 'The Two Kings', with its 'laceratingly direct imagery' (Foster, p. 520), 'September 1913' and 'A Coat', Yeats sought to find a new voice that was both personal and political, contemporary but aware of the past, free from 'single intellectualized positions, so that [he could] grasp the full complexity of life' (Stead, p. 31). The early twentieth-century Yeats was, then, one of Eliot's 'poets': a writer wrestling with the 'complexity' of the world (1953, p. 118), but also, like Joyce, fighting language.

In your essays, you have to follow certain rules and meet various expectations – quoting from and analysing the primary texts is vital – but you do have some freedom. If, for example, you are answering a general question about First World War poetry, feel free to escape the net of the canon* of Owen, Rosenberg, and Sassoon; if you are analysing *The Good Soldier*, there is no harm in linking it to Conrad and Impressionism; if you are writing on a theme or an issue – epistemology, religion, marriage, death, the role of women, the influence of the War, and so on – take untrodden critical paths, make fresh connections between the primary texts. In short, show off your sensitivity to language and your willingness to offer new ideas. It is what the writers you are studying did.

Criticism and Literary Theory

When you move away from the primary texts and begin to think about the secondary sources you might read to broaden and refine your ideas, a good place to start for 1901–1945 is the non-fiction of the writers you are studying. As mentioned above, this was the age of literary 'movements, magazines and manifestos' (see Bradbury and McFarlane), with many authors discussing and writing about writing. (For an excellent compendium of manifestos, magazine articles, prefaces, and extracts from longer works, look at *Modernism: An Anthology of Sources and Documents* (Kolocotroni *et al*)). From 1904 onwards, Ford, for example, published critical and theoretical essays, book reviews, 'revaluations' of literature, 'literary portraits', and 'literary causeries' (see his *Critical Essays*), many of which contain arguments about why English literature needed to change, develop, free itself from the Victorian period, but also ideas about how it could go about doing so. His non-fiction not only helps us better understand the experimentation of his own poetry and fiction, it sheds light on the position of the dissatisfied English writer at the beginning of the century. His reviews of and articles on various groundbreaking publications, such as *Des Imagistes* (1914), the Vorticist* periodical *Blast* (1914–15) and *Ulysses*, also help us understand why they were groundbreaking, why they were part of a seismic shift in English letters.

Other single-author collections include T. S. Eliot's *Selected Prose* (which reprints many of the seminal essays first collected in *The Sacred Wood: Essays on Poetry and Criticism* (1920)) and Virginia Woolf's *Selected Essays*. Eliot's 'The Metaphysical Poets' (1921) contains his quotation about poets having to 'be *difficult*' (p. 118). 'Tradition and the Individual Talent' (1919) contains his now famous statement: 'Poetry is not a turning loose of emotion, but an escape from emotion; it is not the expression of personality, but an escape from personality' (p. 30). Other modernists were also interested in authorial impersonality. As Ford puts it: 'the author must learn to suppress himself' (1924, p. 194). Or as Joyce puts it, via Stephen Dedalus in *A Portrait of the Artist as a Young Man*, regarding the 'dramatic form', the form to which Joyce was working towards: 'The artist, like the God of the creation, remains within or behind or beyond or above his handiwork, invisible, refined out of existence, indifferent, paring his fingernails' (p. 181). In *'Hamlet'* (1919; 'Hamlet and His Problems' in *The Sacred Wood*), Eliot proposes that:

> The only way of expressing emotion in the form of art is by finding an 'objective correlative'; in other words, a set of objects, a situation, a chain of events which shall be the formula of that *particular* emotion; such that when the external facts, which must terminate in sensory experience, are given, the emotion is immediately evoked. (1953, pp. 107–08)

This can be linked to Ford's and the Imagist's* interest in rendering 'concrete objects' to arouse in the reader 'certain emotions' (Ford 2002, p. 156), but also to modernist authorial impersonality.

There are many connections between Joyce (whose *Portrait* can be considered as a quasi-literary manifesto – at least for himself) and Woolf – most notably their use of free indirect style*, interior monologue* and stream of consciousness* – but Woolf had reservations about *Ulysses*. In 'Modern Fiction' (1919; a revised version of 'Modern Novels'), she praises Joyce's attempt to 'reveal the flickerings of that innermost flame which flashes its messages through the brain' (2008, p. 10), but suggests that the novel is too narrow in focus, too 'centred in a self [Leopold Bloom] which [. . .] never embraces or creates what is outside itself or beyond'; 'much of life is excluded or ignored' (pp. 10, 11). Woolf is also unsure about the novel's 'indecency' (p. 10; see also Ford's defensive '*Ulysses* and the Handling of Indecencies' (1922), in Ford 2002). Woolf's essay gets us thinking about Joyce's fiction – what it does and perhaps does not do – and we can either agree or disagree, but it also gives us a route into Woolf's fiction: what it does and perhaps does not do. When studying *Mrs Dalloway* (1925), for example, or *To the Lighthouse* (1927), you might think about how the novels 'reveal the flickerings of that innermost flame'; whether Woolf's avoidance of 'indecency' (*Ulysses* is scatological and sexually explicit) is a limitation; and whether or not Woolf can be accused, as she accuses Joyce, of excluding aspects of life (what is omitted by artists – authors and painters – is almost as interesting as what is included, especially regarding sex, class, and contemporary events).

We do not have to agree with authors' statements about writing – not even their own – nor do we have to agree with critics. You should approach secondary texts as you do primary: with a judgemental eye. Critics, like authors, are just offering over interpretations, and you should never unquestioningly regurgitate their opinions. A quick example to show you why can be given using two pieces on *The Good Soldier*; note their titles, in the appendices of the Norton Critical Edition of the novel: 'Dowell as Untrustworthy Narrator', by Grover Smith; 'Dowell as Trustworthy Narrator', by Paul B. Armstrong. Smith gives his interpretation of Dowell; Armstrong gives his. Who is right, who is wrong? That is for you to decide after you have returned to the novel. And you might, of course, decide that they are both correct. As Frank Kermode writes of *The Good Soldier*: 'We are in a world of which it needs to be said *not* that plural readings are possible (for this is true of all narrative) but that the *illusion of the single right reading is possible no longer*' (1995, p. 336).

There are incontestable facts and there are contestable interpretations and opinions. In 1988, Christopher Ricks published *T. S. Eliot and Prejudice*, which contains a chapter contemplating Eliot and anti-Semitism. In 1995, Anthony Julius published *T. S. Eliot, Anti-Semitism, and Literary Form* (and a revised edition in 2003), in which he argues that Ricks failed to properly 'engage with Eliot's anti-Semitism' (p. 10). It is not a fact that Ricks' and Julius' opinions are incontestable. In an astute observation regarding critics arraigning Eliot and Pound 'on the grounds of anti-Semitism, fascism and misogyny', Jason Harding has said:

> This abeyance of sympathy marks the current unwillingness to read these poets any longer on their own terms, or in the light of the formalist* and ahistorical terms laid down by the New Critics*; although some opponents have arguably been too eager to unmask illiberal opinions before allowing the poetry to speak with its full complexity of tone and nuance. (p. 231)

There are several points here worth keeping in mind when you go to the library to read a pile of secondary texts. Criticism goes through phases, fashions: there is a 'current unwillingness' in much critical writing on Eliot to do what New Critics* used to do: to consider only the text itself. There is an 'abeyance of sympathy', and rightly so. If our interpretations of texts are affected by 'sympathy' (or liking, or hate) for the author, what we write about them will be skewed. For example, in his postcolonial* essay 'An Image of Africa: Racism in Conrad's *Heart of Darkness*' (1977), Chinua Achebe asserts that 'Conrad was a thoroughgoing racist' (p. 8). I have written against this opinion, but not so vehemently and unselfconsciously that I was unaware that my interpretation of *Heart of Darkness* might be 'skewed by my relationship with Conrad, who I do not like to think was racist, and by my ethnic and cultural make up' (Chantler, p. 48). Similarly, in *T. S. Eliot*, Craig Raine argues against Julius' damning of Eliot, and one is probably inclined to agree with his more sensitive approach to the poems, but it is just an approach, no doubt influenced by Raine's relationship with Eliot, whom he considers a 'genius' (p. xix).

New Historicism (see 'Criticism and Theory' in 'The Romantic Period') and cultural materialism* remind us that textual analysis is never impersonal, objective, or ahistorical; it is always personal, subjective, and of its time (see Selden and Widdowson). As Frank Kermode writes: 'We bring ourselves and our conflicts to words, to poems and pictures [. . .]; and thus we change the poems and the pictures' (1991, p. 432). It is wise, though, to *try* to allow the poem, play, short story or novel to 'speak with its full complexity of tone and nuance', while being aware of our contemporary eyes, before adopting (if you feel it necessary) the narrowing lens of a particular critical or theoretical approach. If, for example, you give a feminist* reading of a novel by Conrad, Ford or Joyce, you will no doubt raise many pertinent points about the representation of men and women, and say something about patriarchal* structure, but not only will you be interpreting the text exclusively, rather than inclusively, you might be manipulating the text for your own critical ends. Nina Pelikan Straus, for example, in a vehemently feminist* reading of *Heart of Darkness*, is so passionate and biased that her claims about the novel are unconvincing – and convincing your readers is, of course, the key aim of literary criticism.

Primary texts should always come first. Work out how they work, just as a botanist, for example, would work out how a flower works, and reach your own conclusions about, for example, the representation of women. Once you have done this, see what criticism there is and what theoretical approaches you might use, but only ever to illuminate the primary text's full and beautiful complexity, never to distort or manipulate it for your own critical/personal/ political ends.

 T. S. Eliot's Poetry

'We can only say that it appears likely that poets in our civilization, as it exists at present, must be *difficult*' (Eliot 1953, p. 118). T. S. Eliot was one of those poets. I remember first reading 'The Love Song of J. Alfred Prufrock' (1917) and *The Waste Land* (1922) for a seminar when I was an undergraduate and being baffled by them. I liked them – they were compelling, dark, at times darkly funny – but I knew I did not fully 'get' them, and I still do not, not really. If you read Critic X, he will probably imply that he does, as will Critic Y and Critic Z. If you then compare what they are saying, you will see that X, Y, and Z have not really pinned down the poems, they are just trying to. Frank Kermode's statement about *The Good Soldier* applies: 'the *illusion of the single right reading is possible no longer*' (1995, p. 336).

This section will focus on 'Prufrock', partly to get a grasp on some of the things that make it '*difficult*', partly to help you when analysing Eliot's other poems, but also to help you develop your close reading skills, which may be used when studying any poetry of the period. The poem opens:

> Let us go then, you and I,
> When the evening is spread out against the sky
> Like a patient etherised upon a table;
> Let us go, through certain half-deserted streets,
> The muttering retreats
> Of restless nights in one-night cheap hotels
> And sawdust restaurants with oyster-shells:
> Streets that follow like a tedious argument
> Of insidious intent
> To lead you to an overwhelming question . . .
> Oh, do not ask, 'What is it?'
> Let us go and make our visit. (2002, p. 3, ll. 1–12)

If you are unsure who Prufrock is addressing (who the 'you' is) and are uncomfortable with the voice (surely no one says to another person, 'Let us go then, you and I'), then you are right to be.

Robert Langbaum is not unsure: 'Prufrock is clearly speaking for his own benefit. Yet he does not, like the soliloquist*, address himself; he addresses his other self – the "you" of the first line' (p. 190). We should be wary of such assertiveness. John Carey is more circumspect: 'Who are the "you" and "I" at the poem's start [. . .]? Are they Prufrock's two selves? And which two selves? Is he looking at his reflection in a mirror before going out?' (p. 33). Carey knows that the questions are 'unanswerable because the poem designedly withholds the information needed to answer them'; 'We cannot tell what happens in "The Love Song of J. Alfred Prufrock" ' (p. 33).

Perhaps Prufrock is talking to/at himself, which in its oddness would constructively distance him further from the reader (the poem is, in part, about alienation). Perhaps he is practising a speech intended for someone else but cannot keep to the point, which would further the poem's interest in the divide between formal (contrived and concealing) speech and honest expression. But perhaps Prufrock is not speaking. Because the poem is considered by most critics to be a dramatic monologue*, so has an auditor (even if it is Prufrock), speech has tended to be prioritized over thought and writing.

Why cannot the poem be a modernist stream of consciousness* soliloquy*? It is possible. But the rhyme, the repetition, the tendency to slip into iambic* metre* ... Perhaps Prufrock is writing – the knowing literariness of the poem's title certainly prompts one to think about the written – and can thus be connected to modernist scribe narrators such as Dowell in *The Good Soldier*. Whether speaking, thinking, or writing, Prufrock/'Prufrock' has already got us to think about Eliot's (and other modernists') interest in the self and voice: one of the difficult things about *The Waste Land*, for example, is knowing who is speaking, who 'I' and 'you' are, and whether the self/voice is bounded or blurred (see Levenson 1992, p. 171).

'When the evening is spread out against the sky.' If read literally, this line is confusing: an 'evening' (whatever that means) cannot be 'spread out against the sky'. If read metaphorically, it is still confusing, because the conceptual image cannot be imagined. The simile (an excellent tool to help oneself be understood) does not help: 'Like a patient etherised upon a table'. Imagining an anaesthetized person, pre- or post-operation, does not clarify the image of the evening. F. R. Leavis has commented on the poem's 'oddness of imagery' (Southam, p. 120), and he is right. But we need to think about *why* Eliot, who could have made Prufrock make sense, chose 'oddness' over clarity.

Hugh Kenner has said that 'Eliot deals in effects' (Southam, p. 128): we get a sense, a feeling, of meaning 'rather than meaning itself' (p. 131). 'Let us go then, you and I, / When the evening is spread out against the sky / Like a patient etherised upon a table': we are alienated, confused, perhaps troubled; there is a sense of bleakness and dark foreboding; the simile jars, cuts, but *we* are not etherized. We feel, and we feel like Prufrock.

We also need to consider to what extent Prufrock (not Eliot) is in control of what he is saying/thinking/writing. In a detailed discussion of the simile, A. David Moody argues that 'Prufrock's wit has found an image to express his own state'; 'He surely knows what he is doing in deflecting the sentimentality of evening – and the invitation to the reader – into a pathetic fallacy* to end them all' (p. 32). Moody's Prufrock is a knowing and sensitive user of words; he also seems to be a writer with an imagined reader. Does Prufrock know what he is doing? Perhaps; perhaps not. It does not matter. What matters is that the poem denies a *'single right reading'*. Prufrock might think that he can be 'pinned' down by critical 'eyes' (ll. 58, 55); 'Prufrock' proves otherwise. Perhaps, then, the poem is in part about our desire to pin down people and texts – Prufrock and 'Prufrock' – and how doing so denies the complexity of people and texts.

After the simile, Prufrock suggests that 'you and I' go 'through certain half-deserted streets, / The muttering retreats / Of restless nights in one-night cheap hotels / And sawdust restaurants with oyster-shells'. Why he suggests this journey, it is not possible to say; like the simile, the seedy, unromantic urban landscape perhaps suggests a dark side, an alternative view that usually remains unseen. Perhaps it suggests something about Prufrock's inner landscape. Perhaps it is an 'objective correlative' (Eliot 1953, p. 107) to evoke in the reader Prufrock's emotions.

Craig Raine has said that the 'restless nights in one-night cheap hotels' is 'a memory' (p. 68), but there is nothing in the poem that confirms this, and Raine does not ponder, as you would do in an essay, why Eliot gives Prufrock a past with such nights in it and why Prufrock remembers them at this point in the poem. One of Eliot's biographers, Lyndall Gordon, has written that 'Eliot wrote the poem just before his return to Boston, his thoughts turning to the social ordeals of the Beacon Hill drawing-room and solitary walks past Boston's sawdust restaurants with oyster shells' (p. 66). The drawing room belonged to Adeleine Moffatt: 'Again and again in his student poems [. . .] Eliot caricatured his embarrassing friendship with an emotional older woman, Adeleine Moffatt, who used to serve tea to Harvard men in a home crowded with bric-à-brac, behind Boston's State House' (p. 37). Gordon does what many biographers, of Eliot or any author, seem to like to do: to close down the openness of the text. Prufrock becomes a Bostonian who is similar to Eliot (how similar, we will never know, and we should not care); the woman in the poem becomes Adeleine Moffatt; the room in which the women 'come and go' (l. 13) becomes Moffatt's drawing room. Not only is this tedious and reductive, it does not help us get to grips with how the poem works and what it is about.

Textual openness gives us a certain interpretative freedom – 'gaps' in the text, to use Wolfgang Iser's term (p. 299), which may be filled by the reader – but we should not take liberties with that freedom: the text has 'limits' (Iser, p. 296), beyond which we make absurd claims.

Regarding 'In the room the women come and go / Talking of Michelangelo' (ll. 13–14), for example, much can be (and has been) said. You might discuss, for example, the coming and going, which perhaps suggests that the conversation lacks depth (the women are not sitting and pondering), but so too does Prufrock's shallow observation. You would also want to say something about the use of the vague ('the women') and the specific ('Michelangelo'), and what this might suggest, perhaps about the women, perhaps about Prufrock. You could also consider how form probably influences our sense of the tone and understanding of the content: the metre* and rhyme, which are not far off a limerick's, seem to imply mocking humour; the women are trivializing and in turn are being trivialized by Prufrock. You might then link this to the same couplet two stanzas later (ll. 35–36), the repetition of which seems unnecessary. Perhaps Prufrock thinks the women's talk is unnecessary. Perhaps the repetition says more about Prufrock than it does about the women. You could also say something about the couplet being a fragment and perhaps link this to the fragmentary structure of the poem. Fragmentation, as we have already seen, connects much modernist writing, from *The Waste Land*'s 'These fragments I have shored against my ruins' (p. 69, l. 431) to Ford's individual 'losing more and more the sense of a whole' (1911, p. 62).

Drawing on Gordon's biography, Michael Hollington has said that this 'great unheroic couplet [. . .] is perhaps the best entrée into the psychological problematics of Eliot's early American exposure to art and culture'; 'He wanted to wrest back the control and destiny of culture from such female culture vultures' (pp. 133, 34). For Anthony Julius, the couplet is 'a defensive gesture in a poem dramatising male panic about women'; 'Prufrock' is a 'misogynistic' poem (pp. 22, 65). John Carey focuses on the 'odd' coupling of 'In' with 'come and go' – 'What is meant by coming and going *in* is not clear, and cannot, of course, be clarified': the couplet 'offers a phantom meaning which dissolves when the reader tries to isolate it' (p. 33).

The couplet is a 'gap', and Carey correctly acknowledges it as such. Hollington and Julius do not: they are on the edge of, if not beyond, the text's 'limits', and their arguments are suspicious. In your assignments, you must, as I said earlier of the key aim of literary criticism, convince. Quote and analyse the primary text in detail; discuss, consider, ponder; offer multiple interpretations; resist pinning down if doing so denies complexity. When studying Eliot's poetry, indeed all texts, be like Prufrock: aware that things are complicated and complicated for many reasons.

 ## Virginia Woolf's *Mrs Dalloway*

Both formally and thematically, *Mrs Dalloway* (1925) speaks to many of the issues discussed in this chapter. It is certainly a novel that seeks to deal with the complexity of existence. In this case study, I will focus particularly on the ways in which Woolf is interested, like other writers of this period, in trying to depict the processes of human consciousness. Modernist writing can sometimes be difficult to understand due to its formal complexity; the aim of the section is to think about the complexity of Woolf's novel as a way of helping you to think more broadly about how to approach modernist writing in general.

In the section on 'Historical Context', I quoted from Woolf's 1919 essay 'Modern Fiction', in which she considers the enormous variety and complexity of the 'impressions' received by 'an ordinary mind on an ordinary day', like 'an incessant shower of innumerable atoms' (2008, p. 9). These obviously include external sensory data (what we see, hear, touch, feel, smell), but also internal data (memories, ideas, feelings). Literature has always tried to find ways of representing individual experience, but for writers like Woolf and Joyce it was increasingly apparent that conventional forms of narrative did not adequately address the ways in which the mind actually worked. This was much more than simply a formal problem. After all, if 1901–1945 was a period of epistemological uncertainty, and if communal truths were becoming increasingly pressurized and difficult to sustain, then the question of how to represent individual subjective experience – and how to relate the experiences of separate individuals – was bound to become urgent. For the fiction writer, the first decision is whether to try to represent the self through a first-person narrative ('I thought') or a third-person narrative ('he thought'). The problem with the first person is that it may place too much weight on a single person's experience so as to be unable to reflect the full complexity of life. The problem with the third person is that it may falsely imply that individual experiences are easily comprehended by some objective, external viewpoint. The solution that Woolf found was to write a novel in the third person, but to make great use of free indirect style* to show what her characters are thinking.

Earlier writers, such as Jane Austen, had used free indirect style* to represent characters' thoughts (see 'The Romantic Period'), but this was an occasional device; in *Mrs Dalloway* it is used continually, so that there is a great deal of slippage between the thoughts of particular characters and the impersonal narrative voice. Furthermore, the novel 'moves fluidly between characters', which 'requires the reader to adjust his/her interpretive strategies in view of the multivalence of the narrative point of view' (Hanson, p. 57). Reading *Mrs Dalloway* can be demanding because of these shifts of perspective: we not only have to make sense of the experiences we are reading about, but also work out whose experiences they are. A quick look at the opening lines of the novel should clarify this point:

> Mrs Dalloway said she would buy the flowers herself.
>
> For Lucy had her work cut out for her. The doors would be taken off their hinges; Rumpelmayer's men were coming. And then, thought Clarissa Dalloway, what a morning – fresh as if issued to children on a beach.
>
> What a lark! What a plunge! For so it had always seemed to her (p. 3)

The first sentence, telling us about the novel's protagonist*, is likely to be from the perspective of an omniscient narrator. But what about the next two? It seems that we are hearing Mrs Dalloway's voice. She is worrying about the party and using names without needing to explain them (an omniscient narrator would normally tell the reader who Lucy and Rumpelmayer are). The fact that Woolf omits 'Mrs Dalloway thought' from either of these sentences adds to the energy and immediacy of writing and provides us with quick, fluent access to Mrs Dalloway's subjective perspective. The fourth sentence moves away from free indirect style*, providing a conventional tag – 'thought Clarissa Dalloway' – that helps us to get our readerly bearings. But in the next paragraph we go directly into Mrs Dalloway's consciousness again, and as we read on it becomes clear that we are moving backwards in time to her memories of being eighteen. This opening, therefore, reflects how the human mind jumps swiftly and continually, backwards and forwards, between past ('so it had always seemed') and future ('Rumpelmayer's men were coming').

There is much more to be said about this opening, and about the technique of free indirect style* and its association with the modernist stream of consciousness*; a useful discussion can be found in Lodge 1992 (pp. 42–45). Now, though, I want to consider a different passage that also exemplifies Woolf's technique of depicting consciousness. I earlier described how the First World War shocked and disturbed writers of the period, causing them to question fundamental categories and distinctions. This is apparent in the character of Septimus Warren Smith, whose narrative runs alongside that of Mrs Dalloway, intersecting at the end of the novel when she hears at her party about his death. For the patriarchal* ruling classes, represented by the doctors Holmes and Bradshaw, Septimus is a rather weak delusive, someone who has failed to deal with life in a mature and rational way. And yet his 'madness' is portrayed sympathetically by Woolf and represented as far preferable to the coercive, controlling pursuit of 'divine proportion' (p. 84) by men like Bradshaw. We first encounter Septimus in Regent's Park with his wife Lucrezia. Holmes' claim that that her husband 'was a little out of sorts' (p. 18) contrasts ironically with Septimus' highly sensitized, epiphanic sense of beauty and revelation. Whereas other characters see an aeroplane writing in the sky and interpret the letters differently, Septimus is not interested in the words at all, but filled with a sense of 'unimaginable beauty' (p. 19). A 'nursemaid' tells Rezia that the plane is advertising toffee, and Septimus has the experience that her rasping voice 'can quicken trees into life' (p. 19). Although he tries to ignore the thrilling rising and falling of the elm trees, he is unable to resist:

> But they beckoned; leaves were alive; trees were alive. And the leaves being connected by millions of fibres with his own body, there on the seat, fanned it up and down; when the branch stretched he, too, made that statement. The sparrows fluttering, rising, and falling in jagged fountains were part of the pattern; the white and blue, barred with black branches. Sounds made harmonies with premeditation; the spaces between them were as significant as the sounds. A child cried. Rightly far away a horn sounded. All taken together meant the birth of a new religion – (p. 19)

Clearly here we are getting Septimus' perspective, but it is not written in the first person. The unstated tag for the whole passage is 'Septimus thought' or 'Septimus imagined'. A simple response to this passage would be that, due to the mental illness caused by the war, Septimus is hallucinating. He is imagining connections that are not really there, losing a clear sense of his own identity, finding a false 'pattern', 'premeditation' and 'significan[ce]' in phenomena that are in fact meaningless. Bradshaw would call it 'not having a sense of proportion' (p. 82). Septimus' conclusion that what he believes he is seeing, hearing, and feeling means 'the birth of a new religion' may seem to be the absurd fantasy of a delusive with a Christ complex. The mundane sounds of the child crying and the horn sounding may serve to undercut the rapture of the rest of the passage. And yet it has an undeniable power, which comes at least in part from the use of free indirect style*. Septimus' voice becomes one with the narrative voice, and therefore his perspective on the world impresses itself on to the mind of the reader. Statements such as 'sounds made harmonies with premeditation' are given much more weight without the attachment of a tag. However, through this third-person perspective we also have immediate access to Septimus' complex emotions, emphasized by the syntactical complexity and sound patterns of the prose, and we are offered some insight into his sense of beauty and revelation. In contrast, Woolf does not give us any real insight into the consciousnesses of Holmes and Bradshaw (the novel's villains).

We have seen in this chapter how modernist writers are troubled by individual identity (see, for example, the discussion of 'Prufrock', above). Septimus' sense of a blurring between himself and the natural world therefore may not be a sign of madness, but an articulation of the instability of the self that affects us all. As Clare Hanson points out, this blurring is integral to the form of *Mrs Dalloway*:

> The movements between characters, and elsewhere in the text between focalised narrative and passages of omniscient description or commentary, [. . .] make it difficult for the reader to locate the source of any given thought or construction of 'reality' in the text. This in turn calls into question the usefulness of the category of the 'character', or autonomous 'full' subject, for the reader of *Mrs Dalloway*. (p. 58)

This is a useful way of thinking not just about Woolf's novel, but about modernist writing in general. The most significant texts of this period tend to be suspicious of preconceived categories and forms, particularly the notion of a single objective 'reality' that can easily be represented by literature. As we have seen, this leads to innovative, experimental writing that can be fluid, fragmented, ambiguous, and, yes, difficult. And yet, as I argued above, writers of the period are still trying to understand a complex world, even if such an understanding can only ever be limited, provisional, and constantly changing; this attitude, which we might call a sort of pessimistic optimism, seems to me to be the best critical approach to take to modernist texts.

Further Reading

Bradbury, Malcolm, and James McFarlane (eds) (1991), *Modernism 1890–1930*. London: Penguin. One of the best surveys of the period; you will find particularly useful the opening essay, 'The Name and Nature of Modernism', and the extended sections: 'A Geography of Modernism'; 'Literary Movements'; 'The Lyric Poetry of Modernism'; 'The Modernist Novel'.

Davis, Alex, and Lee M. Jenkins (eds) (2007), *The Cambridge Companion to Modernist Poetry*. Cambridge: Cambridge University Press. A decent overview; includes chapters on: 'The Poetics of Modernism'; 'Pound or Eliot: Whose Era?'; 'Yeats, Ireland and Modernism'. Also contains 'Guide to Further Reading'.

Levenson, Michael H. (1992), *A Genealogy of Modernism: A Study of English Literary Doctrine 1908–1922*. Cambridge: Cambridge University Press. One of the best discussions of early modernism. Conrad and Ford figure strongly in the first two sections; there is a detailed look at Imagism*; the chapter on Eliot's *The Waste Land* is not only useful for understanding the poem but also other modernist writing.

Nicholls, Peter (1995), *Modernisms: A Literary Guide*. London: Macmillan. Note the plural in the title: *Modernisms*. An insightful and refreshing study that embraces the diversity of the subject.

Shiach, Morag (2007), *The Cambridge Companion to the Modernist Novel*. Cambridge: Cambridge University Press. A good overview; includes chapters on: 'Modernists on the Art of Fiction'; 'James Joyce and the Languages of Modernism'; 'Tradition and Revelation: Moments of Being in Virginia Woolf's Major Novels'. Also contains 'Further Reading'.

Stead, C. K. (1980), *The New Poetic: Yeats to Eliot*. London: Hutchinson. An influential and accessible study first published in 1964; full of useful quotations from, and insightful discussions of, Yeats, Eliot, and the Imagists*.

'The First World War Poetry Digital Archive': http://www.oucs.ox.ac.uk/ww1lit/. Oxford University's online repository of over 4,000 items of text, images, audio, and video.

'The Modernist Journals Project': http://dl.lib.brown.edu:8081/exist/mjp/index.xml. An excellent resource for early twentieth-century literary magazines; look particularly at *Blast*, *The English Review*, *Poetry*, and *The New Age*.

Do not forget to keep a record of *all* the texts and websites you look at when researching for an assignment: you will need to list them in your bibliography.

10 Literature 1945–1990

William Stephenson

Chapter Overview

Historical Context

Between the end of the Second World War and the collapse of the Soviet Bloc, English literature reflected the rapid and sometimes difficult changes that were occurring in people's lives in a period of instability and tension. On a global scale, this tension was best illustrated by the stand-off between the two nuclear-armed superpowers, the USA and USSR, that became known as the Cold War, or in a more graphic formulation, the Balance of Terror.

Britain played a declining role in this new bipolar world. After the upheavals of the Blitz and the sustained U-boat blockade which left her infrastructure in tatters, the battering of her armed forces after six years of battle, and the deaths of nearly half a million of her soldiers and civilians, she was in no position to lead an empire. One by one, British colonies became independent, while retaining ties with the former imperial power through the Commonwealth, an affiliation of postcolonial* states. Although Britain's military and economic dominance receded, its cultural hegemony arguably remained: 'in most post-colonial* nations [...] the nexus of power involving literature, language, and a dominant British culture' remained strongly resistant to change (Ashcroft *et al*, p. 4). This led to successive waves of immigration, as Commonwealth citizens from the West Indies, Pakistan,

India, and other former colonies saw a better future for themselves in the UK.

At home, Britain entered a phase of post-war reconstruction. This was ideological as well as physical: the Labour Party, elected by a landslide in 1945, proceeded to set up the infrastructure of state support for the individual that became known as the Welfare State (the blueprint for which had been drawn up even as the war was being fought, in the 1942 Beveridge Report). Perhaps the most significant outcome of the Welfare State for the arts, including literature, was the establishment of the Arts Council in 1945, and the BBC Third Programme in 1946: 'the condition of culture [became] in substantial part a responsibility of the state' (Sinfield, p. 56). Literature had gained a powerful new patron, but one with its own agenda and set of standards: thus at the same time as being funded by state arts organizations and disseminated by the education system, literature became partly *determined* by these institutions, which had their own overt or hidden criteria of excellence (see Sinfield, pp. 56–62).

Despite this subtle extension of state control, censorship of fiction and the theatre was far lighter than ever before by the end of the 1960s. D. H. Lawrence's modernist novel *Lady Chatterley's Lover* (written in 1928) was the subject of a prosecution for obscenity in 1960. The novel was declared not obscene, and therefore British publication was finally permitted. This in effect allowed writers to depict sexuality frankly; furthermore, the Theatres Act of 1968 removed the Lord Chamberlain's power to censor plays in advance of production.

Gender, as well as sexuality, was becoming the topic of increasingly free expression. The women's movement stood at its strongest since the days of the suffragettes: books like Kate Millett's *Sexual Politics* and Germaine Greer's *The Female Eunuch* (both 1970) articulated the aspirations of a new generation of educated and ambitious women who would no longer accept second place in the male-dominated literary-critical institution or in patriarchal* culture as a whole. Gay and lesbian rights emerged as public issues, leading to the effective decriminalization of male homosexuality in England in 1968.

In this new world of relatively free speech, assertions of the rights of women and sexual dissidents were paralleled by a corresponding questioning of class assumptions, particularly in relation to culture. By the 1960s, '[t]he insistence on a categorical distinction between high and popular culture came to be regarded as the "un-hip" assumptions of an older generation' (Storey, p. 158). The Beatles, for instance, had their album covers designed by 'serious' artists such as Peter Blake and Richard Hamilton, used classical instrumentation and arrangements on their records (as well as referencing older popular traditions such as music-hall), and openly acknowledged their debt to other cultures, particularly American black music and the Indian classical tradition: 'Forever seeking new stimuli, they experimented with everything from tape-loops to drugs and chance procedures borrowed from the intellectual avant-garde*' (MacDonald, p. 10). There was a growing sense that art was no longer the privilege of an isolated elite and that ordinary people could aspire to it. Talent and work, rather than status or connections, were increasingly believed to be the keys to success. All this can be seen as part of the emergence of postmodernism* (see below), the dominant cultural movement of the period, that was, in its 1960s phase, 'in part a populist attack on the elitism of modernism' (Storey, p. 156).

By the 1980s, however, the Welfare State had begun to break up. The economic turmoil of the 1970s, where Britain was immobilized by the oil crisis of 1973, the miners' strikes of 1972 and 1974, and a series of industrial disputes culminating in the so-called 'winter of discontent' of 1978–79, led to the election of a Conservative government headed by Margaret Thatcher. The Conservatives attracted skilled working-class voters who had traditionally supported Labour but who switched their allegiance as part of the working population's new-found assimilation of 'capitalist values; of individualism, egoism and economic calculation' (Marshall *et al*, pp. 6–7). Thatcher's policies were designed to encourage this: they included tax cuts, significant reductions in educational and welfare budgets, withdrawal of some state benefits, selling council houses to tenants, the privatization of a number of public utilities nationalized by the Labour government in the 1940s, and the reduction of state regulation in many areas, particularly the financial markets.

As Britain lost its empire and the Welfare State rose and declined, the dominant cultural tendency of the period gradually emerged: postmodernism*. The term has a number of competing definitions. Clearly, though, it means 'after modernism': postmodernism* was a reaction to the modernist movement that had dominated the previous half-century (see the previous chapter). Postmodernism* has been characterized as loss of belief in the grand narratives (for example Christianity) which had, in the past, given Western culture a stable centre: Jean-François Lyotard has argued in *The Postmodern Condition* that 'Simplifying to the extreme, I define *postmodern* as incredulity toward metanarratives' (p. xxiv). Jean Baudrillard has argued that postmodern society is that in which people's lives are dominated by images that feed off and represent one another, rather than any clear or stable reality underlying them, as was the case in the past. The image is so all-pervading and dominant that 'it has no relation to any reality whatsoever: it is its own pure simulacrum' (p. 6), a condition Baudrillard has called hyperreality*. Alternatively, postmodernism* may result from the decentering* of the imperial, nationally based monetary system of the early twentieth century. Money now has no real loyalty to any empire or nation state: globalization* enables investment and work to be transferred across the world instantly, at least in theory. Thus in Fredric Jameson's memorable phrase, postmodernism* is merely 'the cultural logic of late capitalism' (p. 1).

Whatever the causes of postmodernism* may have been, its art appeared at first glance conservative when compared to the groundbreaking experiments of high modernism. Where the artists of 1901–1945 favoured commitment to a personal vision and a radical break with the past, postmodernist* writers preferred ironically distanced reproductions of traditional forms and were often content to participate in the market through adopting accessible, populist styles and devices. In the canonical modernist poem *The Waste Land* (1922), T. S. Eliot offered a collage of quotations and images rather than a coherent narrative: the closing statement of his poem, 'These fragments I have shored against my ruins' (l. 431), was a response to a fractured reality. Eliot's poem implied a conservative philosophy underpinning a radical aesthetic: the need to maintain the integrity of the artist's vision by presenting it in fragments in an era when, after World War One, merely to extend the complacent, coherent surface of Victorian and Georgian literature would have been impossible. By contrast, late twentieth-century postmodernist* work reproduced this surface with irony. John Fowles' novel *The French Lieutenant's Woman* (1969), for instance, offered a pastiche* of sources, such as Victorian novels and academic history, but only as part of a direct imitation of Victorian realist* narrative form that appeared relatively conventional when set against Eliot's poetry or the groundbreaking experiments in prose of other modernist artists like James Joyce. Similarly, Angela Carter's *The Bloody Chamber* (1979) reworked folk tales and often radically revised their content, but did not depart significantly from their formal conventions. Where modernism shattered the past, postmodernism* copied it in quotation marks.

When we read a text from 1945–1990, then, it is important at degree level to bear in mind the text's relationship to its context: the Cold War, the rise and decline of the Welfare State, the women's movement, postmodernism*, and so on. The best way to do this is to find out *exactly* when the text was published and when it was written (which may have been a great deal earlier). Then find out as much as possible about what was happening at that time, in politics, law, social and sexual morality, the struggles for gay rights and women's liberation, education, and so on. What references, direct or indirect, does the text make to social and cultural change? Does it embrace or resist such change (or ambiguously do both)? What points can you make, based on solid historical evidence (for example, documents from the time, or books by later historians), that will support the points you are making in your essay?

Key Authors and Texts

Many new novels of the period featured upwardly mobile and/or working-class protagonists*: John Braine's *Room at the Top* (1957), Alan Sillitoe's *Saturday Night and Sunday Morning* (1958), and Kingsley Amis' *Lucky Jim* (1954) were significant examples. These narratives enacted the struggles of socially ordinary young people (especially men) in the post-War years, and recast the modernist *Bildungsroman** or tale of personal growth, such as D. H. Lawrence's *Sons and Lovers* (1913) and James Joyce's *A Portrait of the Artist as a Young Man* (1916), in terms of post-war social conditions. The main aspiration of the 1950s protagonists* was not so much the modernist one of breaking free from social constraint to express a personal vision, as the postmodernist* one of conquering the system on its own terms while exposing it to irony. In accordance with this, the prose of the 1950s novelists listed above was conservative and realistic* in comparison to the experimental syntax of Joyce or the Freudian rhythms of Lawrence.

Women writers of the period were finding their own ways to develop the novel form, though not always with feminism* in mind or with female protagonists*. Iris Murdoch wrote a number of significant texts addressing existentialism*, such as *The Sea, The Sea* (1978), about a male writer looking back on his career. Other important women novelists of the period were: Doris Lessing, winner of the Nobel Prize in 2007, who illuminated the inner life of a woman writer in her best-known novel, *The Golden Notebook* (1962); Margaret Drabble, who explored the theme of the educated woman who becomes a single mother by choice in *The Millstone* (1965); and Drabble's sister A. S. Byatt, who wrote in her first novel, *The Shadow of the Sun* (1964), of a woman's struggle to emancipate herself from patriarchy* in the form of a dominant father.

Byatt's literary career arguably culminated in the postmodernist* historical romance* *Possession* (1990), winner of the Booker Prize for that year, a complex interweaving of the lives and loves of two Victorian poets and their contemporary biographers. This was part of a trend towards the self-conscious reworking of the past through historical fiction that aimed to recreate earlier times plausibly and yet also to draw attention to its own artificiality. The critic Linda Hutcheon called this type of writing 'historiographic metafiction'* (p. 105). Other examples were John Fowles' *The French Lieutenant's Woman* (1969), an ironic but affectionate reworking of the conventions of Victorian fiction, and J. G. Farrell's *The Siege of Krishnapur* (1973; winner of the Booker Prize), a witty but politically penetrating dissection of British imperialism* in India.

Not all the novelists of the period made overt political statements, or used a historical setting; some preferred indirect comment or symbolism*. A significant example was the Nobel Prize winner William Golding, whose first novel *Lord of the Flies* (1954) became a mainstay of the British education system and is still often taught and set for exams. The tale of a group of school-boys stranded on a desert island who attempt to create a functioning society which rapidly degenerates into savagery, *Lord of the Flies* has been seen as a universal allegory* of innate human evil, a historically specific comment on World War Two, or in the words of the novelist Ian McEwan, as an exposé of 'a thinly disguised boarding school' (cited in Boyd, p. 10).

Other important novelists in the second half of the period (roughly 1970 on) also used the symbolic* rather than realistic* mode, but preferred to connect this to direct social and political commentary through the style that became known as magical realism*. Angela Carter (see the 'Case Study', below) wrote complex allegories* of feminism* based on Gothic* and romance* modes. The Indian-born Salman Rushdie made a huge impact with his second, Booker Prize-winning novel *Midnight's Children* (1981), which was partly a postcolonial* allegory* of the growth of India as an independent nation.

Philip Larkin was one of the most important poets of the post-war period. He was associated with the anti-Romantic, anti-modernist, formally conservative group of poets known as the Movement, who were brought together in Robert Conquest's defining anthology *New Lines* (1956). Larkin recycled nineteenth-century forms using twentieth-century content, minimizing the importance of his own age's debt to modernism (see the previous chapter). Although he began writing under the influence of the great modernist W. B. Yeats, Larkin would engage, in a way Yeats would never have wanted to, with the banality of everyday life. 'Lines on a Young Lady's Photograph Album' (1955) links poetry to photography, the art 'that records / Dull days as dull, and hold-it smiles as frauds, / And will not censor blemishes' (Larkin, p. 71). This encapsulates the acerbic honesty of Larkin's best writing, and the anti-modernist realism* of the Movement.

Larkin was asked to be Poet Laureate* in 1984, but was too ill to accept, and the post was taken by one of his most significant successors, Ted Hughes, who appeared along with some other post-Movement poets in A. Alvarez's anthology *The New Poetry* (1962). Hughes was much more comfortable with myth*, symbol*, and nature than Larkin and the Movement had been. His early poem 'Hawk Roosting' exemplifies this: 'There is no sophistry in my body: / My manners are tearing off heads' (Alvarez, p. 179). Hughes moved on to produce *Crow* (1970), a book which created an archetype* out of a humble carrion bird. Hughes' reputation rests mainly on his early work, though there was considerable critical acclaim for *Birthday Letters* (1998), where he broke a long silence to publish his explorations of his controversial relationship with his first wife, the American poet Sylvia Plath.

Seamus Heaney (winner of the Nobel Prize in 1995) is probably the most significant successor to Larkin and Hughes, though his cultural context and subject matter are very different. In his early work, such as *Death of a Naturalist* (1966), Heaney, like Hughes, often depicted rural, natural objects and animals in relatively conservative verse forms. Gradually Heaney's focus shifted to the political and social world around him, on which he commented in later volumes like *North* (1975), where sacrificed bodies excavated in an archaeological dig are made to stand for victims of the Northern Irish Troubles, in a 'primordial peaty cocktail' of history, sex, and violence that some feminist* readers have found disturbing (Gregson, p. 129). Heaney's work in this period exemplifies a creative tension between myth* and context, or between archetype* and instance.

Heaney and many other significant poets of the 1970s and 1980s are collected in Blake Morrison and Andrew Motion's anthology *The Penguin Book of Contemporary British Poetry* (1982). These include Tony Harrison, whose work engages head-on with the divisive role of class in British society. Harrison's 'Marked with D', for instance, ironically alludes to the children's rhyme of 'Pat-a-Cake Baker's Man' to create an elegy* to his cremated baker father, whose insignificant life is now 'smoke, enough to sting one person's eyes / and ash (not unlike flour) for one small loaf' (Morrison, p. 49). Also anthologized by Morrison and Motion are Paul Muldoon and Derek Mahon, Irish successors to Heaney whose complex work recalls the allusiveness of modernism, but retains a postmodernist* playfulness. Mahon's 'A Disused Shed in County Wexford' daringly elegizes the 'Lost people of Treblinka and Pompeii' by symbolizing them in the form of mushrooms growing in the shed of the title (Morrison, p. 80). Muldoon's narrative poem* 'Immram' follows the protagonist* on a knockabout ride through American pool-halls and hotels, full of intertextual* allusions* including Homer, Shakespeare, the Beat poets, and Bob Dylan. Irishness is situated comically in biblical terms: 'the Irish, the American Irish, / Were really the thirteenth tribe, / The Israelites of Europe' (Morrison, p. 149).

One of the strongest and most influential movements in drama after the war years was the theatre of the absurd*, which abandoned realism* to present allegorical* or symbolic* plays that engaged with the idea that human life is fundamentally absurd in the sense of comically pointless. Samuel Beckett was one of absurdism's* most important exponents: indeed, he was arguably the greatest dramatist writing in English (and French) since the War. His most famous play *Waiting for Godot* (1953) is discussed in the 'Case Study' below: like most of his other work, it is farcical yet bleak. Other significant plays by Beckett include *Endgame* (1957) and *Not I* (1973).

Harold Pinter is possibly Beckett's most significant successor. Pinter's version of absurdism*, unlike Beckett's, emerges from a distinctly English context, ridden by the dialects and class structures of his native country. *The*

Dumb Waiter (1960), for instance, enacts the meeting of two working-class friends and workmates, Ben and Gus, who turn out to be assassins waiting for a victim. In a situation reminiscent of the plight of Vladimir and Estragon in *Waiting for Godot*, they wait in a room, receiving cryptic orders from a man upstairs, via the dumb waiter (or miniature kitchen lift) of the title.

Not all playwrights situated themselves in the absurdist* tradition. Others chose to write in a more realistic* mode (sometimes called 'kitchen sink drama'), often working in direct reaction to the bourgeois, metropolitan content of much popular theatre. Perhaps the best known is John Osborne, whose most famous play, *Look Back in Anger* (1956), is set entirely in a squalid flat in a Midland city. The protagonist* Jimmy Porter, who, like Kingsley Amis' Lucky Jim, 'hungers for power from the position of social inferiority' (Elsom, p. 72), was the most significant of the discontented stage youths who, along with their playwright creators, became known as the 'Angry Young Men'. (The group also included Arnold Wesker and the novelists Kingsley Amis and Alan Sillitoe.) Porter's on-stage violence, coarseness, and abuse of others were seen as a breakthrough: the theatre was at last holding up a mirror to the people of its time, rather than offering a pale, repressed, over-civilized caricature.

Osborne's play was partly a social critique: other dramatists of the period continued to view British society critically, but moved on from the angry young men of Osborne's time, often through representing the problems befalling women. Caryl Churchill interrogated Thatcherism and feminism* in *Top Girls* (1982). The play portrayed the newly conspicuous career women of the 1980s, and suggested the family cost of their ambition. Churchill's socialism was further developed in *Serious Money* (1987), a play written in verse that satirized capitalism, and was highly appropriate in the context of the stock market crash of that year. The plays of David Hare include *Plenty* (1978), the story of a woman who, having risked her life as a spy in World War Two, finds herself disillusioned by 'the conventionally deferential pursuit of self-interest' expected of her after the War (Rabey, p. 113). *Plenty* addresses the fragile conventions of Britain in an atmosphere of crumbling social cohesion.

Other playwrights embraced the postmodernist* values of self-reflexivity and playfulness. Tom Stoppard wrote *Rosencrantz and Guildenstern Are Dead* (1966), a reworking of Shakespeare's *Hamlet* from the viewpoint of two minor characters. In a move typical of postmodernist* literature, the text comments on the past and interrogates the literary canon* by centring itself on characters taken from the margins of a significant intertext. However, Stoppard's play is not a rebellion against Shakespeare: like Estragon and Lucky in *Waiting for Godot*, the two noblemen have no control over their destiny, and end up dying as they do in *Hamlet*.

When we study the prose, poetry, or drama of the period at degree level, we should not take a text in isolation, as if it exists in a vacuum, set apart from other literature. It is difficult to write well about John Osborne's plays, for instance, without knowing something about who influenced him (both in terms of playwrights he wanted to imitate, and the conservative, staid theatre he wanted to reject) and about the group critics believe he helped to create, the Angry Young Men. This will mean finding out something about the social context as well (see 'Historical Context', above). In short, what made Jimmy Porter (and Osborne) so angry? Why did other writers and their characters share this emotion?

Criticism and Literary Theory

The early Cold War years found literary criticism slowly developing from the Formalism* and liberal humanism* initiated by the American New Critics* before the war, and championed in varied form by leading British formalists* such as F. R. Leavis, I. A. Richards, and William Empson. These critics argued for the relative autonomy of the work of art, and against the use by the critic of background information or contextual knowledge. They saw the critic's role as 'to determine what is actually *there* in the work of art' (Leavis, p. 225), irrespective of the critic's taste or ideology, or the author's intent. Leavis marginalized the historical and social contexts of writing and reading, asserting that meaning was objectively present in the language of the text itself (the words on the page).

The reliance on objective meaning began to unravel in the mid- to late-1970s, when a few British critics studied the new philosophy and criticism in vogue in France, and brought them to the UK in the face of considerable resistance. The cause of so much controversy was poststructuralism* – a school of critical thought derived from the philosophy of thinkers such as Roland Barthes and Jacques Derrida, that argued, essentially, that the text could be read neither as an autonomous aesthetic object (the 'well-wrought urn' of liberal humanism*) nor as the communicative act of an author (a vehicle for the author's 'message' or 'voice') because language itself did not describe the world but was self-referential and fundamentally unable either to represent or make present the object(s) which it described.

Barthes expressed the new philosophy in his essay 'The Death of the Author' (1968), where he argued that the author was no longer the single source of meaning that unified the text. He replaced the author with the reader (not a real person, but a concept): 'a text's unity lies not in its origin but in its destination' (p. 148). Thus texts were now open to multiple interpretation – or decentred*. Barthes advocated that the author-centred term 'work' should be replaced by the more neutral 'text': the text, unlike the work, 'is

189

structured but off-centred, without closure', because it is part of language, 'a system with neither closure nor centre' (p. 159). The text is not a simple utterance by one person, but is reformulated by Barthes as 'a tissue of quotations drawn from the innumerable centres of culture' (p. 146). Thus it is constituted by its references to other texts – its intertextuality*.

The shift from work to text led to the type of reading known as deconstruction*. In his book *Of Grammatology* (1967), Derrida outlines how in a deconstructive reading, the text's patterns of meaning are worked out, but the text is also read against the grain, for those unintended suggestions or meanings that may appear without the author's knowledge or that of his/her original audience. The aim is to create 'a signifying structure that critical reading should *produce*' (p. 158). This stands in complete contrast to the hitherto dominant model of critical reading, enshrined in the position of Leavis. The deconstructive critic must *make* meaning, rather than detect it. Deconstruction* makes texts signify by tracing the relationship between the areas of the text's language inside and outside the author's control. Not surprisingly, then, the text is usually read as fragmented and self-contradictory, however unified it appears on the surface.

After the initial shock of the introduction of poststructuralism* and deconstruction*, they began to take hold, firstly within academic research, then graduate seminars and finally undergraduate courses in literary theory. The revolutionary ideas imported in the late 1970s had, within a decade or fifteen years, become the norm. This enabled many existing critical movements to gain from deconstructive thought and adapt themselves accordingly, and allowed many new offshoots of poststructuralism*.

Feminism*, for instance, responded in a number of ways, one of which was the contestation of previously accepted models of woman as clearly opposed to and separate from man but occupying much the same territory. A number of schools of thought arose that sought either to make a radical break with patriarchy* and with male views of the world, by treating 'woman' as a philosophical category rather than as a reference to real females, or to refocus reading on women's texts and female experience, almost marginalizing patriarchy* by ignoring it. These two schools became known roughly as French and Anglo-American feminism* respectively, though many members of each did not belong to the respective nationalities. A key idea of the French feminist* tendency was *écriture féminine*, loosely translated as 'women's writing'. This did not refer to all texts produced by women, but to a style of writing that was allegedly innately female because it refused to conform to patriarchal* structures of grammar and syntax, and instead overflowed with what was seen as a characteristically exuberant, unstructured energy. Hélène Cixous' essay 'The Laugh of the Medusa' both argued for this writing and exemplified it: 'I, too, overflow; my desires have invented new desires, my body knows unheard-of songs' (p. 226).

The Anglo-American school, by contrast, tended to focus not so much on the theoretical concept of 'woman' but on the possibilities offered by studying actual women, particularly their writing. This led to the construction of gyno-criticism*, a school of reading looking at gynotexts or texts centred on women, their lives and views of the world. Elaine Showalter defined gyno-criticism's* assumptions: 'all writing by women is marked by gender' and 'is always "bitextual", in dialogue with both masculine and feminine literary traditions' (p. 4) and thus it should be read 'as a gendered discourse' (p. 5). Both these feminist* schools of criticism emerged from the poststructuralist* assumption that in the late twentieth century, liberal humanism* was no longer an adequate approach to literature, because the 'human' values it claimed to espouse were actually male (not to mention heterosexual, white, Euro-American, bourgeois, and privileged).

While feminism* was undergoing its own evolution, other branches of criticism were emerging, with equally challenging results. At the University of Birmingham, Stuart Hall and his colleagues founded the Centre for Contemporary Cultural Studies, which drew on earlier studies of culture by Raymond Williams and others in order to use critical methodology to engage not with a sealed canon* of 'great literature' but with *all* cultural products, including, for instance, television and advertising. Elsewhere, figures such as Homi Bhabha and Henry Louis Gates Jr. began deconstructing texts in terms of their references to 'race', nation, and otherness. In *Culture and Imperialism* (1990), Edward Said famously wrote that Jane Austen's *Mansfield Park* could not be read without considering the economic dependence of its heroine and her friends upon the slave plantations owned by Sir Thomas Bertram, the senior male character, and therefore the text's 'morality in fact is not separable from its social basis', as 'Austen affirms and repeats the geographical process of expansion involving trade' (including trade in slaves) that underpins that morality (p. 362).

Said's earlier work *Orientalism* (1978) had argued persuasively that depictions of the East in Western literature were based on a long-standing fantasy in which countries such as Turkey, India, and so on (and their people) were constructed according to the West's need to create an Other*. The West constructed the Orient as a projection of everything it believed it was not, and in the process was able to constitute itself as the opposite: so if the Orient was, for example, irrational, lazy, and barbaric, the West was by implication the rational, hardworking, civilizing force that was needed to tame the Orient through colonization. Orientalism* was, in effect, a politicized way of thinking and writing that disguised itself as apolitical: 'a Western style for dominating, restructuring, and having authority over the Orient' (Said, p. 69).

Said, Bhabha, Gates, and others effectively created the literary discipline known as postcolonialism*.

The overall picture, then, of criticism and theory in the late twentieth century is of a liberal humanist* discipline vainly resisting the revolutionary introduction of poststructuralism* and then fragmenting into a number of separate but interlinked sub-disciplines based on related theoretical schools. This neatly matches the emergence of postmodernism* (see 'Historical Context', above): just as barriers between high and low art were being broken down, and diversity and fragmentation were gradually becoming acknowledged as the norm in Western culture, so literary criticism became divided into a number of schools, in which no single movement had an overarching canonical or privileged status.

When we use criticism and theory to look at late twentieth-century texts, it is best to engage *closely* with the ideas of at least one critic. Study Barthes' essay 'The Death of the Author', for instance, and do detailed readings of some of its important points so that you understand what he means. Then work out whether the text you are studying can be read using some of Barthes' ideas. What happens, say, if we look at Angela Carter's *The Magic Toyshop* as 'a tissue of quotations' rather than a straightforward message from the author? I have, to some extent, done this in the 'Case Study' below, when I read the opening page of the novel in terms of the references it makes to other literature. You could take this further by considering the novel as a pastiche* of fairy tale references. Carter no doubt intended some or all of these, but if Barthes is right, we do not know Carter's plans and they need not matter: the text's unity lies in the reader.

 ## Samuel Beckett's *Waiting for Godot*

Beckett's play was first staged in French in Paris as *En attendant Godot* in January 1953. It was subsequently translated by Beckett himself and has been widely performed in English since its first translated production in London in 1955. It is the story of Vladimir and Estragon, two tramps who stand by a tree discussing whether the mysterious Godot will come as promised, or will at least deliver them a message. It was famously described by the French critic Vivian Mercier as a play in which 'nothing happens, twice' (Pattie, p. 74). No significant dramatic action occurs: there is no plot. Instead, Vladimir and Estragon work together like a comic double act, trading complaints, banter and innuendo, 'the comic "cross-talk" [derived by Beckett] from the music hall or the vaudeville' (Lawley, p. 6). The play is based on pointless repetition.

The two tramps watch the bully Pozzo and his slave Lucky arrive and then depart. A boy appears, bringing a message from Godot promising that he will come tomorrow. In the second act of the play, Pozzo and Lucky appear and leave again; the boy makes the same promise; and again Godot does not come.

Waiting for Godot may be read as an existentialist* statement: by exposing the absurdity of Vladimir and Estragon's empty waiting, the play seems to suggest that human identity is constructed through action, and it is everyone's personal responsibility to create their own humanity (thus the two tramps have no identity, as they do nothing). This reading emerges from Beckett's historical context. As a member of the French Resistance during World War Two, he responded very clearly to the dilemma posed for the French people at that time over whether to risk their lives by actively resisting the Nazi occupation or whether to take the safer option of tacit collaboration. The immobility of Vladimir and Estragon suggests that they can be read as *attentistes*, a term meaning 'those who wait', which was used in a hostile way in Resistance circles during the war to describe those who tacitly supported the Nazi regime by not fighting against it (Dukes, p. 30). However, the two tramps may simply be waiting for Godot's order to act, or may be on the run: in *En attendant Godot*, Beckett made Vladimir mention specifically how he and Estragon used to work as grape-pickers for a man named Bonnelly in the village of Roussillon. This is a direct reference to Beckett's own situation after he had fled Paris when his Resistance cell had been betrayed (Lawley, pp. 10–11). In *Waiting for Godot*, though, Beckett deleted the reference to place and employer by having Vladimir fail to remember them, possibly in an attempt to universalize the play, or at least depersonalize it (p. 53).

Perhaps the strongest reference to existentialism* in the play occurs in Act 2, when Pozzo (now blind) is struggling on the floor and calling for help. Vladimir gives a speech advocating action and then turns to Estragon for affirmation of his views. When no answer is forthcoming, Vladimir shifts easily to the opposite tack, qualifying all his previous assertions and making action itself seem pointless:

> Let us not waste our time in idle discourse! [*Pause. Vehemently.*] Let us do something, while we have the chance! [. . .] What do you say? [ESTRAGON *says nothing.*] It is true that when with folded arms we weigh the pros and cons we are no less a credit to our species. (pp. 71–72)

Vladimir eventually resorts to the banal conclusion that they are waiting for Godot to come, and at least they have kept their appointment. He asks Estragon how many people can boast as much, and the laconic reply is

'Billions' (p. 72). Vladimir and Estragon, then, are Everymen in this scene: although they are distinctive characters, they are in some sense supposed to stand for all humans. This might lead to a liberal humanist* reading of the play in which the text attempts to affirm the value of the human condition, by using pointless waiting as the 'dominant metaphor for existence' and yet forcing the audience to empathize with the characters by sharing 'the experience, in real time, of what it is to wait' (Bradby, p. 25).

However, the play parodies* human schemes to make sense of the world, such as philosophy, by recycling them as gibberish. Lucky, Pozzo's slave, is a clapped-out philosopher who nevertheless can be made to think on demand, if he is allowed to wear his hat (another of Beckett's comic uses of stage props). Upon being given the hat and ordered to 'Think!' by Pozzo (p. 35), he launches into the play's one long speech, an incoherent and increasingly deranged unpunctuated monologue that nevertheless tantalizingly gestures towards some semblance of sense:

> in a word for reasons unknown no matter what matter the facts are there and considering what is more much more grave that in the light of the labours lost of Steinweg and Peterman it appears what is more much more grave that in the light the light the light of the labours lost of Steinweg and Peterman that in the plains in the mountains by the seas by the rivers running water running fire the air is the same (p. 37)

The language of Lucky's speech is worth analysing in detail. Firstly, it depends upon repetition: 'the light the light the light' and 'Steinweg and Peterman', when reiterated so often in the quoted passage and elsewhere, cease to become signifiers of enlightenment, knowledge, or religious revelation (light) or of academic weight (Steinweg and Peterman, cited as authorities) but become instead mere sounds, robbed of meaning except as evidence of Lucky's derangement. The unorthodox syntax and punctuation contribute to this. Lucky's speech is one long babble of words. Here the play develops the modernist technique of stream of consciousness* (as, for instance, in 'Penelope', the last chapter of James Joyce's *Ulysses*): 'for reasons unknown no matter what matter the facts are there' cannot, because of its lack of punctuation, make any sense, despite the derivation of its words from the discourse of logic and certainty ('reasons'; 'facts'). Like Godot, meaning is promised by the language, but never appears.

There is also a terrible irony in Lucky's deranged, uncontrolled expansion of thought, when he promises conciseness. The quoted passage begins 'in a word', yet Lucky does exactly the opposite of what this phrase promises (a compression of previously elaborated material); instead, he rambles on continuously. Lucky also suggests his own mysterious sources ('the labours lost'), making his speech almost Gnostic or mystical, as well offering as a joking nod towards Shakespeare's comedy of disguise and mistaken identity, *Love's Labour's Lost*. The quoted passage closes with a statement seemingly about the atmosphere ('the air is the same') yet also offering a subtextual suggestion of the repetition and ultimate meaninglessness of Lucky's efforts (his 'air' or song remains the same throughout, rather than developing a logical argument or progressing a narrative).

Lucky's speech begins with a pseudo-academic declaration of precedence: 'Given the existence as uttered forth in the public works of Puncher and Wattmann of a personal God quaquaquaqua with white beard quaquaquaqua outside time without extension' (p. 36). Lucky seems to propose something about God: that because of previous scholars' work on Him, He may be seen as an individual, but existing eternally. This admirable theological notion is rendered ludicrous by the structure (or lack thereof) of Lucky's utterances. In the middle of Lucky's scrambled attempt at high philosophical discourse comes the farcical detail of the 'white beard', absurd in its isolation, as if facial hair alone could convey authority, like that of a patriarch*; or benevolence, like that of Father Christmas; as if a beard somehow makes God more plausible to those childish enough to believe in Him. The repeated 'quaquaquaqua' alludes to the Latin *qua*, sometimes used in philosophy to mean 'as', to specify a category and its properties (man *qua* man, God *qua* God), but much more obviously, it simulates the quacking of a duck. Thus high and low languages blunder into one another, as academic discourse meets the call of a farmyard animal, and the First Cause meets Santa Claus.

Lucky's speech, when analysed, shows itself to be a parody* of humankind's attempt to make sense of its condition. The play demonstrates a postmodernist* scepticism towards the master narratives, such as Christianity, that had shaped Western culture up to this point (see 'Historical Context', above). The nonsensical games played by the two tramps as they sit and debate what they are doing by the tree dramatize, and parody*, the wider games played in late twentieth-century society to justify any number of political or social positions, postures, and actions.

 ### Angela Carter's *The Magic Toyshop*

The Magic Toyshop (1967) was Angela Carter's second novel. It is the story of Melanie, a girl who finds herself orphaned when her parents die in a plane crash, on the night she tries on her mother's wedding dress, in a symbolic* appropriation of an adult rite of passage. Melanie is then sent to live with her tyrannical uncle, Philip Flower, and his curious family, including his wife, Aunt Margaret, who has not spoken since her marriage to Philip, and Margaret's two brothers, Francie and Finn Jowle. Melanie is shocked by the squalor of Uncle Philip's house, with its lack of hot water and toilet soap, and *The Daily Mirror* as lavatory paper (pp. 55–56). Philip makes Melanie work in his Gothic* and grotesque toyshop, where the line between fantasy and reality is blurred by the uncannily lifelike puppets, with which Philip conducts a perverse 'show'. Philip has designs on Melanie, expressed when his swan puppet simulates sex with her on stage, in a parodic* allusion* to W. B. Yeats' modernist poem 'Leda and the Swan' (1923), in which Zeus rapes Leda while in the form of a swan. Melanie discovers that Margaret has been conducting an incestuous affair with Francie, her brother, all along. At the climax of the novel, Philip finds out about the affair and burns the toyshop down; Melanie escapes the fire and is possibly about to begin a relationship with Finn. As the toyshop burns, Carter implies new worlds of possibility, through an intertextual* reference to the well-known final line of Keats' Romantic sonnet 'On First Looking into Chapman's Homer' (1816): 'they faced each other in a wild surmise' (p. 200).

Such 'surmise' may not be merely personal or sexual. What is important is not that Melanie may now escape with Finn, but that she has, for the first time in her life, a degree of control over her own future. This means that the text can be read 'as a metaphor of English identity in the post-war period' (Gamble, p. 45). Should Melanie, like Britain, continue to think of herself in the old terms (as obedient bourgeois daughter; as sex object in patriarchal* games) or cast for herself a new identity, now that her old world has literally burned down? Sarah Gamble situates the novel in its intended social context, referring to Carter's comment that Melanie's adolescence was supposed to take place at the same time as her own, in the 1950s, 'at the fag-end of the Stafford Cripps era' of post-war reconstruction through self-imposed austerity (Moira Waterson, cited in Gamble, p. 29). In entering the squalor of her new house, Melanie is symbolically ejected 'out of the state of unknowing that characterised the children of Carter's generation who had no memory of life before the war' (Gamble, p. 31). Thus Carter's novel, though neither autobiographical nor realistic*, can be historicized: through the juxtaposition of Melanie's rich childhood and her impoverished adolescence, it re-enacts the dialogue of nostalgia and aspiration being played out in 1950s Britain.

The novel is not, of course, a straightforward social document. It develops a complex series of allusions* to represent Melanie's internal divisions and her displaced identity, as well as to explore the conflict between feminism* and patriarchy*. Melanie is internally displaced before she ever reaches Uncle Philip's house. Doubling and disguise appear on the very first page, which bears close analysis. Melanie looks in the mirror, exploring her identity and her body. An allusion* to John Donne's love poem 'Elegy 19: To His Mistress Going to Bed' (1669) is mixed with references to colonialist exploration, and to depictions of women in Pre-Raphaelite art:

> The summer she was fifteen, Melanie discovered she was made of flesh and blood. O, my America, my new found land. She embarked on a tranced voyage, exploring the whole of herself, clambering over her own mountain ranges, penetrating the moist richness of her secret valleys, a physiological Cortez, da Gama or Mungo Park. For hours she stared at herself, naked, in the mirror of her wardrobe [. . .]. She also posed in attitudes, holding things. Pre-Raphaelite, she combed out her long, black hair [. . .]. (p. 1)

Melanie here places herself as both explorer and explored continent. The quotation from Donne ('O, my America'), originally intended as a lover's metaphor for his newly discovered mistress (her mind and soul, but chiefly her body), is appropriated by Melanie to become a declaration about herself. Her voyage (again a reference to colonialist exploration) is 'tranced', meaning both performed in semi-hypnotic state and entranced or enchanted. The voyage metaphor is then replaced by an image of land-bound exploration, which begins to become literal; Melanie does not quite clamber over mountains, but she does physically explore her own newly mature female body; 'ranges' suggests breasts and 'secret valleys' the vulva (whose 'richness' implies fertility as well as 'moist' sexual arousal). Curiously, the narrator calls Melanie a 'physiological' rather than 'sexual' explorer; her movements are detached, undertaken partly in a spirit of enquiry, rather than simply autoerotic, although 'penetrating' carries clear masturbatory overtones. Just as important as sexuality is self-image; Melanie stares at herself, unclothed, in her *wardrobe* mirror; thus a piece of furniture containing clothing (connoting decorum and social roles) is, in a gesture of self-liberation, made to become the reflector of Melanie's excited celebration of her own nudity.

Despite her new feeling of freedom, Melanie is not, in a sense, alone at this point. She carries with her the baggage of all the education she has accumulated, which makes her see her own nakedness and sexual potential through a series of allusions* and models that are chiefly male. The references to Cortez and other explorers suggest Freud's infamous remark, first published in 1926, that 'the sexual life of adult women is a "dark continent" for psychology' (p. 124), which carried unintended overtones of colonialism and racial prejudice, as well as the sexism of seeing women as an unknown Other*. The narrator's cultural references are to men: to writers, artists, and explorers who shaped images of women and of unknown lands, and conflated the two. The novel is awkwardly gynotextual* here: it dramatizes a young woman's encounter with her body and her sexuality in solitude (through Melanie's implied masturbation) but does so in terms of the male models of women imposed by artists such as Donne and the Pre-Raphaelites.

After reading *Lady Chatterley's Lover*, Melanie 'secretly picked forget-me-nots and stuck them in her pubic hair' (p. 2). Melanie decorates herself like D. H. Lawrence's Constance Chatterley, allowing herself to make a bucolic, fertile space of her own body and to imply a bond with a lover (through 'forget-me-not') who does not in fact exist. The novel also directly refers to a novel that had been allowed publication only seven years before (see 'Historical Context', above). Melanie thus becomes a metonym* for literature in the 1960s, which, like her, was newly discovering its freedom and sexuality, thanks to a reopening of a connection with the past (a modernist novel of sexuality, and a tradition of eroticism stretching from the Renaissance onwards).

Melanie imagines that she is married, having used the net curtain to make temporary nightgowns suitable for her wedding night. 'She conjured [her husband] so intensely to leap the spacetime barrier between them that she could almost feel his breath on her cheek and his voice husking "darling" ' (p. 2). Here she seeks to force herself into a major patriarchal* institution, marriage, by sheer effort of will. Her vision of her husband is couched not in the high literary terms we have had so far (Donne, modernism) but in the languages of popular romance* (his husky breath, the whispered endearment) and science fiction (the 'spacetime barrier').

Thus Melanie dances gaily between conventions. After allusions* to the 'high' art of the Renaissance and to modernism she imitates the 'low', popular art of her own time. Melanie is clearly very well read for a girl of fifteen, but she shows no sense of seeing popular genres as inferior. Instead, her taste is flexible, catholic, and postmodern*. She eagerly juxtaposes Mills and Boon with metaphysical* conceit*, just as the postmodernist* art that was emerging in the 1960s happily blurred 'serious' and popular genres. However, unlike a postmodernist* writer, she does this not in the name of an ironic appropriation of these traditions but in a spirit of joyous self-contemplation, as she forgets the fantasy of the husband 'in sudden absorption in the mirrored play of muscle as she flexed her leg again and again' (p. 2). Melanie moves her limbs repeatedly, looking at herself both as a lover might, and as an artist might. Her discourse is both aesthetic and autoerotic. Quite appropriately, she is absorbed not in her own flesh but in its 'mirrored play': in a game based on an image, or a simulation of herself. Although a direct reference to Baudrillard is not intended, the novel gestures towards the hyperreal* (see 'Historical Context', above).

From the very opening of the novel, Carter's language, when analysed, shows a rich ambiguity. Melanie defines and explores herself, forging an autoerotic bond with her own body of which feminists* like Hélène Cixous would be proud ('The Laugh of the Medusa' is partly a celebration of female masturbation), but she does so in terms set out for her by men. Close reading of the novel's language and careful tracing of its intertextual* references allow the reader to discover this paradox* in the opening page, which sets the tone for the novel's ambiguous relationship with feminism*.

Further Reading

Bennett, Andrew, and Nicholas Royle (2009), *An Introduction to Literature, Criticism and Theory* (fourth edition). Harlow: Pearson Longman. Well-written and wide-ranging, this will help you consider further such issues as: 'Character'; 'Sexual Difference'; 'God'; 'The Postmodern'. 'Further Reading' ends each chapter.

Brannigan, John (2003), *Orwell to the Present: Literature in England, 1945–2000*. Basingstoke: Palgrave Macmillan. Will help your understanding of the relationship between texts and historical contexts; covers numerous authors, from the 'Angry Young Men' to Angela Carter. Includes an annotated bibliography.

Corcoran, Neil (1993), *English Poetry since 1940*. London: Longman. An excellent overview; includes chapters on: 'A Movement Pursued: Philip Larkin'; 'The Poetry of Northern Ireland: Seamus Heaney, Michael Longley, Derek Mahon'; 'Towards the Postmodern?'. 'General Bibliographies' is split into: 'Critical Works'; 'Bibliographies and Reference Books'; 'Literary, Historical, Political and Cultural Contexts'; 'Anthologies'.

Gregson, Ian (2004), *Postmodern Literature*. London: Arnold. An accessible introduction to the subject; chapters cover a range of subjects, including: 'Postmodern Language'; 'The Postmodern Self'; 'Postmodern Genres'; 'Postmodern Gender'. Includes '1945–1998: Timeline of Key Events and Publications' and 'Suggestions for Further Reading'.

Head, Dominic (2002), *The Cambridge Introduction to Modern British Fiction, 1950–2000*. Cambridge: Cambridge University Press. A decent overview; includes chapters on: 'The State of the Novel'; 'Class and Social Change'; 'Gender and Sexual Identity'; 'Country and Suburbia'.

Padley, Steve (2006), *Key Concepts in Contemporary Literature*. Basingstoke: Palgrave Macmillan. No matter which 1945–1990 authors you are studying, you will find this useful, an accessible introduction to: 'Contexts: History, Politics, Culture'; 'Texts: Themes, Issues, Concepts'; 'Criticism: Approaches, Theory, Practice'.

'The Po-Mo Page: Postmodern, Postmodernism, Postmodernity': http://www9.georgetown.edu/faculty/irvinem/theory/pomo.html. A succinct overview; supplement it with more detailed discussions, such as those in the books listed above.

'The Stanford Encyclopedia of Philosophy: Postmodernism': http://plato.stanford.edu/entries/postmodernism/. A more discursive overview of postmodernism, with a bibliography.

Do not forget to keep a record of *all* the texts and websites you look at when researching for an assignment: you will need to list them in your bibliography.

199

11 Literature 1990–The Present

William Stephenson

Chapter Overview

Historical Context

1989, like 1789, was a year of revolution. The Berlin Wall that divided Communist and NATO-controlled zones of the city was breached in a popular uprising; in 1990, Germany became unified for the first time since World War Two. The ground for anti-Communist revolt had been strengthening for some time: in the late 1980s, under the leadership of Mikhail Gorbachev, the Soviet Union undertook a programme of *glasnost* (openness), through which the censorship and social controls characteristic of the past were gradually removed, including those on literature: thousands of previously banned books were republished. Another central feature of Gorbachev's reform programme was *perestroika* (economic restructuring) in which the running of businesses in capitalist fashion was gradually made possible. This put the Soviet economy under massive strain, and eventually led to an attempted military coup in 1991. Boris Yeltsin, Gorbachev's successor, held off the military and was able to continue the process of reform, leading to the dissolution of the Union in the same year.

The largest part of the former Soviet Union is now known as the Russian

Federation, after various republics of the USSR, notably the Ukraine, broke away to become independent. Satellite Communist regimes were overthrown, either fairly peacefully, as in the electoral defeat of General Jaruzelski in Poland in 1989, or by bloodier means, as in the armed revolt which led to the execution of President Ceausescu in Romania in the same year. The process was reminiscent of Britain's loss of empire several decades earlier, but conducted much more quickly. This led some Western intellectuals, notably Francis Fukuyama (1992), to suggest not only that Western democracy had triumphed but also that it had proved itself the ultimate governmental form, or '(in another celebrated phrase) the "only game in town" ' (White, p. 72).

The weakness of the triumphalist 'end of history' thesis was made apparent almost immediately by the exposure of the soft underbelly of the Western democracies: their need for energy, and their dependence on non-Western, often undemocratic partners to supply it. In 1990, President Saddam Hussein of Iraq invaded the neighbouring emirate of Kuwait and seized control of its oilfields. After refusing demands from the USA and United Nations to withdraw, Hussein was faced with a USA-led coalition army that liberated Kuwait in 1991 and drove deep into Iraq, but stopped short of overthrowing his regime and eventually withdrew. Eleven years later, in 2002, the USA claimed that it had intelligence to the effect that Hussein had weapons of mass destruction (chemical, biological, and potentially nuclear arms) and was planning to use them. The USA assembled another coalition army and invaded Iraq again in 2003. Hussein was captured and executed, and the West gained effective control of Iraq's substantial oil reserves. No weapons of mass destruction were found. At the time of writing (mid-2008), the coalition still has a significant military presence in Iraq and is attempting to return control of the country to Iraq's armed forces in the face of fierce resistance from a number of insurgent groups including Al Qaida.

Al Qaida, roughly translated as 'The Base', is the most significant enemy the USA has had to face since the collapse of the Soviet Bloc. It is both a form of anti-Western ideology ('the base' in the sense of a theory or intellectual structure derived from certain branches of Islamic fundamentalism) and an international, multi-cellular affiliation of terrorist groups (Al Qaida has maintained a network of bases, or training camps). Although the organization has been responsible for a number of atrocities throughout the world, its most significant and deadly attack on the West so far was launched on 11 September 2001 (a date now usually referred to by the American ordering of 9/11). Four teams of Al Qaida suicide commandos hijacked US domestic flights and proceeded to pilot them into three targets: the Pentagon and the two towers of the World Trade Center in New York (a fourth plane, after heroic resistance from the passengers and crew, crashed before reaching its target). All the hijackers and nearly 3,000 innocent people were killed, including the passengers and crew of all four flights. This atrocity has had incalculable cultural impact thanks to the huge visibility and the unexpected and gruesome nature of the attack, although the death toll was small compared to the 84,389–92,067 documented civilian deaths in the Iraq war up to early 2008, and the almost certainly much greater number of unreported deaths (Iraq Body Count, 2008). 9/11 and Iraq are the most visible nodes of a wider network of conflict. In response to the attack, President George W. Bush declared the War on Terror, in which he vowed to pursue the enemies of the USA to the bitter end, using 'every resource at our command' to disrupt and defeat 'the global terror network' (Bush, p. 3).

The War on Terror is partly a cyber war, fought on the new technological battlefield of the internet. Terrorist organizations find recruits, and broadcast film of atrocities, via this medium. The internet (a.k.a. the net, the world wide web, or cyberspace) has reported and has driven world conflicts in this period but has also been the engine of peaceful social change. The net began as 'a decentralized computer network for the U. S. Army, moved on to become an academic worldwide information communication system, and eventually came to encompass almost every aspect of our daily existence' (Amichai-Hamburger, p. v): it is now 'the freest, most lightly regulated, most international communications system in the history of mankind' (Graham, p. 23). Messages can be exchanged; conversations held; virtual goods such as text, sound, music, film, and so on, can be broadcast and exchanged in the form of computer files; and physical goods bought and sold. The internet 'brings together the features of a vast library, a gigantic picture gallery, a worldwide noticeboard' (Graham, p. 23). In theory the net's scope as a forum and marketplace is global, though in practice it is dominated by the richest parts of the world, Europe and North America. The net is changing the way literature is written and disseminated, and will continue to do so. In a world where books can be composed, edited, advertised, bought and then read online, no paper text actually need exist. In the first decade of the twenty-first century, print is still the main medium in which literature exists, but in the future this may be very different.

The internet has had subtle, possibly profound effects on human interaction and subjectivity. People can now meet and converse online using created identities or avatars, which may differ radically from their off-line selves. Experimentation with different appearances, genders, sexualities, ethnicities, and so on is happening on an unprecedented scale in the virtual environment, in a way that is beginning to modify social relationships within and around literature, and to shift the relationship of author and reader. One example of such a shift, based on experimental sexuality, is 'slash', a genre of prose fiction written by fans of novels, films and TV series (such as the *Harry Potter* novels and *Star Trek*), and published on dedicated websites. In 'slash' stories, the characters and background world of the original text are used, but an imaginary homosexual relationship is created between two characters (who are usually heterosexual males in the original). The style and content of 'slash' varies from romance* (a sort of cyberspace Mills and Boon) to hardcore pornography. Paradoxically, most of the writers and consumers of 'slash' fiction are not homosexual men but heterosexual women.

As people have begun to redefine their relationship to traditional subject positions (gender roles, class identities, ethnicities, modes of consumption), so they have begun to rethink their relationship to the non-human world. This re-evaluation has been urgently needed, as the issue of ecology, and potential global disaster, has become of critical concern in the 1990s and beyond. Although the environmentalist movement has a long history, its arguments have gained new urgency with the revelation that the world is warming up year by year, almost certainly because of human activities such as the burning of fossil fuels that produce carbon dioxide and other gases that prevent the earth from losing heat. The consequences of climate change are potentially cataclysmic and are at the very least extremely significant. This has led to the rise of a number of intellectual and political movements dedicated to averting ecological disaster: some of these advocate a 'managerial approach to environmental problems', believing that the challenges raised by global warming can be met without major social change, whereas others argue that for human existence on the planet to be sustainable, there must be 'radical changes in our relationship with the non-human natural world, and in our mode of social and political life' (Dobson, p. 2).

Literature, as always, has sought to respond to the urgent issues of its time, but has often done so by indirect, metaphorical means: Pat Barker's *Regeneration* (1991), for instance (see the 'Case Study', below), is ostensibly about World War One, but in the context of the 1991 Gulf War has been read as a comment on the contemporary world. Likewise, Jo Shapcott's poem 'Phrase Book' (see 'Key Authors and Texts', below) addresses the Gulf War indirectly through the fractured monologue of one participant, rather than offering propaganda.

When we read contemporary literature at degree level we must take into account not only its direct references to current events but also the indirect impact of these events. How are the form and content of novels, plays or poems affected by ecological concerns or the threat of terrorism? How has new technology influenced the vocabulary and imagery writers are able to use? Are authors or characters simply products of their time, or do they have a role in creating it? Again, as with studying any other historical period, look for actual documents of the time (books, broadcasts, websites) which provide concrete, quotable evidence of the context from which the text has emerged. It is usually best to research carefully the exact years in which a book was written and published, rather than to rely on generalizations.

Key Authors and Texts

One of the most significant war novelists of the last twenty years has been Ian McEwan. Although his career began before 1990, some of his best known work, notably *Atonement* (2001), has been published since. In *Atonement*, the young Briony Tallis incriminates an innocent family friend, Robbie, in the mistaken belief that he has raped her cousin. Briony later becomes a writer, and narrates the war experiences of Robbie and his reconciliation with his girlfriend, Briony's sister Cecilia: however, the whole narrative may be Briony's literary fantasy, an effort in words to atone for her earlier fatal misunderstanding. McEwan's novel suggests, against poststructuralism*, that writing does not in fact constitute the world but is a weak substitute for it, and implies, in the context of the Gulf Wars, that literature cannot change the political world, only comment on it at a significant remove. McEwan's earlier novel of conflict, *The Innocent* (1990), is set during the Cold War. The novel's strained personal relationships are a microcosm of the destructive tensions between declining and emergent superpowers. The novel ends with the protagonist's* hope that he and his German ex-girlfriend will visit the Berlin Wall together 'before it was all torn down' (p. 303). McEwan here addressees the actual destruction of the Wall in 1989, but also hints that the entire Cold War world was being torn down, for which the Wall was a metonym*. *Atonement* and *The Innocent* suggest that literature can reconstruct past history imaginatively, but can also use historical settings to comment on present events, whether intellectual (the critical debate about poststructuralism* in the 1990s; see 'Criticism and Literary Theory', below) or political (the implosion of the Communist regimes, and the alleged 'end of history').

Other novelists of the 1990s and twenty-first century have very different concerns, but their work, like McEwan's, comments on the social tensions of the time. Clearly there are far too many writers to mention, so here, and in the paragraphs below on poetry and drama, I will concentrate on a few representative examples.

Jeanette Winterson began her literary career with *Oranges are Not the Only Fruit* (1985), an autobiographical novel detailing the difficulties faced by a lesbian adolescent in a small northern town, brought up by intensely religious foster parents. Winterson has gone on to compose other novels such as *Written on the Body* (1992), whose narrator's gender is never determined, despite his/her relationships with lovers of both sexes. Rather than being pigeonholed as a 'lesbian writer', Winterson uses the novel form to destabilize received ideas

of gender and sexuality in a way that aligns her work with queer theory*
(see 'Criticism and Literary Theory', below).

David Mitchell's most important novels are probably *Ghostwritten* (1999)
and *Cloud Atlas* (2004), which both use a structure of interlocking fragments
each with a different narrator and in the style of a different genre. The poly-
phonic narratives of *Ghostwritten* and *Cloud Atlas*, although hugely ambitious,
suggest not the construction of a new form (the same structure had been
used by modernists, such as James Joyce in *Ulysses*, published in 1922; or
postmodernists*, such as John Fowles in *A Maggot*, published in 1985),
but modernism's and postmodernism's* refinement and assimilation into
the mainstream. The work of the vastly talented Mitchell is thus typical of
the literary world since 1990, which is engaging with modernist *and* postmodernist* forms as received ideas of the past that can be reworked.

Irvine Welsh has gained notoriety since the publication of *Trainspotting*
(1993). Narrated using a stylized version of Scottish dialect, *Trainspotting* is
the account of a group of heroin addicts in the housing estates of Edinburgh.
The novel is an exposure of the dystopian underside of the Thatcherite
project of consumerism, free enterprise, and the erosion of communitarian
values. *Trainspotting* has been attacked for allegedly glamorizing drug abuse,
especially since the film adaptation of the novel (with the same title) was
released in 1996; but to write in Scottish dialect about a group of thieves and
junkies did not, at the time, seem remotely like a commercial proposition
(Morace, p. 86). Welsh's work engages with the Thatcherite erosion of the
Welfare State, giving a voice to the victims of the social policies of the 1980s
and 1990s.

Carol Ann Duffy (see the 'Case Study', below) is the best-known English
poet at present. Her nearest rival is probably Simon Armitage, whose work,
like Duffy's, uses familiar words in unfamiliar ways to disturb preconceptions. One of the poems in his second collection, *Kid* (1992), has the following
title and first line: 'The Metaphor Now Standing at Platform 8 / will separate
at Birmingham New Street' (p. 51). Here, Armitage combines the familiar
language of train announcements with a witty, reflexive comment on the role
and function of poetry; his metaphor doesn't just turn one thing into another,
it has a driver, a dead man's handle and a buffet car in the centre. Instead of a
refreshment trolley, poets 'will troubadour the aisle reciting their short but
engaging pieces' (p. 52).

Poets since 1990 have tried to open up a dialogue with traditional forms,
without slavishly copying past rules: 'Good new poetry traditionally keeps
up a live conversation with two things at once: the real world now, and other
poems, past poems' (Padel, p. 22). In 'Fiction and the Reading Public', Sean
O'Brien writes:

You read, and then you go to sleep:
That's work's permission to be dead.
And while you sleep you watch them pulp
Whole libraries you have not read. (Hulse *et al*, p. 193)

The jaunty iambic* tetrameter* and ABAB rhyme scheme are intended as a joke: they fit the ironic tone of the content. If meant seriously, they would reduce the poem to doggerel. The content of the stanza, of course, is partly a comment on how the modern reader or writer ('you') can imagine whole traditions ('libraries') destroyed that have been marginalized or bypassed. The poem's form enacts this process, giving the tetrameter* form 'permission to be dead' and yet reproducing it mockingly, much as a poet of an earlier generation, Philip Larkin, did in his notorious 'This Be The Verse', whose carefully scanned opening line, 'They fuck you up, your mum and dad' (p. 180), might be read as an oblique comment on the anxiety of influence, of the poet's oedipal relationship with tradition, as much as a direct reference to the negative influence of parents.

Other poets have engaged directly with the tense political situation evolving around them, without always sacrificing subtlety or writing propaganda. Jo Shapcott, for instance, in the title poem of her collection *Phrase Book* (1992), writes:

I am expecting a gentleman (a young gentleman,
two gentlemen, some gentlemen). Please send him
(them) up at once. This is really beautiful.

Yes, they have seen us, the pilots, in the Kill Box
on their screens (Hulse *et al*, p. 204)

The scrambled syntax of most of the poem prevents it from becoming a simple polemic against the 1991 Gulf War. The speaker is 'an Englishwoman' (p. 204) in a foreign country under attack, probably by USA or coalition forces (Iraq, then?) but little else of her immediate situation is clear. The lines about the 'gentlemen', where the noun shifts uneasily from singular to plural, suggest the speaker is learning a new language, as if English has an awkward grammar still to be mastered. The poem mimics the phrase books of the title, which reproduce key snippets of language, in various grammatical forms, for tourists. The speaker, then, may be impersonating an Englishwoman in an attempt to gain asylum, or exemption from attack; she may also be thoroughly decentred* by the experience of war, her identity fragmented by literal and/or metaphorical bombardment.

The poem also mimics the digitally fragmented, televised, simulatory nature of the electronically fought and mediated war. As Jean Baudrillard controversially put it, the Gulf conflict was not a war in the conventional sense of the term, but a postmodernist* collage of images. Weapons were detonated but war in the conventional twentieth-century sense was buried, 'whether in the concrete and sand Iraqi bunkers or in the Americans' electronic sky, or behind that other form of sepulchre, the chattering television screens' (p. 63; see the 'Literature 1945–1990' chapter on hyperreality*).

This sense of polemical urgency was often matched in the theatre. The most controversial plays since 1990 have made the most vivid connections with the playwrights' social contexts. One of the most significant dramatists has been Sarah Kane, whose plays range from the controversial *Blasted* (1995) to the cryptic *Crave* (1998) and posthumously performed *4.48 Psychosis* (2000). *Blasted* begins with a scene of attempted seduction in a hotel room, but then transgresses the limits of realism* when a soldier with a sniper's rifle enters the room, and the scene appears to be transported to a contemporary battle zone. The play includes (in no particular order) on-stage nudity, masturbation, oral sex, urination, anal rape, and the eating of eyes and a baby, so its controversy is perhaps not surprising. What is more significant is Kane's impact on contemporary theatre, and her relationship to her context. The transformation of the hotel room into a war zone was partly an attempt to defamiliarize the Bosnian war of the early 1990s, to bring it home to the audience and away from the simulatory procession of images offered by the media (see the account of Jo Shapcott, above), so that those murdered and systematically raped during the conflict become not mere images, but people like the audience, speaking English, living in Leeds.

Blasted suggests the audience's complicity not only in this war but also in the sexualized violence of contemporary culture. As Kane herself commented of the relationship between the situation in the hotel room and Bosnia, 'one is the seed and the other is the tree. I do think that the seeds of full-scale war can always be found in peace-time civilisation' (Saunders, p. 39). For instance, Kane makes the journalist Ian, himself a rapist, dictate a story of the murder and rape of a British backpacker, in the titillating, sensationalist style of a tabloid newspaper. Kane claimed she took the story directly from *The Sun* tabloid, only changing the names and a few details (Saunders, p. 52).

Kane has influenced an emerging generation of dramatists, such as Mark Ravenhill (see Aleks Sierz's *In-Yer-Face Theatre*). His work seems equally to court controversy. His play *Shopping and Fucking* (1996) created administrative problems for the theatre producing it because a 'nanny' computer program, of the sort designed to protect children from unsuitable internet sites, refused to accept the title (Ravenhill, p. ix). Like *Blasted*, the play has on-stage drug abuse and other potentially shocking acts. Again, more significant than this is its social commentary on a post-Thatcherite, post-Welfare State world of unchecked corporate power, where consumerism has replaced any political or religious consensus. The personal and the material (or the emotional and the physical) are blurred throughout the play: at one point the heroin addict Mark claims he has learned in therapy that 'emotional dependencies' are 'just as addictive' as the heroin he is taking (Ravenhill, p. 17). The play envisages a bleak future lying in wait, where human activity is reduced to 'Shopping, Television' (p. 89).

Contemporary writers cannot be studied alone. They influence each other and are influenced by their times, and in some cases actively seek to change their society. Sarah Kane's references to the Bosnian conflict in *Blasted*, for instance, can be connected either to *Shopping and Fucking*'s attack on consumerism (which, like a dictatorship, requires ideological control, with advertising as its propaganda), or to the work of Jo Shapcott, who attempts to bring the Gulf War home by writing as if English civilians are involved, or to Ian McEwan's account of American manipulation of the English protagonist* in *The Innocent*. The point is not to turn your essay into a simple attack on or defence of the current government, or to be distracted from the essay question by commenting generally on international affairs, but to show through careful analysis and research how your chosen text is written in a particular period of history (the present). Like citizens of so many past eras, contemporary writers and readers are shaped by, and resist, larger political and historical forces.

Criticism and Literary Theory

Since 1990, poststructuralism* and literary theory have become so much the norm in universities and on undergraduate courses that a backlash has occurred, with some commentators proclaiming the death of theory (or fervently hoping to bring it into being). A number of critics have suggested that poststructuralism* was always misguided and is redundant, among them Valentine Cunningham, who suggests that language cannot, as poststructuralist* theory claims, be separated from its referents and treated as a self-contained system: 'Words point to things – even invisible things, like God or toothache or epistemology' (p. 20). In his polemic *Therrhoea and After*, Raymond Tallis argues: 'The conclusion that all signs, not merely linguistic ones, lack signifieds is the inescapable reduction to absurdity' of Jacques Derrida's arguments (p. 28).

Cunningham's and Tallis' arguments are themselves abstract and theoretical, perhaps as much as the poststructuralist* ones they aim to refute. In fact, as this suggests, theory has not died but has mutated and evolved in the university classroom. Poststructuralism* never was a monolith: it was, at its simplest, a convenient catch-all label for the practice of critics influenced by

Derrida, Roland Barthes, and other French writers of the 1960s and 1970s. Since the 1990s, many literary critics have outgrown or discarded that influence, but theorists are hardly reverting to liberal humanism* *en masse*. Instead, postmodernism* 'has itself come to represent an increasingly vexed issue', as has poststructuralism* (Tew, p. 20). Postmodernism* is no longer seen as an automatically appropriate description of the dominant cultural movement of our time. Instead, some commentators are asking what lies beyond it and whether it is now obsolete. This applies to writers as much as critics: 'Many novelists are increasingly responding to postmodernism* and challenging its self-determining features, and in fact have baulked at its restrictive interpretative code' (Tew, p. 10). The example Philip Tew gives is A. S. Byatt's historical romance* *Possession* (1990), some of whose characters are literary scholars who find the postmodernist* and ultra-theoretical interpretations of their Victorian subject matter by other academics too limiting (see the 'Literature 1945–1990' chapter).

The debate goes both ways. Just as theory is now being put to the test, so is the assumption that 'great' literature, or even literature itself, deserves special privilege. For instance, thanks to cultural materialist* criticism of his work, Shakespeare is no longer *unquestionably* the greatest writer in English, but neither has he been demoted to the equivalent of, say, a hack who churns out badly-written romances* or thrillers. Instead, critics have sought to examine the mechanisms and power relations through which his greatness was created and sustained: this is even more relevant because of Shakespeare's continuing popularity. Alan Sinfield, for instance, has attempted in his critique of *Othello* to point to what he sees as the 'racism and sexism in the play' that emerges not from Iago's character but 'the Venetian culture' of the text (p. 745). To see racism and sexism in Shakespeare is not to travesty him as politically incorrect, but to refuse to take for granted the humanistic picture of Shakespeare as the promoter of universal values and truths. Instead, his plays not only engage critically with such problems as racial and sexual discrimination, but also to some extent reflect the values of their age, which may be chauvinistic or xenophobic: 'In my view, when traditional critics perceive Shakespearean women characters in terms of stereotypes, they are often more or less right' (p. 748).

Seeing Shakespeare as sexist is not entirely new. Feminist* critics have always been sceptical about the canon* of 'great' male writing. However, in the late twentieth and early twenty-first centuries, the canon* of *theory* came into question too. Many feminists* were critical of the masculine orientation of theory (the theorist as investigating subject, intellectual explorer confronting the past, by default male). This was a construction which applied, despite its best intentions, to some theories written by women, including some feminism*: Hélène Cixous, for example, has sometimes been mistaken for a patriarchal* male writer by undergraduate students, who assume that her declaration that women's writing is full of flow, excess, and irrationality is innately sexist (see the account of 'The Laugh of the Medusa' in the 'Literature 1945–1990' chapter). Some feminists* of the 1990s and after began to look for a post-feminist* position that engaged critically with previous versions of feminism*, for instance by shifting the agenda 'from debates around equality to a focus on debates around difference' (Brooks, p. 4), including differences between women, rather than simply between the two genders. Thus feminism* began to diversify: black, lesbian, and non-Western women, for instance, began to resist what they perceived to be the default assumption of much earlier feminist* writing that a woman was, unless otherwise specified, white, heterosexual, and European or American. This diversification of feminism* did not involve simply erasing earlier Anglo-American and French schools of thought (see the 'Literature 1945–1990' chapter), but sought to reform them, just as theory rethought past ideas without making them cease to exist.

Since 1990, the term post-feminism* has been used in another way, to refer to the acceptance by some women of traditional gender roles due to the belief, promoted by sections of the media (including some literature), that the equality sought by earlier feminists* has been achieved. Critics have exposed this assumption as false: this form of post-feminism* coincided with a moment when 'acclaimed feminist* studies demonstrate that not only have women's real advancements been limited, but also that there has been a backlash against feminism* of international significance' (Coppock *et al*, p. 3). Thus post-feminism* might have signified a new non-sexist world in magazines, television programmes, and novels, but was possibly a means of concealing the continuing relegation of women to secondary roles.

The 1990s saw another significant development in gender studies with the emergence of queer theory*. This was a body of ideas championed by a critical school that aimed to examine literature from the perspective of gay and lesbian rights, and/or to destabilize gender and sexuality in the text, using deconstruction* (see the 'Literature 1945–1990' chapter) in order to suggest the sexual contradictions and flux at the heart of seemingly stable, 'straight' texts. Judith Butler, in *Gender Trouble: Feminism and the Subversion of Identity* (1990), argued that gender was performative*, meaning created by actions (signs, gestures, rituals, dress codes) rather than inborn. Butler questioned the feminist* distinction between the female (innate, biological sex) and the feminine (a series of behavioural norms attached to the female by patriarchy*), by arguing that *both* were culturally constructed. Butler was sometimes misread by enthusiasts who took her work to mean that gender was now a matter of choice, of self-conscious theatrical display: Butler's work, though, makes clear the extent to which gender norms are powerfully enforced by social codes, and cannot be transgressed on a whim.

Another prominent queer theorist* is Eve Kosofsky Sedgwick, whose works include *Between Men: English Literature and Male Homosocial Desire* (1985) in which she argued that the classic love triangle of two men and a woman was in fact a patriarchal* rivalry between the two men, in which the woman was secondary, a mere signifier of the two men's deeper desire for one another as rivals. This desire was homosocial*, meaning a form of same-sex bonding that was not sexual but had the potential to become so. In her later book *Epistemology of the Closet* (1990), Sedgwick argued that literature and society have been shaped by a crisis of definition: heterosexuality is the basis of most literary plots and social structures (marriage, the family) but depends for its existence on homosexuality, the Other* which it is not, but which must exist in awkward symbiosis with it.

Ethnicity or 'race', particularly racial otherness, has been another significant area of study since 1990. Postcolonial* studies became part of the mainstream in the period. It is regularly the subject of modules on undergraduate courses in literature, and a number of introductory textbooks have appeared on it (for example, McLeod 2000; Loomba 2005), following the foundational work of leading figures such as Edward Said (see the 'Literature 1945–1990' chapter). Since its arrival, postcolonialism* has diversified, with the emergence of a more generalized ethnic studies (not linked necessarily to the colonial) seeking to study ethnicity in literature, and to make the question of 'race' problematic. The new scholarship focuses on 'scientific evidence to the effect that biological genetic differences did not sort themselves out into evenly distinguishable "races" ' (Rivkin and Ryan, p. 961). Instead, ethnicity is treated as a social and historical construct, often using poststructuralist* theory.

When we write essays on contemporary literature using criticism and theory, it is always worth reading the criticism carefully and using whole essays as much as we can, rather than just sound-bites or snippets from textbooks. Judith Butler's *Gender Trouble*, for instance, would help a great deal in a reading of Jeanette Winterson or Sarah Kane, but only if we take the time to understand what Butler is saying (that gender is not just a performance; it is actually *created*, rather than just copied, through actions that may be theatrical). The closer your reading of the theory you use, as well as of your literary text, the better. This might also mean treating your theory sceptically, by asking questions of it and sometimes refusing to accept its assumptions; your chosen novel, poem, or play might offer evidence that your chosen critic or theorist is not always right.

211

Pat Barker's *Regeneration*

Pat Barker's 1991 novel uses real people as its protagonists*, but shows the reader that it is making up a story about them; it is an example, then, of historiographic metafiction* (see the 'Literature 1945–1990' chapter). As Barker's 'Author's Note' warns, 'Fact and fiction are so interwoven in this book that it may help the reader to know what is historical and what is not' (p. 251). In real history, the poets Wilfred Owen and Siegfried Sassoon met at Craighlockhart Hospital during World War One. Sassoon helped Owen revise some of his manuscripts* there. Barker dramatizes this encounter: when analysed, her version shows how, for the protagonists* and for the reader, present and past, and memory and language, mix ambiguously.

Owen is trying to revise a poem, and ignore the distracting world around him, chiefly the wind. The irony is that while doing so, he is trying to find the perfect word to describe shells passing over, which make a sound somewhat like the wind. So to try to remember the past, Owen ignores the clues all around him in the present. However, the two worlds cannot be separated as easily as Owen thinks. Sassoon thinks the right word should be 'hiss' rather than 'wail'. Sassoon's demonstrative point made to Owen, 'I hear hissing', is highly ambiguous (p. 142). It seems to mean 'my experience of war tells me "hissing" is the right word for the poem', but could also mean 'because of the wind, I can hear hissing now: I am reliving the memory'. Thus Sassoon is, by implication, blurring his traumatic memory of bombardment with his present circumstances.

In keeping with this, Barker's narrative allows the wind around Owen's room to wail (like the shells in Owen's draft of the poem) and crack branches 'like rifle fire' (p. 142). On a symbolic* level, then, the wind could refer to the war itself, raging outside, totally outside the poets' control. However, the sounds also have personal meanings. After going to bed that night, Sassoon hears a tapping noise he heard before when talking to Owen, and finds it 'impossible not to think of the battalion' (p. 143). The sound offers an associative link to the soldiers he has to care for on the Front. It is the tapping, which has no clear cause, that sets this process in train: it is 'a distinct, purposeful sound, quite unlike the random buffeting of the wind' (pp. 142–43). Analysis of this passage suggests that Barker is using the example of Sassoon and the sounds as an analogy for how the mind seeks meaning (the 'purposeful' tapping reminds him of the battalion) in the middle of chaos (the 'random' wind). A parallel might be drawn here with the image of the train in Carol Ann Duffy's sonnet 'Prayer' (see the 'Case Study', below).

The passage shows that not only is Owen's poetry affected by war and created through the connotations of words, so too, in Freudian theory, is the mind, which draws on a number of associations (or links between memories and words or sounds) to interpret events. Owen's and Sassoon's doctor, W. H. R. Rivers (another of *Regeneration*'s characters who existed in real history) was aware of this. He used psychoanalysis*, then a new and controversial discipline, to encourage the traumatized officers not to forget their dreadful experiences, but to remember them, thus overcoming repression* and allowing the mind to encompass what had happened. As Rivers concludes, he is teaching his patients the value of recollection, including admitting to weakness and showing symptoms like tears. This goes completely against their upbringing: 'They'd been trained to identify emotional repression* as the essence of manliness' (p. 48).

This can be seen through close analysis of the passage where Rivers hypnotizes the traumatized officer Billy Prior for the first time and Prior recalls the hitherto repressed memory of finding a severed eye in his hand and asking himself, 'What am I supposed to do with this gob-stopper?' (p. 103). This, it seems, was the immediate cause of Prior's inability to speak when admitted to the hospital; the eye is like a large round sweet, or gob-stopper, but is also the catalyst that stops Prior's mouth, rendering him unable to speak, through a classically Freudian associative link between eye, sweet, and muteness. Prior has difficulty facing this, and repeatedly butts Rivers in the chest 'hard enough to hurt. [. . .] It was the closest Prior could come to asking for physical contact' (p. 104). Prior's butting of Rivers reminds the doctor 'of a nanny goat on his brother's farm, being lifted almost off her feet by the suckling kid' (p. 104). Rivers realizes he is a 'male mother' to his patients, but (in an anticipation of late twentieth-century scepticism about gender stereotypes) decides he dislikes the term, because he 'distrusted the implication that nurturing, even when done by a man, remains female' (p. 107).

The nanny goat image is, as Rivers believes later, 'ridiculous' (p. 107), but it also suggests more than Rivers seems to notice. The image implies that it is in fact the mother (Rivers) who is more moved by the experience than the kid (Prior), who also appears stronger, because powerful enough to lift the larger animal almost off her feet. The image allows Rivers to remember an earlier patient who was 'like Prior. The same immensely shrewd eyes. X-ray eyes. The same outrageous frankness' (p. 107). Rivers sees his bond with these men as one of nurturing, but is annoyed at the association of nurture and femininity. He wishes to remain a man, within the context of a close bond with another man. In short, there is a strong homosocial* undertone here of which Rivers seems unaware. Prior's head, when butting Rivers, has phallic parallels, suggesting a symbolic* form of sexual assault. Prior's face, after he withdraws his head, is 'blind and slobbery' (p. 104), again implying a phallus.

Prior's 'outrageous frankness' is closely linked to his eyes, which Rivers is careful to see not as attractive but as like an X-ray: penetrating. Just before the butting incident, Prior has told Rivers that his nightmares 'get muddled up with sex' (p. 100), but Rivers misses this cue.

The point of such an analysis of the novel, which detects sexuality in a seemingly non-sexual scene, is not to force on to the material a simple correspondence of symbol* and underlying cause in order to conclude that Rivers is really homosexual or that Prior really wants to seduce or rape him. Rather, the novel is subtly pointing to the ways in which the male bonds in the novel are homosocial* (and thus potentially homosexual), in ways which even the most sophisticated and forward-thinking characters, like Rivers, are unaware. Part of the reason for this lack of awareness (or lack of ability to admit it) is historical, connected to the social context of the setting of the novel and the social context in which it was written and read (that of the late twentieth century, which would tend to seek sexuality in situations where, eighty years before, it might not be seen, even among those who had read Freud).

The novel can, here and elsewhere, be read through queer theory* (see 'Criticism and Literary Theory', above) as it presents sexuality, as well as gender, as unstable and contingent upon history. Sassoon's friend, the poet Robert Graves, refers to how a former lover, though only 'in an entirely honourable, platonic' way (p. 203), has been arrested for soliciting, and 'since that happened my affections have been running in more normal channels. [. . .] I'd hate you to think I was homosexual *even in thought*' (p. 199). The ex-boyfriend's arrest is the catalyst for Graves' decision to embrace heterosexual courtship: quite understandably he does not want to be persecuted for his choice of partner, and is convincing himself he is now 'normal'.

The conversation concludes with a carefully placed remark from Graves: his former partner is to be sent to Rivers 'To be cured' (p. 199). Graves seems, at this point, to have subscribed to the idea that homosexuality is a disease. Many of Barker's readers may find such a notion antiquated or offensive; but rather than anachronistically attacking Graves as homophobic, the novel aims to show how his view of homosexuality emerges out of his historical context. During the war, men faced death together daily, creating strong homosocial* desires (male bonding) but did so in an army whose hierarchies and, therefore, military discipline would, it was believed, have been severely undermined by homosexual behaviour.

When doing detailed close reading of *Regeneration* and thinking about how best to interpret it, keep in mind that it foregrounds the 'cultural tensions' heightened by the war, raising 'questions about duty, authority, psychology, gender, homosexuality, class, love, memory, the value of individual life, and the value of the imagination' (Westman, p. 25) and implies that all of these are as relevant nearly one hundred years later, in an age riven by its own cultural and military conflicts.

 ## Carol Ann Duffy's Poetry

The sonnet 'Prayer' from *Mean Time* (1993) 'draws together many of Duffy's preoccupations: desire, loss, [. . .] nostalgia for a lost childhood, the urge to name and the absence of words with which to name' (Rees-Jones, p. 49). The poem begins by suggesting that although 'we cannot pray', sometimes 'a prayer / utters itself' (p. 127, ll. 1–2). This declaration is followed by two surreal images: a woman lifts her head 'from the sieve of her hands' (l. 3) to stare 'at the minims sung by a tree' (l. 4). Presumably the singing tree is uttering the prayer, and the woman is lifting her head from her hands (thus symbolically hauling herself out of despair) by paying attention to it. The hands are a 'sieve' because of the gaps in the woman's fingers, through which something must be draining, perhaps the woman's hope, if the image is pursued to its conclusion. 'Minims' is a curious word to use when 'songs' or 'verses' might have made more sense. Duffy probably chose the word because of its alliterative qualities and its sense of murmuring (perhaps as in the rustling leaves of a tree) through the 'm' sounds. However, 'minim' has two other properties: in music, a minim is a long note that lasts two beats of a bar, and in the singular, the word is a palindrome (it is spelt the same backwards). Thus the image suggests symmetry and unity: two moments (beats) are united in one long sound, which has a certain self-contained, reversible form. This might imply something worthy of the woman's attention, a well-wrought natural prayer that will resist or reverse the despairing drainage implied by 'sieve'. Duffy's poem here also harks back to the Romantics with its implication that godliness can be found in nature.

The next stanza adds an image whose trochaic* rhythm complements its meaning. Sometimes a man will hear 'his youth / in the distant Latin chanting of a train' (ll. 7–8). In this case, the image is one of a man-made rather than natural substitute for religion: the train, a machine, is the associative link which binds the man to his culture, his classical education, and thus his childhood. Again, there is a surrealist undertone: the train, not the man, is chanting Latin. It is the man, though, who makes the voiceless sounds of the train speak: the image points to the human capacity for making meaning out of chaos, of which religion is one example (see also the analysis of *Regeneration* above).

The third stanza continues in this vein, though it begins with the exhortation

'Pray for us now' (l. 9). This suggests a Catholic church service, specifically the Litany of the Blessed Virgin Mary, but the poem does not make clear to whom the line is addressed (Nature? Everyone? Mary?). The reader is left to decide as the sonnet concludes in Shakespearean fashion, with a remarkable rhyming couplet: 'Darkness outside. Inside, the radio's prayer – / Rockall. Mallin. Dogger. Finisterre' (ll. 13–14). Here, the mass media – specifically, the BBC Radio 4 Shipping Forecast – becomes the social glue knitting the community together in the absence of faith. Just as importantly, the poem does not actually quote the forecast (which would supply wind speeds and directions after each of the names of the regions of the sea) but abbreviates it to the names themselves. The reader is invited to fill in the gaps in the poem (or as a reception theorist might say, concretize* it) with reference to their own presumed immersion in the secular British culture from which Duffy emerges. The allusion* to the forecast is not intended to be hard for the reader to work out (unlike those, say, in Duffy's modernist predecessors such as T. S. Eliot): the forecast is widely followed by large numbers of non-seagoing listeners, despite its irrelevance to their lives. As Radio 4's controller Mark Damazer pointed out, the forecast 'scans poetically. It's got a rhythm of its own. It's eccentric, it's unique, it's English' (2007).

In this sense the forecast is like poetry (which might be another, hidden subject of 'Prayer'), and in particular Duffy's poetry. Whether in metre or in free verse, her work's appeal to a wide readership is rooted not only in its engagement with current social concerns, such as the position of women, but also in its adroit manipulation of popular culture. Duffy's *Selected Poems* juxtaposes two short pieces, '$' and 'Liverpool Echo', both from Duffy's first full-length collection, *Standing Female Nude* (1985). Both poems address how popular music is recalled and reproduced.

'$' is a compilation of clichés taken from songs, mostly rock'n'roll standards of the 1950s. The opening line, 'A one a two a one two three four' (p. 18, l. 1), mimics the count-in used to give a band the correct tempo and starting point; it also recalls the opening seconds of the Beatles' first LP, *Please Please Me*, released in 1963. As a whole, the poem seems meaningless: it is simply eight lines of the nonsense syllables used to fill in between the lyrics on hit singles. However, the title suggests that the poem could be read as a satirical comment on the shoddy goods that gullible people will pay for, echoing Max Horkheimer and Theodor Adorno's early twentieth-century analysis of the culture industry as a system of mass deception, through which the proletariat is hoodwinked and socially controlled by the bourgeoisie, via a series of mass-marketed, standardized products whose 'specific content [. . .] is derived from [invariable types] and only appears to change. The details are interchangeable' and in any case are merely 'ready-made clichés to be slotted in anywhere' (Horkheimer and Adorno, p. 1244).

Conversely, the poem could be read as a celebration of the sort of popular culture which is mindless in the best possible sense: allowing joyful, uninhibited fun through the dissolution of the downwardly imposed limits of acceptable grammar, meaning, and behaviour. The poem's surreal, sometimes hilarious juxtapositions help to prevent any simple logic from developing. 'Boogie woogie' (l. 2) may have been an early twentieth-century style of rhythmic piano playing, and a euphemism for sex, but in the scrambled, nonsensical context of Duffy's '$' it means more than just these. It immediately follows the opening line's count-in, indicating a context of rehearsed, performed music, and is juxtaposed with 'chou chou cha cha chatta / noogie' (ll. 2–3), presumably a reference to 'The Chattanooga Choo-Choo' (a 1940s song about a train, popularized by Glenn Miller). The juxtaposition indicates the wider, pop-cultural context in which syllables are manipulated for rhythmic effect, as well as retaining the innuendo of the original expression.

On the opposite page from '$' in *Selected Poems* is 'Liverpool Echo', a very different poem about the past. It is formally more conventional than '$', as it is a sonnet with a regular rhyme scheme. Without ever naming the group, the poem is clearly about the relationship of the Beatles to Liverpool, a city 'which cannot say goodbye' (p. 19, l. 8). The references to death in the poem could be an extended metaphor for the economic decline of Liverpool in the 1970s and 1980s, or for the break-up of the Beatles, or could be allusions* to the actual death of John Lennon, who was assassinated in 1980. People wait outside the Cavern Club, the old haunt of the Beatles, 'as if nostalgia means you did not die' (l. 4). The fans are compared to 'litter on the water' floating outside the club (l. 13). Tonally, the poem achieves a complex balance between elegy* and social comment, between acknowledging the nostalgia of Liverpool and critiquing it.

'Liverpool Echo' is quite the opposite of '$' in its lack of quotation of the past: its only direct reference to the Beatles' music is to '*Ain't She Sweet*' (l. 7), a song the band performed early in their career but which was in fact a cover version. '$', though, quotes the lyrics of a number of different artists, omitting all the words that make sense, and directly recycles them, forming a pastiche* of meaningless fragments that nevertheless hints at logic through its title and its juxtapositions. '$' is a postmodernist* collage, an appropriation of the past with affection but also playful irony (see the 'Literature 1945–1990' chapter). 'Liverpool Echo', by contrast, with its ambiguous sympathy towards Liverpudlians' fond illusion of personal bonding with the Beatles, in which 'everybody has an anecdote / of how they met you' (ll. 9–10), reflects a modernist nostalgia for order in a broken, dysfunctional world, even as the Beatles are shown never to appear except in the form of a jukebox recording of a song they never wrote.

Duffy's poetry is often taught and read because of its feminist* concerns, its use of dramatic monologue* and its engagement with unconventional sexuality (Duffy is openly lesbian). Here, I have deliberately avoided these issues to suggest instead how close analysis of her work reveals its complex, ambiguous relationship to popular culture, which is, like religion, a machine of mass deception and yet also a source of comfort and even transcendence. In Duffy's universe, even a tree or a radio can utter a prayer.

Further Reading

Barry, Peter (2009), *Beginning Theory: An Introduction to Literary and Cultural Theory* (third edition). Manchester: Manchester University Press. A comprehensive and accessible introduction; primary texts are used throughout to show the theories in practice. Includes chapters on: 'Feminist Criticism'; 'Lesbian/Gay Criticism'; 'Postcolonial Criticism'. Contains an annotated 'Further Reading'.

Bentley, Nick (ed.) (2005), *British Fiction of the 1990s*. London: Routledge. A wide-ranging introduction; includes chapters on: 'Mapping the Millennium: Themes and Trends in Contemporary British Fiction'; 'Science and Fiction in the 1990s'; ' "Fascinating Violation": Ian McEwan's Children'; 'Pat Barker's Vanishing Boundaries'.

Bickley, Pamela (2008), *Contemporary Fiction: The Novel since 1990*. Cambridge: Cambridge University Press. An informative and lively book, the two long discursive chapters – 'Reading Contemporary Fiction'; 'Approaches to the Texts' – will help further your understanding of the period and hone your close reading skills. Concludes with: 'Critical Approaches'; 'How to Write About Contemporary Fiction'; 'Further Reading'; 'Glossary'.

Brinton, Ian (2009), *Contemporary Poetry: Poets and Poetry since 1990*. Cambridge: Cambridge University Press. In the same series as Bickley's *Contemporary Fiction*, the two discursive chapters are: 'Approaching Contemporary Poetry'; 'Approaching the Texts'. Concludes with: 'Critical Approaches'; 'How to Write About Contemporary Poetry'; 'Books About Poetry'; 'Glossary'.

Broom, Sarah (2005), *Contemporary British and Irish Poetry: An Introduction*. London: Palgrave Macmillan. Covers a wide range of key subjects – class, race, gender, subjectivity, and so on – and an interesting selection of poets, including Patience Agbabi, Moniza Alvi, Armitage, Ciaran Carson, Carol Ann Duffy, Jackie Kay, and Benjamin Zephaniah.

Sierz, Aleks (2001), *In-Yer-Face Theatre: British Drama Today*. London: Faber and Faber. A groundbreaking introduction to playwrights such as Sarah Kane, Mark Ravenhill, Patrick Marber, and Martin McDonagh. Contains extracts from interviews with the authors and a useful bibliography.

'Contemporary Writers in the UK': http://www.contemporarywriters.com/. Search for the author you are studying; gives brief biographies and critical overviews, and selected links.

The *Guardian*: http://www.guardian.co.uk/. Search for articles by and reviews of the authors you are studying; you might also look at the *Observer, The Daily Telegraph*, and *The Times*.

Glossary of Terms

This glossary is designed to help you engage with *Studying English Literature* by defining some of the key terms used. You are advised, however, to buy a separate glossary, which will cover many more terms and go into greater detail than we have been able to do here. We particularly recommend *The Oxford Dictionary of Literary Terms* (2008) by Chris Baldick.

absurdism The belief that human existence is absurd in the sense of comical and pointless, lacking any meaning. This leads to absurdist literature, in particular the theatre of the absurd.

allegory The telling of one story in the guise of another, in which each main element of the new story corresponds to an element in the original story.

alliteration The repetition of consonantal sounds in two or more nearby words; usually these sounds come at the start of a word or of a stressed syllable.

allusion A reference to something, perhaps a person or an event, but particularly to another work of literature, usually indirectly so that the reader is assumed to share the knowledge of an unspecified source; nearly all works of literature allude to other works of literature but some do so extensively.

apostrophe An address to an inanimate object, or an absent person.

archetype An original and unique model or pattern on which other phenomena are based, or by which they are influenced.

avant-garde The leading edge of any artistic movement; art that sets out to challenge existing rules or preconceptions of what is acceptable.

ballad A popular narrative poem*, normally associated with oral transmission.

bathos Typically, the movement from something sublime* or elevated to something ridiculous, ordinary, or mundane.

Bildungsroman The German term for the 'novel of development' or education.

blank verse Unrhymed iambic pentameter*.

caesura A pause, usually near the middle of a line of verse, often marked by punctuation.

canon In literature, this is used to refer to the texts judged to be worthy of study by critics, academics, and other authority figures. The canon is constantly changing, and in recent years has become considerably more inclusive.

catharsis A term from Aristotle used to describe the purging or working-through of strong emotions, perhaps by watching characters in whom we have an emotional investment experience something terrible on stage.

chiasmus A pattern having the structure ABBA, where the sequence of words or ideas is reversed in two parallel clauses, as in Alexander Pope's criticism of a tasteless garden with its 'Trees cut to Statues, Statues thick as trees' (*Epistle to Burlington*, l. 120).

comedy of manners A genre focusing on the behaviour of middle- or upper-class people in domestic life.

conceit Derived from the Latin word for 'concept', the word came to be applied to an extended, elaborate metaphor, simile or analogy; it is particularly associated with the metaphysical poets*.

concretization The filling in of gaps in the text by the reader; for example, imagining the colour of the cat in the sentence 'the cat sat on the mat'.

cultural materialism While not ignoring the structure and language of a work, cultural materialists locate it in a specific cultural and historical moment.

decadence In the late nineteenth century, a term associated with art-for-art's sake and the French symbolist movement.

decentred A postmodernist* term meaning 'without a stable centre or clear organization'. Used to describe self-contradictory texts after deconstructive reading, or characters who do not have a clear sense of self, or any situation after previously accepted hierarchies have collapsed.

deconstruction A type of reading that aims to break down the patterns of meaning set up by the text, and to point out the text's inconsistencies, paradoxes*, and flaws.

dramatic monologue A poem where a fictional speaker addresses an audience.

écriture féminine 'Women's writing' or 'feminine writing': a French feminist* term referring not to writing by females, but to the sort of text that breaks down received patriarchal* ideas of grammar, syntax, etc. in order to 'flow' in what is allegedly a distinctly female way.

elegy A piece of writing, most often a poem, which mourns the loss of someone or something. If a piece of writing is 'elegiac', it is profoundly sombre.

ellipsis The omission of certain words, to be taken as understood, particularly used in poetry to create compactness (and sometimes complexity).

epic Originally a long narrative poem* depicting the deeds of heroes and often recounting the founding myth* of a people or nation. Later the term has also been applied to novels depicting historical events or developments.

epistolary Relating to or denoting the writing of letters ('epistles') or literary works in the form of letters; an epistolary novel is presented as a series of letters.

eponymous A term used to describe a match in a title and a specific name; a work that is named after someone or something (*King Lear* and *Macbeth* are 'eponymous' plays).

existentialism A philosophy that largely evolved in France after World War Two, which argued that people were formed by their actions rather than any pre-existing 'essence'. Each person is responsible for creating themselves through what they choose to do.

farce Comedy without having recourse to wit or intellectual complexity, which is solely designed to produce laughter.

feminism In general, the global movement to promote the rights of women. In literary criticism, it is reading that examines the status of women, the role of femininity and the power of patriarchy* in the text.

fin de siècle Literally 'end of the century', a term usually associated with the Decadent* movement at the end of the nineteenth century.

foot A unit of poetic metre*, containing two or three syllables.

Formalism The literary critical school that argues that literature evolves not through historical change but with reference to other literature that came before it: thus literature should be studied for its form.

free indirect discourse/style A form of writing that conflates characters' thoughts and utterances with a third-person narrative voice.

globalization The tendency for the world in the late twentieth and twenty-first centuries to become increasingly similar due to the spread of late capitalist ideology, especially that of the United States of America.

Gothic Refers broadly to fiction, particularly popular in the Romantic period, that seeks to produce fear and suspense. Many Gothic novels use medieval settings and present innocent young women beset with dangers, secrets, and supernatural phenomena.

gynocriticism A branch of feminist* criticism that seeks to read texts in terms of women's experience rather than as a challenge to patriarchy*. Texts that are centred on such experience are *gynotexts*.

heroic couplets Traditionally, in English poetry, a sequence of couplets rhymed in pairs (AA, BB, CC, DD, etc.) using iambic pentameter*.

heteronormative An ideology which proposes that a heterosexual lifestyle is 'normal' and that a homosexual one is deviant.

homosocial Desire between members of the same sex that is not sexual, but has the potential to become so (e.g. intense male bonding).

hyperbole Exaggeration or overstatement for emphasis or rhetorical effect.

hyperreality The condition in which the seemingly 'real' world is actually composed of images that refer only to each other, rather than to a pre-existing reality.

iamb A metrical foot* with an unstressed syllable followed by a stressed syllable.

iambic pentameter Referring to a verse form that uses the rhythm of the iamb* five times in each line.

Imagism An influential poetic 'movement' inaugurated by the publication of *Des Imagistes* (1914), which included poems by, among others, Richard Aldington, H. D. (Hilda Doolittle), F. S. Flint, Ford Madox Ford, James Joyce, and Ezra Pound.

imperialism The ideological project that justifies the economic takeover of foreign countries (colonialism) because of the allegedly superior culture and technology of the invading (imperial) power.

interior monologue The imitation in prose of a character's actual thought processes, often written with little or no grammatical structure.

intertextuality The presence of other texts in the text under discussion, regardless of the intent of the author. Thus a text's intertexts can include not only those deliberately referred to by the writer, but also those whose structures, stock devices or even exact words are copied or varied in the text.

Jacobean A period of history spanning the reign of James I (1603–1625).

liberal humanism The school of criticism that believes that literature conveys timeless, universal human values. It tends also to argue that literature is above politics and each text should be read as an autonomous aesthetic object, without reference to social considerations such as gender or class.

libertine A libertine is someone typically defined as leading a dissolute and sexually promiscuous lifestyle, with little or no regard for moral or religious codes. 'Libertinism' also implies 'freethinking' in matters of religion and conduct.

lyric A short poem giving thoughts and/or feelings of a single speaker.

magical realism The genre of fiction that narrates magical or impossible events as if they are quite normal and everyday.

manuscript Usually a hand-written version of a text, either a completed text or a draft of a text, and therefore (usually) written before publication.

masque A visually rich court entertainment produced in England in the sixteenth and seventeenth centuries, presenting a simple plot based on allegorical or mythical figures with limited dialogue, music, and dancing.

melodrama Literally, drama with music. Associated with nineteenth-century theatre and characterized by heightened emotion, sensational plots, and unsubtle characterization.

metafiction Fiction that treats literature, storytelling, and the composition of literature as a central topic: often novels about novelists writing novels.

metaphysical poetry Poetry that employs complex, extended figures of speech called conceits*. The effect of metaphysical poetry comes from the use of this unusual imagery to explore themes such as romantic love, religious experience, and personal identity.

metonymy A figure of speech in which a term is substituted for something close to it; for example, referring to the police as 'the law'.

metre The scheme of versification in any given poem, referring to the pattern of stresses that constitutes the regular rhythm (e.g. iambic pentameter*).

mock-epic A style of writing that models the treatment of ordinary, everyday, or relatively trivial subjects on the epic* in order to ridicule them.

mock-heroic A style of writing that treats ordinary, everyday, or relatively trivial subjects as if they are worthy of heroic treatment; closely associated with the mock-epic*.

myth A story, usually about origins, shared by a community. It seeks to explain otherwise mysterious phenomena in a narrative structure where supernatural beings have a direct involvement in human affairs.

narrative poem A poem that tells a story, such as Coleridge's 'The Rime of the Ancient Mariner' (a ballad*) or Byron's *Don Juan* (a mock-epic*).

New Criticism A mid-twentieth-century, originally American, 'movement' in literary criticism that promoted detailed textual analysis divorced from biography or historical context.

Orientalism The construction by Western writers of a version of the East (the Orient) that reflects the need to create an Other* that is allegedly everything the West is not (e.g. lazy, decadent, sensual).

Other Whatever is not the self, or is the opposite to it. Thus the Other to a white male character might be black and female.

ottava rima An eight-line stanza with the rhyme scheme abababcc.

oxymoron A verbal paradox* or opposition; a contradiction in terms.

paradigm A foundational or archetypal example of something; a model of its kind.

paradox An apparently self-contradictory statement, idea, or concept.

parody A comic imitation.

pastiche A piece of writing that imitates the writing of another author or authors by using the words and expressions that typify the style of the original, often for purposes of comic parody*.

pathetic Arousing pity or sadness; related to pathos*.

pathetic fallacy The attribution of human feelings and responses to objects, natural phenomena or animals.

pathos The feeling of pity or sorrow evoked by a text.

patriarchal A social structure which places the man/father ('patriarch') in a position of authority and power; hence, the dominant rule of men over women (on a domestic or broader political level); often used in feminist* criticism.

performative Refers to a thing or state that is created through speech and/or action, as in the statement 'I now pronounce you man and wife' that creates a marriage.

peripateia A term from Aristotle used to describe a switch in the action; a reversal of fortune.

periphrasis Sometimes known as 'circumlocution', periphrasis uses more words than are strictly necessary and approaches its subject indirectly or obscurely (in a 'roundabout' way).

personification A figure of speech that gives human traits to animals, objects, or ideas.

phallocentric Obsessed with or centred on the penis (phallus); seen from the perspective of the male and male sexuality, particularly in the construction of meaning; a term often used in feminist* criticism.

Poet Laureate A poet appointed by the government or monarch, who is expected to write poems to commemorate State occasions and other significant national events.

postcolonialism The school of literary criticism that reads texts from the colonial period or after (e.g. from British India or India after independence), seeking to investigate how colonialism was maintained, resisted, or overcome. Usually examines constructions of imperialism*, ethnicity, and 'race'.

post-feminism Either: (a) a new movement or 'wave' within late twentieth and early twenty-first century feminism* that seeks to question the assumptions of previous generations of feminists in order to take the women's movement forward, or; (b) the media-fuelled assumption that the 'battle' for equal rights between the sexes has been won, and that women can therefore occupy traditional gender roles.

postmodernism A term with several competing definitions (see '1945–1990: Historical Context'), but which refers to the dominant cultural movement of the late twentieth century, that came after modernism and reacted to it.

poststructuralism The school of literary criticism based on late twentieth-century French philosophy (see '1945–1990: Criticism and Literary Theory') that seeks to read a text through breaking down the linguistic and conceptual structures it appears to set up. Usually this involves blurring seemingly clear binary oppositions such as: male/female, living/dead, good/evil.

protagonist The main character in a literary text.

psychoanalysis The so-called 'talking cure' initiated by Sigmund Freud in the late nineteenth century, in which patients were encouraged to talk about their experiences, dreams, memories, etc. so that repressed material could be uncovered and mental illness cured.

queer theory Theory that reads literature and other cultural production either from the perspective of gay and lesbian rights, or to affirm a gay or lesbian tradition, or with a view to destabilizing gender and sexuality in the text and seeing the paradoxes or contradictions within 'straight' narratives.

realism The attempt to portray human existence accurately, usually associated with the depiction of everyday life in nineteenth-century fiction, drama, and painting.

repression In Freudian psychology, the removal of unwanted or threatening material to the unconscious, so that the ego (conscious mind) remains unaware of it.

romance Originally a long narrative poem* with its origins in the medieval period and revived in the Renaissance. Rooted in the chivalric, courtly love tradition, it depicted a knightly lover undergoing a series of trials in a quest for his love to be requited by an unattainable woman. Sometimes used more broadly (in contrast with realism*) to refer to fiction with a tendency to escapism and/or fantasy.

satire A mode of personal, social, or political critique, satire is typified by indirect methods, seeming, for instance, to condone and approve of that which it (really) deplores.

sensation novel A popular genre in the 1860s, which generally involved crime, scandal, and intrigue.

sensibility A term associated particularly with eighteenth-century literature and philosophy, which suggests an individual's capacity to sympathize with the sufferings of others and/or to be affected by the beauties of art, literature, and landscape.

social-problem novel Victorian novels depicting the problems of industrialization (sometimes known as the 'industrial novel'), such as class conflict, working conditions in factories, and the living conditions of the poor.

soliloquy A speech spoken by a character who believes him or herself to be firmly out of earshot of anybody. The character is meant to be unaware of the presence of the theatre audience too, and so the thoughts that are spoken can, in most cases, safely be presumed to be 'true' or innermost thoughts.

stream of consciousness Narrative that attempts to follow the thoughts of a character, giving the reader access to private opinions, emotions, etc. as the character registers them. Usually more structured than interior monologue*, it generally relies on orthodox grammar and syntax.

structuralist A structuralist believes that texts can be grouped according to those narrative structures that they have in common.

Sublime, the An awe-inspiring quality in art or landscape that initially overcomes the self but eventually leads to its empowerment.

symbol A symbol is an image that can have a number of possible meanings, some of which may never be made clear, and which often gives a sense of cohesion to the literary work.

syntactic inversion An inversion of standard word order, for instance putting the adjective after the noun (as in the example 'kings barbaric' for the normal 'barbaric kings').

tautology Unnecessary repetition of words or phrases in close proximity.

tetrameter A pattern of four metrical feet*.

theatre of the absurd See *absurdism*.

trimeter A pattern of three metrical feet*.

trochee A metrical foot* containing a stressed syllable followed by an unstressed syllable.

utopian A utopia is an idealized state, often having perfect qualities. Its opposite is a 'dystopia', a nightmarishly chaotic imagined universe.

Vorticism An artistic and literary 'movement' emanating from the periodical *Blast: The Review of the Great English Vortex* (1914–15). It published work by, among others, T. S. Eliot, Ford Madox Ford, Wyndham Lewis, and Ezra Pound.

zeugma A device where one word is applied in two completely different senses, as in Pope's 'stain her Honour, or her new Brocade', where the verb 'stain' is applied literally to the noun 'Brocade', but metaphorically to the noun 'Honour'.

References

Introduction

Primary Texts

Lawrence, D. H. (2007), *Selected Stories*. London: Penguin.

Shakespeare, William (1995), *Twelfth Night, or What You Will*. Ed. Roger Warren and Stanley Wells. Oxford: Oxford University Press.

Silkin, Jon (ed.) (1996), *The Penguin Book of First World War Poetry* (second edition). London: Penguin.

Woolf, Virginia (1992), *To the Lighthouse*. Ed. Margaret Drabble. Oxford: Oxford University Press.

Secondary Texts

Attridge, Derek (2004), *The Singularity of Literature*. London: Routledge.

Baldick, Chris (2008), *The Oxford Dictionary of Literary Terms* (third edition). Oxford: Oxford University Press.

Culler, Jonathan (2000), *Literary Theory: A Very Short Introduction*. Oxford: Oxford University Press.

Lennard, John (2005), *The Poetry Handbook: A Guide to Reading Poetry for Pleasure and Practical Criticism* (second edition). Oxford: Oxford University Press.

QAA (2000), 'Subject Benchmark Statements: English'. http:www.qaa.ac.uk/academicinfrastructure/benchmark/honours/English.asp#6 (accessed 17 October 2008).

Part I Studying Shakespeare

Shakespeare and the Renaissance

Primary Texts

Bacon, Francis (2002), *Francis Bacon: The Major Works*. Ed. Brian Vickers. Oxford: Oxford University Press.

Elizabeth I (2000), *Elizabeth I: Collected Works*. Ed. Leah Marcus, Janel Mueller, and Mary Beth Rose. Chicago: University of Chicago Press.

Machiavelli, Niccolò (1988), *The Prince*. Ed. Quentin Skinner and Russell Price. Cambridge: Cambridge University Press.

Montaigne, Michel de (1958), *The Complete Essays of Montaigne*. Ed. Donald M. Frame. Stanford: Stanford University Press.

Shakespeare, William (2002), *The Complete Sonnets and Poems*. Ed. Colin Burrow. Oxford: Oxford University Press.

Shakespeare, William (2007), *Complete Works*. Ed. Jonathan Bate and Eric Rasmussen. London: Macmillan/RSC.

Secondary Texts

Borges, J. L. (1964), *Labyrinths: Selected Stories and Other Writings*. Ed. Donald A. Yates and James E. Irby. New York: New Directions.

Burckhardt, J. (1990), *The Civilization of the Renaissance in Italy*. Harmondsworth: Penguin.

The Comedies

Primary Text

Shakespeare, William (2007), *Complete Works*. Ed. Jonathan Bate and Eric Rasmussen. London: Macmillan/RSC.

Secondary Texts

Barber, C. L. (1959), *Shakespeare's Festive Comedy: A Study of Dramatic Form and Its Relation to Social Custom*. Princeton: Princeton University Press.

Freedman, Barbara (1991), *Staging the Gaze: Postmodernism, Psychoanalysis, and Shakespearean Comedy*. Ithaca: Cornell University Press.

MacCary, W. T. (1985), *Friends and Lovers: The Phenomenology of Desire in Shakespear ean Comedy*. New York: Columbia University Press.

Maslen, R. W. (2005), *Shakespeare and Comedy*. London: Thomson Learning.

McDonald, Russ (ed.) (2004), *Shakespeare: An Anthology of Criticism and Theory*. Oxford: Blackwell.

Miola, R. (1994), *Shakespeare and Classical Comedy: The Influence of Plautus and Terence*. Oxford: Clarendon Press.

Muir, Kenneth (1979), *Shakespeare's Comic Sequence*. New York: Barnes and Noble.

Salingar, Leo (1974), *Shakespeare and the Traditions of Comedy*. Cambridge: Cambridge University Press.

Traub, Valerie (1992), *Desire and Anxiety: Circulations of Sexuality in Shakespearean Drama*. London: Routledge.

The Tragedies

Primary Text

Shakespeare, William (2007), *Complete Works*. Ed. Jonathan Bate and Eric Rasmussen. London: Macmillan/RSC.

Secondary Texts

Alfar, Cristina León (2003), *Fantasies of Female Evil: The Dynamics of Gender and Power in Shakespearean Tragedy*. Newark: University of Delaware Press.

Bradley, A. C. (1905), *Shakespearean Tragedy: Lectures on 'Hamlet', 'Othello', 'King Lear' and 'Macbeth'*. London: Macmillan.

Frye, Northrop (1957), *The Anatomy of Criticism*. Princeton: Princeton University Press.

Knight, G. Wilson (2001), *The Wheel of Fire: Interpretations of Shakespearian Tragedy*. London: Routledge.

Knights, L. C. (1964), 'How Many Children Had Lady Macbeth? An Essay in the Theory and Practice of Shakespeare Criticism', *Explorations: Essays in Criticism Mainly On the Literature of the Seventeenth Century*. Harmondsworth: Peregrine.

Knights, L. C. (1966), *Some Shakespearean Themes and an Approach to 'Hamlet'*. Palo Alto: Stanford University Press.

Loomba, Ania, and Martin Orkin (eds) (1998), *Post-Colonial Shakespeares*. London: Routledge.

McAlindon, Tom (1991), *Shakespeare's Tragic Cosmos*. Cambridge: Cambridge University Press.

Part II Studying Seventeenth- and Eighteenth-Century Literature

Literature 1600–1660

Primary Texts

Andrewes, Lancelot (2005), *Selected Sermons*. Ed. Peter McCullough. Oxford: Oxford University Press.

Bacon, Francis (1996), *The Major Works*. Oxford: Oxford University Press.

Cary, Elizabeth (1995), *The Tragedy of Mariam*, in *Renaissance Drama by Women*. Ed. S. P. Cerasano and Marion Wynne-Davies. London: Routledge.

Dekker, Thomas (1999), *The Shoemaker's Holiday*, in *Renaissance Drama: An Anthology*. Ed. Arthur Kinney. London: Routledge.

Donne, John (1990), *The Major Works*. Ed. John Carey. Oxford: Oxford University Press.

Halkett, Anne (2007), *Lady Anne Halkett: Selected Self-Writings*. Ed. Susanne Trill. Aldershot: Ashgate.

Herbert, George (2007), *The English Poems of George Herbert*. Ed. Helen Wilcox. Cambridge: Cambridge University Press.

Herrick, Robert (1996), *Robert Herrick, Everyman's Poetry*. London: J. M. Dent.

Hutchinson, Lucy (2000), *The Memoirs of the Life of Colonel Hutchinson*. London: Phoenix Press.

Jonson, Ben (1979), *Ben Jonson's Plays and Masques: Texts of the Plays and Masques, Jonson on His Work, Contemporary Readers on Jonson, Criticism*. Ed. Robert M. Adams. New York: Norton.

Jonson, Ben (1996), *The Complete Poems*. Ed. G. Parfitt. London: Penguin.

Lanyer, Aemilia (1993), *Salve Deus Rex Judæorum*. Ed. Susanne Woods. Oxford: Oxford University Press.

Middleton, Thomas (1999), *A Chaste Maid in Cheapside*, in *Renaissance Drama: An Anthology*. Ed. Arthur Kinney. London: Routledge.

Milton, John (2007), *Paradise Lost*. Ed. Barbara Lewalski. Oxford: Blackwell.

Spenser Edmund (2001), *The Faerie Queene*. Ed. A. C. Hamilton, Hiroshi Yamashita, Toshiyuki Suzuki, and Shohachi Fukuda. London: Longman.

Tottel, Richard (1965), *Tottel's Miscellany, 1557–1587*. Ed. H. E. Rollins. Cambridge, MA: Harvard University Press.

Vaughan, Henry (1976), *The Complete Poems*. London: Penguin.

Wroth, Mary (2000), *The Countess of Montgomery's Urania*. Ed. J. A. Roberts. Tempe, Arizona: Medieval Renaissance Text Society.

Wroth, Mary (1995), *Love's Victory*, in *Renaissance Drama by Women*. Ed. S. P Cerasano and Marion Wynne-Davies. London: Routledge.

Secondary Texts

Boucher, Philip. (1992), *Cannibal Encounters: Europeans and Island Caribs, 1492 1763*. Baltimore: Johns Hopkins University Press.

Brooks, Cleanth (1947), *The Well-Wrought Urn: Studies in the Structure of Poetry*. New York: Harcourt Brace.

Burke, Kenneth (1973), *Philosophy of Literary Form* (third edition). Berkeley: University of California Press.

Demara, John G. (1980), *Milton's Theatrical Epic: The Invention and Design of Paradise Lost*. Cambridge, MA: Harvard University Press.

Dollimore, Jonathan (1984), *Radical Tragedy: Religion, Ideology and Power in the Drama of Shakespeare and His Contemporaries*. Chicago: University of Chicago Press.

Fowler, Alastair (ed.) (1970), *Silent Poetry: Essays in Numerological Analysis*. London: Routledge.

Goldberg, Jonathan (1983), *James I and the Politics of Literature: Jonson, Shakespeare, Donne and Their Contemporaries*. Baltimore: Johns Hopkins University Press.

Greenblatt, Stephen (1980), *Renaissance Self-Fashioning*. Chicago: University of Chicago Press.

Hackett, Helen (2000), *Women and Romance Fiction in the English Renaissance*. Cambridge: Cambridge University Press.

Haselkorn, Anne M., and Betty Travitsky (1990), *The Renaissance Englishwoman in Print: Counterbalancing the Canon*. Amherst, MA: University of Massachusetts Press.

Helgerson, Richard (1992), *Forms of Nationhood*. Chicago: University of Chicago Press.

Hyde, Edward (1979), *The History of the Civil Wars and the Rebellion Begun in the Year 1641: A Selection*. Oxford: Oxford University Press.

Krontiris, Tina (1992), *Oppositional Voices: Women as Writers and Translators of Literature in the English Renaissance*. London: Routledge.

Loewenstein, David (1990), *Milton and the Drama of History: Historical Vision, Iconoclasm, and the Literary Imagination*. Cambridge: Cambridge University Press.

Montrose, Louis (1983), ' "Shaping Fantasies": Figurations of Gender and Power in Elizabethan Culture'. *Representations*, 1.2, 61–94.

Schleiner, Louise (1994), *Tudor and Stuart Women Writers*. Bloomington: Indiana University Press.

Sinfield, Alan (1982), *Literature in Protestant England 1560–1660*. London: Croom Helm.

Wiseman, Susan (1998), *Drama and Politics in the English Civil War*. Cambridge: Cambridge University Press.

Literature 1660–1714

Primary Texts

Behn, Aphra (1972), 'On the Death of the Late Earl of Rochester', in *Rochester: The Critical Heritage*. Ed. David Farley-Hills. London: Routledge and Kegan Paul.

Behn, Aphra (1997), *Oroonoko*. Ed. Joanna Lipking. New York: Norton.

Behn, Aphra (1999), *The Rover, or The Banished Cavaliers*. Ed. Anne Russell. Ontario: Broadview.

Congreve, William (1994), *The Way of the World*. Ed. Brian Gibbons. London and New York: A & C Black and Norton.

Defoe, Daniel (1965), *The Shortest Way with the Dissenters*, in *Daniel Defoe*. Ed. J. T. Boulton. London: B. T. Batsford.

Defoe, Daniel (1986), *A Journal of the Plague Year*. Ed. Anthony Burgess and Christopher Bristow. Harmondsworth: Penguin.

Dryden, John (2003), *The Major Works*. Ed. Keith Walker. Oxford: Oxford University Press.

Etherege, Sir George (2005), *The Man of Mode; or Sir Fopling Flutter*, in *Four Restoration Libertine Plays*. Ed. Deborah Payne Fisk. Oxford: Oxford University Press.

Milton, John (1971), *Paradise Lost*. Ed. Alastair Fowler. London: Longman.

Pope, Alexander (1997), *The Poems of Alexander Pope*. Ed. John Butt. New Haven: Yale University Press.

Rochester, John Wilmot, Earl of (1968), *The Complete Poems*. Ed. David M. Vieth. New Haven: Yale University Press.

Swift, Jonathan (2008), *'A Tale of a Tub' and Other Works*. Ed. Angus Ross and David Woolley. Oxford: Oxford University Press.

Secondary Texts

Alsop, Derek (2002), *'That Second Bottle: Essays on John Wilmot, Earl of Rochester*. Ed. By Nicholas Fisher'. *Modern Language Review*, 97.1, 174–75.

Fisher, Nicholas (ed.) (2000), *That Second Bottle: Essays on John Wilmot, Earl of Rochester*. Manchester: Manchester University Press.

Gallagher, Catherine (1998), 'Who was That Masked Woman? The Prostitute and the Playwright in the Comedies of Aphra Behn' (1988), in *Aphra Behn: Contemporary Critical Essays*. Ed. Janet Todd. Basingstoke: Macmillan.

Johnson, James William (2004), *A Profane Wit: The Life of John Wilmot, Earl of Rochester*. Rochester, NY: Rochester University Press.

Montaigne, Michel Eyquem de (1738), *Essays* (fifth edition). Trans. Charles Cotton. 3 vols. London: Bettesworth *et al*.

Owen, Susan J. (ed.) (2001), *A Companion to Restoration Drama*. Oxford: Blackwell.

Thormählen, Marianne (1993), *Rochester: The Poems in Context*. Cambridge: Cambridge University Press.

Todd, Janet (1998), *The Critical Fortunes of Aphra Behn*. Columbia, SC: Camden House.

Literature 1714–1789

Primary Texts

Burney, Frances (2008), *Evelina*. Ed. Edward A. Bloom and Vivien Jones. Oxford: Oxford University Press.

Defoe, Daniel (2003), *Robinson Crusoe*. Ed. John Richetti. London: Penguin.

Fielding, Henry (1980), *Joseph Andrews and Shamela*. Ed. Douglas Brooks-Davies. Oxford: Oxford University Press.

Fielding, Henry (2005), *Tom Jones*. Ed. Thomas Keymer and Alice Wakely. London: Penguin.

Fielding, Henry (2008), *Jonathan Wild*. Ed. Hugh Amory. Oxford: Oxford University Press.

Forster, E. M. (1992), *Howard's End*. Ed. Oliver Stallybrass. Harmondsworth: Penguin.

Gay, John (1986), *The Beggar's Opera*. Ed. Bryan Loughrey and T. O. Treadwell. London: Penguin.

Haywood, Eliza (2000), *Love in Excess*. Ed. David Oakleaf. Ontario: Broadview.

Haywood, Eliza (2004), *Anti-Pamela; or, Feign'd Innocence Detected by Eliza Haywood* and *An Apology for the Life of Mrs Shamela Andrews by Henry Fielding*. Ed. Catherine Ingrassia. Ontario: Broadview.

Horace (1978), *Satires, Epistles and Ars Poetica*. Trans. H. Rushton Fairclough. Cambridge, MA: Harvard University Press.

Johnson, Samuel (2000), *The Major Works*. Ed. Donald Greene. Oxford: Oxford University Press.

Pope, Alexander (1977), *The Poems of Alexander Pope*. Ed. John Butt. New Haven: Yale University Press.

Richardson, Samuel (1980), *Pamela*. Ed. Peter Sabor. Harmondsworth: Penguin.

Richardson, Samuel (1985), *Clarissa*. Ed. Angus Ross. Harmondsworth: Penguin.

Smollett, Tobias (1998), *The Expedition of Humphry Clinker*. Ed. Lewis M. Knapp and Paul-Gabriel Boucé. Oxford: Oxford University Press.

Sterne, Lawrence (2003), *The Life and Opinions of Tristram Shandy, Gentleman*. Ed. Joan and Melvyn New. London: Penguin.

Swift, Jonathan (2005), *Gulliver's Travels*. Ed. Claude Rawson. Oxford: Oxford University Press.

Swift, Jonathan (2008), *'A Tale of a Tub' and Other Works*. Ed. Angus Ross and David Woolley. Oxford: Oxford University Press.

Secondary Texts

Battestin, Martin C. (2000), *A Henry Fielding Companion*. Westport: Greenwood Press.

Carnell, Rachel (2006), *Partisan Politics, Narrative Realism, and the Rise of the British Novel*. Basingstoke: Palgrave Macmillan.

Fairer, David (2003), *English Poetry of the Eighteenth Century 1700–1789*. London: Longman.

Hammond, Brean (2005), *Pope Amongst the Satirists 1660–1750*. Tavistock: Northcote House.

Ingrassia, Catherine (2004), 'Introduction', in Eliza Haywood, *Anti-Pamela; or, Feign'd Innocence Detected by Eliza Haywood* and *An Apology for the Life of Mrs Shamela Andrews by Henry Fielding*. Ed. Catherine Ingrassia. Ontario: Broadview.

O'Gorman, Frank (1997), *The Long Eighteenth Century: British Political and Social History, 1688–1832*. London: Arnold.

Sage, Lorna (ed.) (1999), *The Cambridge Guide to Women's Writing in English*. Cambridge: Cambridge University Press.

Smallwood, Angela J. (1989), *Fielding and the Woman Question: The Novels of Henry Fielding and Feminist Debate 1700–1750*. New York and Hemel Hempstead: St. Martin's Press and Harvester Wheatsheaf.

Spencer, Jane (1986), *The Rise of the Woman Novelist: From Aphra Behn to Jane Austen*. Oxford: Blackwell.

Warner, William B. (1998), *Licensing Entertainment: The Elevation of Novel Reading in Britain, 1684–1750*. Berkeley: University of California Press.

Watt, Ian (1957), *The Rise of the Novel: Studies in Defoe, Richardson, and Fielding*. Berkeley: University of California Press.

Part III Studying Romantic and Victorian Literature (1789–1901)

The Romantic Period

Primary Texts

Austen, Jane (2004), *Pride and Prejudice*. Ed. James Kinsley. Oxford: Oxford University Press.

Burke, Edmund (1990), *A Philosophical Enquiry into the Origin of our Ideas of the Sublime and Beautiful*. Oxford: Oxford University Press.

Butler, Marilyn (ed.) (1984), *Burke, Paine, Godwin, and the Revolution Controversy*. Cambridge: Cambridge University Press.

Byron, Lord (1986), *Don Juan*. Ed. T. G. Steffan, E. Steffan and W. W. Pratt. Harmondsworth: Penguin.

Cox, Jeffrey N., and Michael Gamer (eds) (2003), *The Broadview Anthology of Romantic Drama*. Ontario: Broadview.

Equiano, Olaudah (2003), *The Interesting Narrative and Other Writings*. Ed. Vincent Carretta. Harmondsworth: Penguin.

Shelley, Mary (1999), *Frankenstein; or, the Modern Prometheus*. Ed. D. L. Macdonald and Kathleen Scherf. Ontario: Broadview.

Wordsworth, William (1988), *Selected Prose*. Ed. John O. Hayden. Harmondsworth: Penguin.

Wu, Duncan (ed.) (2006), *Romanticism: An Anthology* (third edition). Oxford: Blackwell.

Secondary Texts

Abrams, M. H. (1971), *Natural Supernaturalism*. New York: Norton.

Bainbridge, Simon (1995), *Napoleon and English Romanticism*. Cambridge: Cambridge University Press.

Barrell, John (1991), *The Infection of Thomas De Quincey: A Psychopathology of Imperialism*. New Haven: Yale University Press.

Bate, Jonathan (1991), *Romantic Ecology: Wordsworth and the Environmental Tradition*. London: Routledge.

Bate, Jonathan (2000), *The Song of the Earth*. London: Picador.

Botting, Fred (1995), *Gothic*. London: Routledge.

Brannigan, John (1998), *New Historicism and Cultural Materialism*. Basingstoke: Macmillan.

Butler, Marilyn (1975), *Jane Austen and the War of Ideas*. Oxford: Clarendon.

Butler, Marilyn (1982), *Romantics, Rebels and Reactionaries*. Oxford: Oxford University Press.

Colley, Linda (1996), *Britons: Forging the Nation 1707–1837*. London: Vintage.

Cox, Jeffrey N. (1998), *Poetry and Politics in the Cockney School*. Cambridge: Cambridge University Press.

Curran, Stuart (1988), 'The I Altered', in *Romanticism and Feminism*. Ed. Anne K. Mellor. Bloomington: Indiana University Press.

Dart, Gregory (1999), *Rousseau, Robespierre and English Romanticism*. Cambridge: Cambridge University Press.

Day, Aidan (1995), *Romanticism*. London: Routledge.

Duckworth, Alastair M. (1971), *The Improvement of the Estate: A Study of Jane Austen's Novels*. Baltimore: John Hopkins.

Ferber, Michael (2005), 'Introduction', in *A Companion to European Romanticism*. Ed. Michael Ferber. Oxford: Blackwell.

Fulford, Tim, and Peter J. Kitson (1998), *Romanticism and Colonialism*. Cambridge: Cambridge University Press.

Higgins, David (2005), *Romantic Genius and the Literary Magazine: Biography, Celebrity, Politics*. London: Routledge.

James, Felicity (2008), *Charles Lamb, Coleridge and Wordsworth: Reading Friendship in the 1790s*. Basingstoke: Palgrave.

Johnson, Claudia (1988), *Jane Austen: Women, Politics and the Novel*. Chicago: University of Chicago Press

Jones, Chris (1993), *Radical Sensibility: Literature and Ideas in the 1790s*. London: Routledge.

Kirkham, Margaret (1983), *Jane Austen, Feminism and Fiction*. Brighton: Harvester Press

Kitson, Peter J. (2007), *Romantic Literature, Race, and Colonial Encounter*. Basingstoke: Palgrave.

Leask, Nigel (1992), *British Romantic Writers and the East: Anxieties of Empire*. Cambridge: Cambridge University Press.

Levinson, Marjorie (1986), *Wordsworth's Great Period Poems*. Cambridge: Cambridge University Press.

Lovejoy, Arthur (1924), 'On the Discrimination of Romanticisms'. *PMLA*, 39.2, 229–53.

McCalman, Iain (ed.) (1999), *An Oxford Companion to the Romantic Age*. Oxford: Oxford University Press.

McCusick, James (2000), *Green Writing: Romanticism and Ecology*. New York: St Martin's Press.

McGann, Jerome J. (1983), *The Romantic Ideology*. Chicago: University of Chicago Press.

Mellor, Anne K. (1988), *Mary Shelley: Her Life, Her Fiction, Her Monsters*. London: Routledge.

Mellor, Anne K. (1993), *Romanticism and Gender*. London: Routledge.

Pittock, Murray (2008), *Scottish and Irish Romanticism*. Oxford: Oxford University Press.

Roberts, Warren (1979), *Jane Austen and the French Revolution*. London: Macmillan.

Ross, Marlon B. (1989), *The Contours of Masculine Desire: Romanticism and the Rise of Women's Poetry*. New York: Oxford University Press.

Russell, Gillian, and Clara Tuite (2006), *Romantic Sociability: Social Networks and Literary Culture in Britain, 1770–1840*. Cambridge: Cambridge University Press.

Ruston, Sharon (2007), *Romanticism*. London: Continuum.

Said, Edward (1978), *Orientalism*. London: Routledge.

Said, Edward (1993), *Culture and Imperialism*. London: Chatto and Windus.

Thompson, E. P. (1991), *The Making of the English Working Class*. Harmondsworth: Penguin.

Treadwell, James (2005), *Autobiographical Writing and British Literature 1783–1834*. Oxford: Oxford University Press.

Trumpener, Katie (1997), *Bardic Nationalism: The Romantic Novel and the British Empire*. Princeton: Princeton University Press.

Wellek, René (1949), 'The Concept of "Romanticism" in Literary History'. *Comparative Literature*. 1.1/1.2, 1–23/147–72.

The Victorian Period

Primary Texts

Abrams, M. H. (ed.) (2006), *The Norton Anthology of English Literature*. 2 vols. New York: Norton.

Brontë, Charlotte (2006), *Jane Eyre*. Ed. Stevie Davies. London: Penguin.

Brontë, Emily (2004), *Wuthering Heights*. Ed. Pauline Nestor. London: Penguin.

Collins, Wilkie (2003), *The Woman in White*. Ed. Matthew Sweet. London: Penguin.

Darwin, Charles (1998), *The Origin of the Species*. Ed. Gillian Beer. Oxford: Oxford University Press.

Dickens, Charles (1996), *Great Expectations*. Ed. David Trotter and Charlotte Mitchell. Harmondsworth: Penguin.

Dickens, Charles (2007), *Hard Times*. Ed. Graham Laws. London: Penguin.

Dickens, Charles (2003), *Oliver Twist*. Ed. Philip Horne. London: Penguin.

Gaskell, Elizabeth (1996), *North and South*. Ed. Patricia Ingham. Harmondsworth: Penguin.

Hardy, Thomas (1890), 'Candour in English Fiction'. http://pages.ripco.net/~mws/candour.txt (accessed 9 August 2008).

Wilde, Oscar (2000), *The Importance of Being Earnest and Other Plays*. Ed. Richard Allen Cave. Harmondsworth: Penguin.

Secondary Texts

Beer, Gillian (1983), *Darwin's Plots: Evolutionary Narrative in Darwin, George Eliot and Nineteenth-Century Fiction*. Cambridge: Cambridge University Press.

Brantlinger, Patrick (1988), *Rule of Darkness: British Literature and Imperialism, 1830–1914*. Ithaca: Cornell University Press.

Gallagher, Catherine (1985), *The Industrial Reformation of English Fiction: Social Discourse and Narrative Form from 1832–1867*. Chicago: University of Chicago Press.

Gilbert, Sandra, and Susan Gubar (1979), *The Madwoman in the Attic: The Woman Writer and the Nineteenth-Century Literary Imagination*. New Haven: Yale University Press.

Kaplan, Cora (2007), *Victoriana: Histories, Fictions, Criticism*. Edinburgh: Edinburgh University Press.

Kucich, John (2006), *Imperial Masochism: British Fiction, Fantasy and Social Class*. Princeton: Princeton University Press.

Levine, George (1981), *The Realistic Imagination: English Fiction from 'Frankenstein' to 'Lady Chatterley'*. Chicago: University of Chicago Press.

Miller, D. A. (1988), *The Novel and the Police*. Berkeley: University of California Press.

Raby, Peter (1995), *'The Importance of Being Earnest': A Reader's Companion*. New York: Twayne.

Sedgwick, Eve Kosofsky (1993), *Between Men: English Literature and Male Homosocial Desire*. New York: Columbia University Press.

Sedgwick, Eve Kosofsky (1995), *Epistemology of the Closet*. Harmondsworth: Penguin.

Showalter, Elaine (1991), *Sexual Anarchy: Gender and Culture at the Fin de Siècle* London: Bloomsbury.

Spivak, Gayatri Chakravorty (1985), 'Three Women's Texts and a Critique of Imperialism'. *Critical Inquiry*, 12, 243–61.

Sutherland, John (1995), *Victorian Fiction: Writers, Publishers, Readers*. Basingstoke: Macmillan.

Williams, Raymond (1970), *The English Novel from Dickens to Lawrence*. Oxford: Oxford University Press.

Wynne, Deborah (2001), *The Sensation Novel and the Victorian Family Magazine*. Basingstoke: Palgrave.

Part IV Studying Twentieth-Century and Contemporary Literature

Literature 1901–1945

Primary Texts

Arnold, Matthew (1993), *Selected Poems and Prose*. Ed. Miriam Allott. London: Everyman.

Beckett, Samuel (2000), *Waiting for Godot* (second edition). London: Faber and Faber.

Conrad, Joseph (2000), *'Heart of Darkness' with 'The Congo Diary'*. Ed. Robert Hampson. London: Penguin.

Eliot, T. S. (2002), *Collected Poems 1909–1962*. London: Faber and Faber.

Ford, Ford Madox (1995), *The Good Soldier*. Ed. Martin Stannard. New York: Norton.

Ford, Ford Madox (1997), *Selected Poems*. Ed. Max Saunders. Manchester: Carcanet.

Joyce, James (1992), *Dubliners*. Ed. Terence Brown. Harmondsworth: Penguin.

Joyce, James (1992), *Finnegans Wake*. London: Paladin.

Joyce, James (2000), *A Portrait of the Artist as a Young Man*. Ed. Jeri Johnson. Oxford: Oxford University Press.

Joyce, James (2000), *Ulysses*. London: Penguin.

Reilly, Catherine W. (ed.) (2007), *Scars upon My Heart: Women's Poetry and Verse of the First World War*. London: Virago.

Rhys, Jean (2000), *Good Morning, Midnight*. London: Penguin.

Silkin, Jon (ed.) (1996), *The Penguin Book of First World War Poetry* (second edition). London: Penguin.

Woolf, Virginia (2000), *Mrs Dalloway*. Ed. David Bradshaw. Oxford: Oxford University Press.

Yeats, W. B. (1996), *The Poems*. Ed. Daniel Albright. London: Orion.

Secondary Texts

Achebe, Chinua (1988), *Hopes and Impediments: Selected Essays 1965–1987*. Oxford: Heinemann.

Booth, Howard J., and Nigel Rigby (eds) (2000), *Modernism and Empire*. Manchester: Manchester University Press.

Bradbury, Malcolm, and James McFarlane (eds) (1991), *Modernism 1890–1930*. London: Penguin.

Carey, John (1992), *The Intellectuals and the Masses: Pride and Prejudice Among the Literary Intelligentsia, 1880–1939*. London: Faber and Faber.

Chantler, Ashley (2008), *'Heart of Darkness': Character Studies*. London: Continuum.

Childs, Peter (2007), *Modernism and the Post-Colonial: Literature and Empire 1885–1930*. London: Continuum.

Drabble, Margaret (ed.) (2000), *The Oxford Companion to English Literature* (sixth edition). Oxford: Oxford University Press.

Eliot, T. S. (1953), *Selected Prose*. Ed. John Hayward. Harmondsworth: Penguin.

Eliot, T. S. (1997), *The Sacred Wood: Essays on Poetry and Criticism*. London: Faber and Faber.

Faulkner, Peter (1985), *Modernism*. London: Methuen.

Ford, Ford Madox (1911), *Ancient Lights*. London: Chapman and Hall.

Ford, Ford Madox (1913), 'Preface', *Collected Poems*. London: Max Goschen.

Ford, Ford Madox (1914), 'Literary Portraits XLVIII: M. Charles-Louis Philippe and "Le Père Perdrix" '. *Outlook*, 34, 174–75.

Ford, Ford Madox (1924), *Joseph Conrad: A Personal Remembrance*. London: Duckworth.

Ford, Ford Madox (2002), *Critical Essays*. Ed. Max Saunders and Richard Stang. Manchester: Carcanet.

Foster, Roy (1997), *W. B. Yeats: A Life: I: The Apprentice Mage: 1865–1914*. Oxford: Oxford University Press.

Frawley, Maria (2008), 'The Victorian Age, 1832–1901', in *English Literature in Context*. Ed. Paul Poplawski. Cambridge: Cambridge University Press.

Gordon, Lyndall (1998), *T. S. Eliot: An Imperfect Life* (revised edition). London: Vintage.

Hanson, Clare (1994), *Virginia Woolf*. Basingstoke: Macmillan.

Harding, Jason (2007), 'Modernist Poetry and the Canon', in *The Cambridge Companion to Modernist Poetry*. Ed. Alex Davis and Lee M. Jenkins. Cambridge: Cambridge University Press.

Hollington, Michael (2007), 'Some Art-Historical Contexts for "Tradition and the Individual Talent" ', in *T. S. Eliot and the Concept of Tradition*. Ed. Giovanni Cianci and Jason Harding. Cambridge: Cambridge University Press.

Iser, Wolfgang (2008), 'The Reading Process: A Phenomenological Approach', in *Modern Criticism and Theory: A Reader* (third edition). Ed. David Lodge and Nigel Wood. Harlow: Pearson Longman.

James, Henry (1995), 'Preface' (1908), *The Portrait of a Lady*. Ed. Robert D. Bamberg. New York: Norton.

Joannou, Maroula (1998), 'Suffragette Fiction and the Fictions of Suffrage', in *The Women's Suffrage Movement: New Feminist Perspectives*. Ed. Maroula Joannou and June Purvis. Manchester: Manchester University Press.

Julius, Anthony (2003), *T. S. Eliot, Anti-Semitism, and Literary Form* (revised edition). London: Thames and Hudson.

Kermode, Frank (1991), *The Uses of Error*. London: Collins.

Kermode, Frank (1995), 'Recognition and Deception', in Ford Madox Ford, *The Good Soldier*. Ed. Martin Stannard. New York: Norton.

Kolocotroni, Vassiliki, Jane Goldman and Olga Taxidou (eds) (1998), *Modernism: An Anthology of Sources and Documents*. Edinburgh: Edinburgh University Press.

Langbaum, Robert (1972), *The Poetry of Experience: The Dramatic Monologue in Modern Literary Tradition*. London: Chatto and Windus.

Levenson, Michael H. (1992), *A Genealogy of Modernism: A Study of English Literary Doctrine 1908–1922*. Cambridge: Cambridge University Press.

Lodge, David (1992), *The Art of Fiction*. Harmondsworth: Penguin.

Lodge, David (1993), *The Modes of Modern Writing: Metaphor, Metonymy, and the Typology of Modern Literature*. London: Edward Arnold.

Lunn, Eugene (1982), *Marxism and Modernism: An Historical Study of Lukás, Brecht, Benjamin, and Adorno*. Berkeley: University of California Press.

Matthews, Steven (2004), *Modernism*. London: Arnold.

Moody, A. David (1979), *Thomas Stearns Eliot: Poet*. Cambridge: Cambridge University Press.

Nietzsche, Friedrich (1998), 'Preface to *Human, All Too Human*' (1878), in *Modernism: An Anthology of Sources and Documents*. Ed. Vassiliki Kolocotroni, Jane Goldman, and Olga Taxidou. Edinburgh: Edinburgh University Press.

Raine, Craig (2006), *T. S. Eliot*. Oxford: Oxford University Press.

Ricks, Christopher (1994), *T. S. Eliot and Prejudice*. London: Faber and Faber.

Saunders, Max (1996), *Ford Madox Ford: A Dual Life*. 2 vols. Oxford: Oxford University Press.

Selden, Raman, and Peter Widdowson (1993), *A Reader's Guide to Contemporary Literary Theory* (third edition). Hemel Hempstead: Harvester Wheatsheaf.

Southam, B. C. (1978), *T. S. Eliot: 'Prufrock', 'Gerontian', 'Ash Wednesday' and Other Shorter Poems: A Casebook*. Basingstoke: Macmillan.

Stead, C. K. (1980), *The New Poetic: Yeats to Eliot*. London: Hutchinson.

Stern, J. P. (1985), *Nietzsche*. London: Fontana.

Straus, Nina Pelikan (1987), 'The Exclusion of the Intended from Secret Sharing in Conrad's *Heart of Darkness*'. *Novel: A Forum on Fiction*, 20.2, 123–37.

Watt, Ian (1980), *Conrad in the Nineteenth Century*. London: Chatto and Windus.

Watts, Cedric (1993), *A Preface to Conrad* (second edition). Harlow: Longman.

References

Wells, H. G. (1916), *What is Coming? A Forecast of Things After the War*. London: Cassell.
Whitworth, Michael H. (ed.) (2007), *Modernism*. Oxford: Blackwell.
Woolf, Virginia (2008), *Selected Essays*. Ed. David Bradshaw. Oxford: Oxford University Press.

Literature 1945–1990

Primary Texts
Alvarez, A. (ed.) (1966), *The New Poetry* (revised edition). London: Penguin.
Beckett, Samuel (2000), *Waiting for Godot* (second edition). London: Faber and Faber.
Byatt, A. S. (1991), *Possession: A Romance*. London: Vintage.
Carter, Angela (1981), *The Magic Toyshop*. London: Virago.
Eliot, T. S. (2002), *Collected Poems 1909–1962*. London: Faber and Faber.
Fowles, John (2004), *The French Lieutenant's Woman*. London: Vintage.
Golding, William (2002), *Lord of the Flies*. London: Faber and Faber.
Heaney, Seamus (2001), *North*. London: Faber and Faber.
Larkin, Philip (1990), *Collected Poems* (revised edition). Ed. Anthony Thwaite. London: Marvell Press, Faber and Faber.
Morrison, Blake, and Andrew Motion (eds) (1982), *The Penguin Book of Contemporary British Poetry*. London: Penguin.
Osborne, John (1978), *Look Back in Anger*. London: Faber and Faber.
Pinter, Harold (1964), *'The Birthday Party' and Other Plays: 'The Birthday Party'; 'The Room'; 'The Dumb Waiter'*. London: Methuen.
Stoppard, Tom (1973), *Rosencrantz and Guildenstern Are Dead*. London: Faber and Faber.

Secondary Texts
Ashcroft, Bill, Gareth Griffiths and Helen Tiffin (2002), *The Empire Writes Back* (second edition). London: Routledge.
Barthes, Roland (1977), *Image-Music-Text*. Trans. Stephen Heath. London: Fontana.
Baudrillard, Jean (1994), *Simulacra and Simulations*. Trans. Sheila Faria Glaser. Ann Arbor: University of Michigan Press.
Boyd, S. J. (1990), *The Novels of William Golding* (second edition). Hemel Hempstead: Harvester Wheatsheaf.
Bradby, David (2001), *Beckett: 'Waiting for Godot'*. Cambridge: Cambridge University Press.
Cixous, Hélène (1986), 'The Laugh of the Medusa', in *Feminist Literary Theory: A Reader*. Ed. Mary Eagleton. Oxford: Blackwell.
Derrida, Jacques (1976), *Of Grammatology*. Trans. Gayatri Chakravorty Spivak. Baltimore: Johns Hopkins University Press.
Dukes, Gerry (2006), 'The Godot Phenomenon', in *Samuel Beckett: 100 Years*. Ed. Christopher Murray. Dublin: New Island.
Elsom, John (1979), *Post-War British Theatre* (revised edition). London: Routledge and Kegan Paul.
Freud, Sigmund (1962), *Two Short Accounts of Pyscho-Analysis*. Trans. James Strachey. London: Pelican.

Gamble, Sarah (2006), *Angela Carter: A Literary Life*. Basingstoke: Palgrave Macmillan.

Gregson, Ian (2004), *Postmodern Literature*. London: Arnold.

Hutcheon, Linda (1988), *A Poetics of Postmodernism: History, Theory, Fiction*. London: Routledge.

Jameson, Fredric (1991), *Postmodernism, Or, the Cultural Logic of Late Capitalism*. London: Verso.

Lawley, Paul (2008), *'Waiting for Godot': Character Studies*. London: Continuum.

Leavis, F. R. (1962), *The Common Pursuit*. London: Peregrine.

Lyotard, Jean-François (1984), *The Postmodern Condition: A Report on Knowledge*. Trans. Geoff Bennington and Brian Massumi. Manchester: Manchester University Press.

MacDonald, Ian (1998), *Revolution in the Head: The Beatles' Records and the Sixties* (updated edition). London: Pimlico.

Marshall, Gordon, David Rose, Howard Newby and Carolyn Vogler (1988), *Social Class in Modern Britain*. London: Unwin Hyman.

Pattie, David (2000), *The Complete Critical Guide to Samuel Beckett*. London: Routledge.

Rabey, David Ian (2003), *English Drama Since 1940*. Harlow: Pearson.

Said, Edward (2001), *The Edward Said Reader*. Ed. Moustafa Bayoumi and Andrew Rubin. London: Granta.

Showalter, Elaine (1989), 'Introduction: The Rise of Gender', *Speaking of Gender*. London: Routledge.

Sinfield, Alan (2004), *Literature, Politics and Culture in Postwar Britain* (revised edition). London: Athlone Press.

Storey, John (1993), *An Introductory Guide to Cultural Theory and Popular Culture*. Hemel Hempstead: Prentice Hall/Harvester Wheatsheaf.

Literature 1990–The Present

Primary Texts

Armitage, Simon (1992), *Kid*. London: Faber and Faber.

Barker, Pat (1992), *Regeneration*. London: Penguin.

Duffy, Carol Ann (1994), *Selected Poems*. London: Penguin in association with Anvil Press Poetry.

Hulse, Michael, David Kennedy and David Morley (eds) (1993), *The New Poetry*. Newcastle: Bloodaxe.

Kane, Sarah (2001), *Complete Plays: 'Blasted', 'Phaedra's Love', 'Cleansed', 'Crave', '4.48 Psychosis', 'Skin'*. London: Methuen.

Larkin, Philip (1990), *Collected Poems* (revised edition). Ed. Anthony Thwaite. London: Marvell Press, Faber.

McEwan, Ian (1991), *The Innocent*. New York: Bantam.

McEwan, Ian (2001), *Atonement*. London: Jonathan Cape.

Mitchell, David (1999), *Ghostwritten*. London: Hodder and Stoughton.

Mitchell, David (2004), *Cloud Atlas*. London: Hodder and Stoughton.

Ravenhill, Mark (2001), *Plays: 1: 'Shopping and Fucking'; 'Faust is Dead'; 'Handbag'; 'Some Explicit Polaroids'*. London: Methuen.

Welsh, Irvine (1994), *Trainspotting*. London: Minerva.

Winterson, Jeanette (1992), *Written on the Body*. London: Jonathan Cape.
Winterson, Jeanette (2001), *Oranges Are Not the Only Fruit*. London: Vintage.

Secondary Texts

Amichai-Hamburger, Yair (ed.) (2005), *The Social Net: Human Behaviour in Cyberspace*. Oxford: Oxford University Press.

Baudrillard, Jean (1995), *The Gulf War Did Not Take Place*. Trans. Paul Patton. Sydney: Power Publications.

Brooks, Ann (1997), *Postfeminisms: Feminism, Cultural Theory and Cultural Forms*. London: Routledge.

Bush, George W. (2001), 'Address to a Joint Session of Congress and the American People' (20 September 2001). http://www.state.gov/coalition/cr/rm/2001/5025.htm [site now discontinued].

Butler, Judith (1990), *Gender Trouble: Feminism and the Subversion of Identity*. London: Routledge.

Coppock, Vicki, Deena Haydon and Ingrid Richter (1995), *The Illusions of 'Post-Feminism': New Women, Old Myths*. London: Taylor and Francis.

Cunningham, Valentine (1994), *In the Reading Gaol: Postmodernity, Texts and History*. Oxford: Blackwell.

Damazer, Mark (2007), http://news.bbc.co.uk/1/hi/entertainment/6940597.stm (accessed 27 October 2008).

Dobson, Andrew (2000), *Green Political Thought* (third edition). London: Routledge.

Fukuyama, Francis (1992), *The End of History and the Last Man*. New York: Free Press.

Graham, Gordon (1999), *The Internet: A Philosophical Inquiry*. London: Routledge.

Horkheimer, Max, and Theodor Adorno (2004), 'The Culture Industry as Mass Deception', in *Literary Theory: An Anthology* (second edition). Ed. Julie Rivkin and Michael Ryan. Oxford: Blackwell.

Iraq Body Count (2008), http://www.iraqbodycount.org/ (accessed 12 November 2008).

Loomba, Ania (2005), *Colonialism/Postcolonialism* (second edition). London: Routledge.

McLeod, John (2000), *Beginning Postcolonialism*. Manchester: Manchester University Press.

Morace, Robert A. (2001), *Irvine Welsh's 'Trainspotting': A Reader's Guide*. New York: Continuum.

Padel, Ruth (2007), *The Poem and the Journey: And Sixty Poems to Read Along the Way*. London: Chatto and Windus.

Rees-Jones, Deryn (2001), *Writers and Their Work: Carol Ann Duffy* (second edition). Tavistock: Northcote House.

Rivkin, Julie, and Michael Ryan (eds) (2004), *Literary Theory: An Anthology* (second edition). Oxford: Blackwell.

Saunders, Graham (2002), *'Love Me or Kill Me': Sarah Kane and the Theatre of Extremes*. Manchester: Manchester University Press.

Sedgwick, Eve Kosofsky (1985), *Between Men: English Literature and Male Homosocial Desire*. New York: Columbia University Press.

Sedgwick, Eve Kosofsky (1994), *Epistemology of the Closet*. Harmondsworth: Penguin.

Sierz, Aleks (2001), *In-Yer-Face Theatre: British Drama Today*. London: Faber and Faber.

Sinfield, Alan (2004), 'Cultural Materialism, *Othello*, and the Politics of Possibility', in *Literary Theory: An Anthology* (second edition). Ed. Julie Rivkin and Michael Ryan. Oxford: Blackwell.

Tallis, Raymond (1999), *Theorrhoea and After*. Basingstoke: Macmillan.

Tew, Philip (2007), *The Contemporary British Novel* (second edition). London: Continuum.

Westman, Karin (2001), *Pat Barker's 'Regeneration': A Reader's Guide*. London: Continuum.

White, Stephen (2001), *Communism and Its Collapse*. London: Routledge.

Index